Find It Fast

IN THE

Bible

Ron Rhodes

This Billy Graham Evangelistic Association
special edition is published with permission
from Harvest House Publishers.

HARVEST HOUSE PUBLISHERS
Eugene, Oregon 97402

Acknowledgments

Kerri, David, and Kylie
Thanks so much for your prayers, support,
and encouragement during the time it took
to write this book.
I so appreciate each of you!

Cover by Terry Dugan Design, Minneapolis, Minnesota

FIND IT FAST IN THE BIBLE

Copyright © 2000 by Ron Rhodes
Published by Harvest House Publishers
Eugene, Oregon 97402

Library of Congress Cataloging-in-Publication Data
Rhodes, Ron
   Find it fast in the Bible/Ron Rhodes.
      p. cm.
   Includes bibliographical references and index.
   ISBN 0-913367-29-X
    1.Bible—Indexes.   I. Title.
  BS432 .R46 2000
  220.3—dc21

Printed in the United States of America.

To my daughter Kylie
with affection

Preface

Find It Fast in the Bible is designed to help you find meaningful Bible verses on a wide variety of issues in a quick and easy way.

Whether you're looking for verses on *growing deeper with God* (faith, prayer, meditation, praise), *understanding emotions* (anger, anxiety, discouragement, jealousy), *prophecy* (the Rapture, Tribulation Period, Second Coming), *angels* (guardians and others), *ethics* (drinking, adultery, divorce), *family* (marriage, parenting), or *general doctrine* (God, Jesus, the Holy Spirit, salvation), this guide provides quick references on these and over 1,000 other relevant topics.

The guide is arranged from A to Z, and under each subject heading you will find short, easy-to-read descriptions of each verse. I pray this book will serve you well as a constant companion in Bible study!

—Ron Rhodes
Rancho Santa Margarita, California
A.D. 2000

Contacting the Author

REASONING FROM THE SCRIPTURES MINISTRIES is a teaching ministry that will help you grow strong in the Word of God and equip you to become knowledgeable in the application of biblical wisdom.

We publish a free newsletter and offer numerous materials (many free) on a variety of relevant issues. If you would like to be on our mailing list, or if we can be of service to you in any way, please do not hesitate to write:

Ron Rhodes
Reasoning from the Scriptures Ministries
P.O. Box 80087
Rancho Santa Margarita, CA 92688

We also have a free Internet newsletter that goes out to thousands of Christians in over 45 countries. If you would like to subscribe, send an e-mail to ronrhodes@aol.com and put "Subscribe" in the body of your e-mail.

Abba

God is our dear Father—Galatians 4:6.
Members of God's family—Romans 8:15.

Ability

Can do all things through Christ—Philippians 4:13.
Divine source of ability—1 Peter 4:11.
Increased abilities through Christ—John 14:12.
Serve according to ability—Acts 11:29.
Special ability to build tabernacle—Exodus 31:3.
Special ability to make priestly garments—Exodus 28:3.

Abomination

Cross-dressing—Deuteronomy 22:5.
Dishonesty—Proverbs 20:23.
Double standards—Proverbs 20:10.
Homosexuality—Leviticus 18:22.
Idolatry—Deuteronomy 27:15.
Occultism—Deuteronomy 18:10,11.
Sacrificing children—Leviticus 18:21.
Sex with animals—Leviticus 18:23.
Sex with close relatives, neighbor's wife—Leviticus 18:6,20.

Abortion

God has a purpose for those in womb—Jeremiah 1:5.
Rights of the unborn—Exodus 21:22,23.
Unborn children are persons—Psalm 51:5; 139:13-16.
Unborn children have consciousness—Luke 1:41,44.

Abstinence from Liquor, Examples of

Daniel—Daniel 1:8.
John the Baptist—Matthew 11:18; Luke 1:15.
Nazirite vow—Numbers 6:3,4.

A

Samson's mother—Judges 13:4,14.
See Alcohol; Intoxication.

Acceptance
Accept all authority—1 Peter 2:13.
Accept both good and adversity from God—Job 2:10.
Accept Christians weak in faith—Romans 14:1.
Accept counsel—Proverbs 4:10.
Accept discipline—Proverbs 19:20.
Accept one another—Romans 15:7.
Accept situation Lord has put you in—1 Corinthians 7:17.
Husbands love and accept your wives—1 Peter 3:7.
Wife, accept authority of husband—1 Peter 3:1.

Accidents
Accident led to Uzzah's death—2 Samuel 6:6,7.
Tower fell and killed people—Luke 13:4.
Unintentional killing—Deuteronomy 19:4-7.
Unintentional sin—Leviticus 4:2,22.

Accomplishment
Accomplish what God calls us to—1 Corinthians 9:24-27.
Can accomplish anything with Christ's help—Philippians 4:13.
Give God glory for accomplishments—Psalm 118:23.
Necessity of being rooted in Christ—John 15:1-8.
Necessity of relationship with Holy Spirit—Galatians 5:22,23.
Think first, then accomplish—Luke 14:28.

Accountability
For use of money—Luke 19:15.
For words spoken—Matthew 12:36,37.
In accordance with level of understanding—1 Samuel 3:7; Luke 12:48.
To God—Ezekiel 18:20; Romans 3:19; 14:12.
See Responsibility.

Accuracy

Accurate measurement—Isaiah 28:17.
Every jot and tittle of Scripture accurate—Matthew 5:17,18.
Jesus a perfect reflection of Father—Hebrews 1:3.
Perfect aim—Judges 20:16.
Scripture words accurate—Matthew 22:41-46.
Singular word in Scripture accurate—Galatians 3:16.
Use accurate scales—Leviticus 19:36; Deuteronomy 25:13; Ezekiel 45:10.
Verb tense in Scripture accurate—Matthew 22:23-33.

Accusations, False

Enemies say evil things—Psalm 41:5.
False accusations—Luke 3:14.
False reports—Exodus 23:1.
Followers of Jesus lied about—Matthew 5:11.
Slanderous gossip—Leviticus 19:16.
See Dishonesty; Innocence; Liars/Lies; Perjury.

Achievement

See Accomplishment.

Adam and Eve

Created by God—Genesis 1:26,27; 2:21,22.
United—Genesis 2:24.
See Fall of Man.

Adolescence

Boy provides bread and fish for Jesus—John 6:9.
Demon-possessed boy delivered—Mark 9:14-29.
Dying girl in need of healing—Luke 8:41-56.
Jesus as a boy—Luke 2:41-52.
See Children.

Adoption into God's Family

By faith in Christ—Galatians 3:26.

Called to take on family likeness—Philippians 2:14,15.
Father allows us into His family—1 John 3:1,2.
Gentiles in God's family too — Ephesians 2:19.
Jesus firstborn of many brothers—Romans 8:29.
Jesus made it all possible—Galatians 4:4,5; Ephesians 1:5.
Jews and Gentiles heirs together—Ephesians 3:6.
Lord disciplines us as His children—Hebrews 12:6-9.
Those led by Spirit are sons of God—Romans 8:14.

Adultery

Abstain from sexual immorality—Acts 15:20.
Adulterer sins in private—Job 24:15.
Adultery forbidden—Exodus 20:14.
Adultery starts in the heart—Matthew 15:19; Mark 7:21.
Adultery with the eyes—Matthew 5:28; 2 Peter 2:14.
Avoid sexually immoral people—1 Corinthians 5:9-11.
Death penalty in Old Testament times—Leviticus 20:10.
Divorce and adultery—Matthew 5:32.
Keep clear of sexual sin—Colossians 3:5; 1 Thessalonians 4:3.
Make a covenant with your eyes to avoid lust—Job 31:1.
Sexual immorality brings judgment—1 Corinthians 10:8.
Sexual immorality emerges from sinful nature—Galatians 5:19.
Sexual intercourse with neighbor's wife forbidden—Leviticus 18:20.
Watch out for immoral women—Proverbs 5:3,4.

Adversary

See Enemies.

Adversity

All of us encounter trouble—Job 5:7.
Builds endurance—Romans 5:3,4.
Cast all anxiety on God—Psalm 55:22; 1 Peter 5:7.
Childbirth painful—Genesis 3:16.

A

Christ gives us rest—Matthew 11:28.

Christ helps us in temptation—Hebrews 2:18.

Count it all joy—James 1:2.

Do not be discouraged if God disciplines you—
Proverbs 3:11,12; Hebrews 12:5,6.

Do not be dismayed—Isaiah 41:10.

Do not be troubled; trust Christ—John 14:1.

Do not worry, Lord will fight for you—Exodus
14:13,14.

Go boldly to throne of grace—Hebrews 4:16.

God brings consolation—Lamentations 3:32.

God brings good out of evil—Genesis 50:20; Romans
8:28; Philippians 1:12.

God encourages us—2 Corinthians 7:6.

God gives rest to the weary—Jeremiah 31:25.

God heals the brokenhearted—Psalm 147:3.

God helps in times of trouble—Psalm 46:1.

God is our refuge—Deuteronomy 33:27; Psalm 9:9.

God is our shepherd—Psalm 23.

God of all comfort helps us—2 Corinthians 1:3,7.

God preserves us—Psalm 138:7.

God strengthens the weak—Isaiah 40:29.

God turns mourning into joy—Jeremiah 31:13.

God will never forsake you—Hebrews 13:5.

God's strength makes up for our weakness—
2 Corinthians 12:9.

Holy Spirit (Comforter) helps us—John 14:16,17.

Life is full of trouble—Job 14:1.

Lord is our helper—Hebrews 13:6.

Present troubles insignificant in view of future glory—
2 Corinthians 4:17.

Pressed, but not crushed—2 Corinthians 4:8.

Share in Christ's sufferings—Romans 8:17.

Suffering can be good for you—Psalm 119:71.

Take courage—James 5:8.

Trials test our faith—1 Peter 1:6,7.

A

Trust Christ, your High Priest—Hebrews 4:15.
Trust God in times of trouble—Psalm 50:15.
We will not drown in deep rivers—Isaiah 43:2.

Prayers in

Arise and rescue me—Psalm 3:7; 17:13; 40:13; 71:4;
119:134; 120:2.
Be merciful—Psalm 25:16; Isaiah 33:2.
Do not abandon me—Psalm 71:9; Jeremiah 17:17.
Do not ignore my cry for help—Psalm 35:17,22; 55:1;
83:1; 109:1.
Do not punish me anymore—Psalm 39:10.
Do not remember sins forever—Isaiah 64:9.
Encourage me by your word—Psalm 119:26-28.
How long will you forget me?—Psalm 13:1.
I come to you for protection—Psalm 7:1.
Let your unfailing love comfort me—Psalm 119:76.
Make your face shine down on us—Psalm 80:3.
Please hurry to help me—Psalm 71:12.
Protect me from plots of the wicked—Psalm 64:2;
119:154; 140:1.
Restore my life again—Psalm 71:20; 119:107.
Rise to my defense—Psalm 35:23; 43:1.
Save me from my enemies—Psalm 9:13,14; 17:14; 71:2.
Snatch me from the jaws of death—Psalm 9:13.
Surround me with tender mercies—Psalm 119:77.

Why God Allows

Brings glory to God—John 9:1-3; 11:1-4; 21:19.
Develops humility—Deuteronomy 8:16.
Discipline by God—1 Corinthians 11:32; Hebrews 12:5.
Drives us to God's Word—Psalm 119:71.
Keeps us from straying from God—Psalm 57:10; Ezekiel
14:11; 1 Peter 5:10.
Makes us more fruitful—John 15:2.
Prevents pride—2 Corinthians 12:7.
Produces glory in us—2 Corinthians 4:17.

10

Proves our character—Deuteronomy 8:2.
Purifies us—Psalm 66:10; Isaiah 1:25.
Tests our faith—1 Peter 1:7.

Advice

Be quick to listen—James 1:19.
Fools think they need no advice—Proverbs 12:15.
Godly person gives wise advice—Psalm 37:30;
    Proverbs 10:31,32.
Listen to God—John 6:45.
Listening makes one wise—Proverbs 19:20.
Obtain guidance—Proverbs 20:18.
Plans fail for lack of counsel—Proverbs 15:22.
Sheep listen to shepherd—John 10:27.
Son listen to your father—Proverbs 1:8; 13:1.
Wise man listens—Proverbs 12:15; 13:10.
Wise person gives good advice—Proverbs 15:7.
Young men should follow advice—Proverbs 7:1,2.

Advocate, Spiritual

Holy Spirit is our advocate—John 14:16.
Jesus is our advocate—1 John 2:1.

Afflicted, Duty to the

Be a Good Samaritan—Luke 10:25-37.
Be kind to despairing friend—Job 6:14.
Be kind to strangers—1 Timothy 5:10; Hebrews 13:2.
Be sympathetic—Philippians 2:1,2.
Feed hungry, clothe naked, visit prisoners—Matthew
    25:31-46.
Share food with the hungry—Isaiah 58:7,10.

Affluence

Abraham was wealthy—Genesis 13:2.
Accumulating wealth, meaningless—Ecclesiastes 4:8.
Can hinder attaining salvation—Matthew 19:16-26.

Do not envy the affluent—Psalm 73:3-28.

Do not store treasures on earth—Matthew 6:19.

False confidence in wealth—Psalm 49:5-8; Proverbs 11:28; Jeremiah 48:7.

God blesses with riches, wealth, honor—2 Chronicles 1:11,12.

Lure of wealth—Matthew 13:22.

Not worth losing one's soul—Matthew 16:26.

Prosperity short-lived—Psalm 37:35,36.

Rich man and Lazarus—Luke 16:19-31.

Solomon was wealthy—1 Kings 10:23.

Store up treasure in heaven—Luke 12:33.

Wealth by unjust means wrong—Habakkuk 2:9.

Wealth can be treacherous—Habakkuk 2:5.

Where your treasure is, there your heart is—Luke 12:34.

Age

Abraham was promised longevity—Genesis 15:15.

Be mindful of how brief life is—Psalm 39:4,5.

Control tongue and live long—Proverbs 13:3.

God has assigned years—Psalm 90:10.

God sovereign over length of life—Job 14:5; Psalm 139:16.

Honor father and mother, live long—Exodus 20:12.

Respect older folks—1 Peter 5:5.

We quickly disappear—Job 14:1,2.

Wicked will never live long—Ecclesiastes 8:13.

Agreeable

Agree wholeheartedly—Philippians 2:2.

Brothers live together in harmony—Psalm 133:1.

Can two walk together without agreeing?—Amos 3:3.

Live in harmony and peace—Psalm 133:1; Romans 12:16; 14:19; 15:5,6.

Stop arguing among yourselves—1 Corinthians 1:10.

A

Agriculture

Allow gleaning; do not harvest all—Leviticus 19:9,10.

Beautiful vineyards—Ecclesiastes 2:4.

Cain, a farmer—Genesis 4:2.

Cultivate Garden of Eden—Genesis 2:15.

Cultivate ground—Genesis 3:23.

Farmers are patient—James 5:7.

Hardworking farmers enjoy their fruit—2 Timothy 2:6.

Honor Lord with best produce—Proverbs 3:9,10.

Lord gives rain—Jeremiah 5:24.

Noah became farmer—Genesis 9:20.

Parable of the sower—Matthew 13:1-23.

Plant a variety of crops—Ecclesiastes 11:6.

Plowing and sowing necessary—Isaiah 28:24,25.

Sow generously—2 Corinthians 9:6.

Alcohol

Aaron and descendants forbidden to drink—Leviticus 10:9.

Abstinence, part of Nazirite Vow—Numbers 6:2,3.

Be filled with Spirit, not drunk on wine—Ephesians 5:18.

Do not carouse with drunkards—Proverbs 23:20.

Do not cause brother to stumble—Romans 14:21.

Helps the dying—Proverbs 31:6.

Jesus turned water to wine—John 2:1-11.

Leads to brawls—Proverbs 20:1.

Leads to incapacitation—Isaiah 28:1,7.

Medicinal purposes—1 Timothy 5:23.

New wine, old wineskins—Matthew 9:17; Mark 2:22; Luke 5:37,38.

Noah got drunk—Genesis 9:20-27.

Older women, not heavy drinkers—Titus 2:3.

Priests must not drink before entering courtyard—Ezekiel 44:21.

Robs people of clear thinking—Hosea 4:11.

Wine is not the way to riches—Proverbs 21:17.

See Abstinence from Liquor, Examples of; Wine.

Alms (Good Deeds)

Do good and share with others—Hebrews 13:16.

Do privately—Matthew 6:1.

Give to the poor—Matthew 19:21; Luke 11:41; 12:33; 1 John 3:17.

Give to those who ask—Matthew 5:42.

Help the poor—Deuteronomy 15:7; Galatians 2:10.

Share food with the hungry—Isaiah 58:7,10.

Share money generously—Romans 12:8.

Support your relatives—Leviticus 25:35.

Use money for good—1 Timothy 6:17,18.

Ambassadors, God's

Messengers for God—Matthew 22:2-14; Luke 1:19; John 1:6.

Paul, God's ambassador in chains—Ephesians 6:20; Philemon 1:9.

We are Christ's ambassadors—2 Corinthians 5:20.

See Ministry; Missionary Work.

Ambition, Warnings Regarding

Better to be a servant—Luke 22:26,27.

Beware of devil's temptations—Matthew 4:3-11.

Do not be concerned about who is greatest—Luke 9:46-48.

Exalted will be humbled—Matthew 23:12.

Gain the world, lose your soul—Matthew 16:26.

Oppression and extortion wrong—Habakkuk 2:6.

Watch out for jealousy—James 4:2.

Watch out for religious hypocrisy—Mark 12:38-40.

Wealth by unjust means wrong—Habakkuk 2:9.

Wealth can be treacherous—Habakkuk 2:5.

Amusement

Can end in sorrow—Proverbs 14:13.
Can lead to evil—Job 1:4,5.
Can lead to poverty—Proverbs 21:17.
Doing wrong considered fun—Proverbs 10:23.
Indulgence characteristic of wicked—Isaiah 47:8;
Titus 3:3.
Meaningless—Ecclesiastes 2:1,2.
See Hedonism; Pleasure, Worldly.

Anatomy

God knit our flesh and bones together—Job 10:11.
God put us together—Psalm 139:13,15.
God's hands constructed us—Psalm 119:73.

Angels

A hundred million—Daniel 7:10.
Believers will judge in future—1 Corinthians 6:3.
Cherubim guards tree of life—Genesis 3:24.
Created prior to creation of earth—Job 38:7.
Do not worship angels—Colossians 2:18; Revelation
19:9,10; 22:8,9.
God commanded and the angels were created—Psalm
148:2,5.
Good angels are "elect" angels—1 Timothy 5:21.
Innumerable—Hebrews 12:22.
Interested in plan of redemption—1 Peter 1:12.
Man a little lower than angels—Psalm 8:5.
Michael is archangel—Jude 9.
Seraphim proclaim God's holiness—Isaiah 6:1-3.
War in heaven—Revelation 12:7.
World will not be ruled by angels—Hebrews 2:5.
See Demons; Satan.

Angel Activities Among Believers

Bring messages—Acts 10:3-33.

A

Escort to heaven at death—Luke 16:22.
Give encouragement—Acts 27:23,24.
Give guidance—Acts 8:26.
Guard and protect—Psalm 91:11; Matthew 18:10.
Protected Elisha—2 Kings 6:15-17.
Shut lion's mouth—Daniel 6:22.
Used by God to answer prayer—Acts 12:5,7-10.

Angel Activities Among Unbelievers

Angel of death—2 Samuel 24:16.
Announce judgments—Revelation 14:6-10.
Execute judgments—Isaiah 37:36; Acts 12:23.
Promote evangelism—Acts 8:26-39.
Rejoice when sinners repent—Luke 15:7.
Restrain wickedness—Genesis 19:10-13.

Nature of

Can take on appearance of humans—Hebrews 13:2.
Distinct from humans—Psalm 8:4,5.
Have emotions—Luke 2:13.
Have intellect—1 Peter 1:12.
Have wills—Jude 6.
Invisible to our eyes—2 Kings 6:17.
Ministering spirits—Hebrews 2:14.
No marriage—Matthew 22:30.
Very powerful—Psalm 103:20.

Ranks of

Archangel—Jude 9.
Cherubim—Genesis 3:22-24.
Chief princes—Daniel 10:13.
Different ranks—Ephesians 3:10; Colossians 1:16.
Guardian angels—Matthew 18:10.
Ruling angels—Ephesians 3:10.
Seraphim—Isaiah 6:1-3.

Related to Jesus

Announced Jesus' birth—Luke 2:9-11.

16

Bow before Christ in heaven—1 Peter 3:22.

Christ above all angelic beings—Ephesians 1:20,21; Hebrews 1:4.

Christ created angels—Colossians 1:16.

Strengthened Jesus after temptations—Matthew 4:11.

Strengthened Jesus in Gethsemane—Luke 22:43.

Will accompany Christ at Second Coming—Matthew 25:31.

Anger

Avoid angry people—Proverbs 22:24,25.

Avoid disputes—Proverbs 17:14.

Be patient—Proverbs 16:32.

Be slow to anger—James 1:19.

Causes quarrels—Proverbs 30:33.

Characteristic of fools—Ecclesiastes 7:9.

Do not sin with anger—Ephesians 4:26.

Elders, not quick-tempered—Titus 1:7.

Fool is quick-tempered—Proverbs 12:16.

Gentle answer turns away wrath—Proverbs 15:1.

Get rid of anger—Ephesians 4:31; Colossians 3:8.

Hothead starts fights—Proverbs 15:18; 29:22.

Jesus on anger—Matthew 5:22.

Love is not easily angered—1 Corinthians 13:5.

Restrain anger—Proverbs 19:11.

Short-tempered people do foolish things—Proverbs 14:17.

Those who control anger are wise—Proverbs 14:29.

Turn from rage and envy—Psalm 37:8.

Wise people keep their cool—Proverbs 29:8,11.

God's

At breaking covenant—Joshua 23:16.

At disobedience—1 Samuel 28:18; Ephesians 5:6.

At sin and greed—Isaiah 57:17; Jeremiah 4:4.

At those who reject truth—Romans 1:18; 2:8; Hebrews 3:10,11.

At wickedness—Psalm 7:11.
At worshiping other gods—Judges 2:12.
Day of the Lord, a day of anger—Isaiah 13:9.
Earth trembles when He is angry—Jeremiah 10:10.
Lasts for only a moment—Psalm 30:5.
Slow to anger—Psalm 86:15; Joel 2:13.

Animals

Adam named—Genesis 2:19,20.
Animals are God's—Psalm 50:10.
Clean and unclean—Leviticus 20:25.
Eating animals for food—Genesis 9:3.
God created animals—Genesis 1:24.
God feeds animals—Psalm 147:9; Matthew 6:26.
God provides for animals—Genesis 1:30.
Pigs, demons cast into—Matthew 8:31,32.
Saved during flood—Genesis 6:19,20.
Wolf and lamb together—Isaiah 11:6.

Anointing

Anointing of Holy Spirit—1 John 2:20.
God anoints with oil of joy—Psalm 45:7.
Healing and anointing with oil—Mark 6:13; James 5:14.
Jesus was anointed with burial spices—Mark 16:1.
Jesus was anointed with perfume—Matthew 26:12; John 12:3.

Anthropomorphisms Used of God

Breathes—Psalm 33:6.
Listens—Psalm 31:2.
Never sleeps—Psalm 121:4.
Not deaf or blind—Psalm 94:9.
Rests—Genesis 2:2,3.
Sees—Genesis 11:5.
Wings—Psalm 36:7; 57:1.

A

Antichrist

Denies Christ—1 John 2:22; 2 John 7.
Denies incarnation—1 John 4:3; 2 John 7.
Destiny is Lake of Fire—Revelation 19:20.
Dominion of, during Tribulation Period—Revelation 13.
Is coming—1 John 2:18.
Man of lawlessness—2 Thessalonians 2:1-10.
Spirit of Antichrist—1 John 4:3.
See Satan; Tribulation Period.

Anxiety

Cast all anxiety on God—1 Peter 5:7.
Do not worry about anything—Philippians 4:6,7.
Do not worry about tomorrow—Matthew 6:31-33.
God will supply all needs—Philippians 4:19.
Hope in God as a cure—Psalm 43:5.

Apathy

Hard hearts—Ezekiel 2:4; Mark 6:52; Ephesians 4:18.
No concern about right and wrong—Ephesians 4:19.
No concern for God or man, a parable—Luke 18:1-5.
Refusal to hear or see—Ezekiel 12:2.

Apologetics

Apollos contended for the faith—Acts 18:24-28.
Be light of the world—Matthew 5:14.
Be ready with answer—1 Peter 3:15.
Be salt—Matthew 5:13.
Contend for the faith—Jude 3.
Paul reasoned with Jews and Gentiles—Acts 17:2;
    18:4,19.
See Doctrine.

Apostasy

Do not be carried away by error—2 Peter 3:17.
Do not turn from God—Hebrews 3:12.
End-times rebellion—2 Thessalonians 2:3.

Idolatrous priests—Zephaniah 1:4.
Many will turn away from truth in last days—1 Timothy 4:1.
Many will turn from Christ—Matthew 24:10,11.
Must serve God with whole heart—1 Chronicles 28:9.
People will reject truth—2 Timothy 4:4.
People will turn from right teaching—2 Timothy 4:3.
Turning from God leads to death—Ezekiel 3:20; 18:24-26; 33:12.

Apostles

Ability to heal—Luke 9:1,2.
Authority to cast out demons—Mark 3:14,15.
Instructed by Holy Spirit—Acts 1:2.
Names of 12 apostles—Matthew 10:2-4.
Performed miraculous signs—Acts 2:43; 5:12.
Powerful witnesses—Acts 4:33.
Proof of apostleship—2 Corinthians 12:12.
Sent out to preach—Mark 3:14.

False

False apostles deceive—2 Corinthians 11:13.
False apostles lie—Revelation 2:2.
False prophets—Matthew 7:15; 24:11; Mark 13:22.
False teachers—Matthew 5:19; 15:9; 1 Timothy 1:7; 4:2; 6:3; Titus 1:11.

Appetite

Esau's hunger led to folly—Genesis 25:29-34.
Feed hungry, clothe naked, visit prisoners—Matthew 25:34-46.
Feed hungry enemies—Proverbs 25:21,22; Romans 12:20.
God fills the hungry with good things—Psalm 107:9.
Jesus fasted 40 days—Matthew 4:2; Luke 4:2.
Lazy person goes hungry—Proverbs 19:15.
Loss of appetite—Job 3:24; Psalm 102:4; 107:18.

Overly concerned for food—Luke 12:22,29.
Share food with the hungry—Isaiah 58:7,10.
Wise person is hungry for truth—Proverbs 15:14.
Workers' appetite—Proverbs 16:26.

A

Appreciation

Appreciate church leaders—1 Thessalonians 5:12,13.
Appreciation for food—John 6:11.
Honest answers appreciated—Proverbs 24:26.
No appreciation shown—Psalm 78:9-21.
See Thankfulness.

Apprehension

Anxious thoughts, God is aware of—Psalm 139:23.
Do not worry—the Lord will fight for you—Exodus
    14:14.
Fear not, God is with you—Psalm 23:4.
God has not given us spirit of fear—2 Timothy 1:7.
Let not your heart be troubled—John 14:27.
There is no fear in love—1 John 4:18.
Whom shall I fear?—Psalm 27:1.

Ararat

Ark rested on—Genesis 8:4.
See Ark, Noah's.

Archangel

Call of archangel—1 Thessalonians 4:16.
Michael would not rebuke devil—Jude 1:9.
See Angels.

Argument

Contentious wife—Proverbs 25:24.
Fools insist on quarreling—Proverbs 20:3.
Job wanted to argue his case—Job 13:3.
Michael argued with Satan—Jude 1:9.

Quarreling, jealousy, outbursts of anger—2 Corinthians 12:20.

Stay away from complaining and arguing—Philippians 2:14.

Stop arguing among yourselves—1 Corinthians 1:10,11.

Troublemaker plants seeds of strife—Proverbs 16:28.

Ark, Noah's

Kept Noah's family and animals safe—Genesis 6:13,14,18-20.

Noah acted in faith in building—Hebrews 11:7; 1 Peter 3:20.

Noah and family saved because of righteousness—Genesis 7:1.

Rested on Ararat—Genesis 8:4.

Ark of the Covenant

Behind inner curtain, Most Holy Place—Exodus 26:33.

Captured—1 Samuel 4:11-22.

Contained stone tablets—Exodus 25:16,21; 40:20.

Description of contents—Hebrews 9:4.

Dimensions of—Exodus 25:10; 37:1.

Remained in Philistia seven months—1 Samuel 6:1.

Sent back to Israel—1 Samuel 6:3,11-13.

Tribe of Levi carried—Deuteronomy 10:8.

Uzzah struck dead for touching—2 Samuel 6:6,7.

Armageddon

Antichrist's campaign into Egypt—Daniel 11:40-45.

Christ returns at height of—Revelation 19:11-21.

Devastating to humanity—Matthew 24:22.

Place of final battle—Revelation 16:14,16.

Siege of Jerusalem—Zechariah 14:2.

See Second Coming of Christ; Tribulation Period; War.

Armor, Spiritual

Clothe yourselves with armor of light—Romans 13:12,13.

Put on all of God's armor—Ephesians 6:11-18.
Put on armor of faith, love, and hope—
1 Thessalonians 5:8.

Army

See Cavalry; Military.

Arrests, Notable

Apostles arrested—Acts 5:18.
Jesus arrested—John 18:12.
John the Baptist arrested— Matthew 14:3; Mark 6:17.
Paul and Silas arrested—Acts 16:19.
Saul sought to arrest Christians—Acts 9:2.
Stephen arrested—Acts 6:12.

Arrogance

Boastful tongue—Psalm 12:3,4.
Do not speak with arrogance—1 Samuel 2:3.
God hates arrogance—Proverbs 8:13.
God will crush arrogance of the proud—Isaiah 13:11.

Ascension of Jesus Christ

See Jesus Christ, Ascension of.

Ashamed

Adam and Eve naked, felt no shame—Genesis 2:25.
After sin, Adam and Eve felt shame—Genesis 3:7,10.
Fool put to shame—Proverbs 3:35.
Judas seized with remorse—Matthew 27:3.
Never be ashamed to tell others about Christ—
2 Timothy 1:8.
No shame to suffer as a Christian—1 Peter 4:16.
Prayer to avoid shame—Psalm 31:1.
Shameful children—Proverbs 17:2.
Sin leads to shame and disgrace—Genesis 3:7;
Proverbs 3:35; 13:5.
See Shame.

Assassination

Commandment against murder—Genesis 9:5; Exodus 20:13; Deuteronomy 5:17.

Cursed is one who kills in secret—Deuteronomy 27:24.

From the heart comes murder—Matthew 15:19; Mark 7:21.

Lord detests murderers—Psalm 5:6.

See Murder.

Assault and Battery

Jesus assaulted—Matthew 26:67; Mark 14:65.

Pregnant women assaulted—Exodus 21:22.

Striking father or mother—Exodus 21:15.

Turn the other cheek—Matthew 5:39.

Two people quarreling—Exodus 21:18,19.

Assurance of Salvation

Assurance based on Scripture—1 John 5:10-13.

Assurance from Christ—John 5:24.

God can keep us from falling—Jude 1:24.

God guards what we entrust to Him—2 Timothy 1:12.

Holy Spirit testifies we are God's children—Romans 8:16.

Jesus intercedes for us—Hebrews 7:25.

Nothing can separate us from God—Romans 8:38,39.

Secure in Father's hand—John 10:29.

We are sealed by Holy Spirit—Ephesians 4:30.

We can be confident—Ephesians 3:12.

Astrology

Astrologers cannot interpret dreams—Daniel 4:7.

Astrologers cannot save you—Isaiah 47:13,14.

Do not try to read future in stars—Jeremiah 10:2.

See Constellations; Occultism.

Astronomy

Glory in sun, moon, and stars—1 Corinthians 15:41.

God created stars—Isaiah 40:26; Amos 5:8.

God made heavens beautiful—Job 26:13; Psalm 136:5.

God provides light by sun and moon—Jeremiah 31:35.
Heavens declare God's glory—Psalm 19:1.
Movement of the stars—Job 38:31,32.
Night sky, God designed—Psalm 8:3.
Northern sky, God spreads out—Job 26:7.
Stars cannot be counted—Jeremiah 33:22.
See Constellations; Interstellar Space; Moon; Stars; Sun.

Atheism

Ask the animals, they will tell you—Job 12:7-9.
Fool says there is no God—Psalm 14:1; 53:1.
God's existence evident in creation—Romans 1:20.
God's truth in human heart proves His existence—
Romans 1:18,19.

Athletics

Archery—Genesis 21:20.
Boxing—1 Corinthians 9:26.
Do not lose race—Philippians 2:16.
Fight a good fight—2 Timothy 4:7.
In race everyone runs, only one gets prize—
1 Corinthians 9:24.
Run with endurance—Hebrews 12:1.
Strain to reach end of the race—Philippians 3:14.
Swimming—Isaiah 25:11.
Wrestling—Genesis 32:24-30.

Atonement

Day of

No work to be done—Numbers 29:7.
Once a year—Exodus 30:10; Hebrews 9:7.
Tenth day after Festival of Trumpets—Leviticus
23:27,28.

Extent of

Christ is Savior of all—1 Timothy 4:10.
Christ made atonement for all—1 John 2:2.

25

Christ made salvation provision for whole world—
2 Corinthians 5:19.

Christ paid price for all men—1 Timothy 2:5,6; 2 Peter 2:1.

See Salvation.

Made by Jesus

Blood confirms New Covenant—Hebrews 9:20.

Died for our sins—1 Peter 3:18.

Made peace—Colossians 1:20.

Once and for all—Hebrews 7:27; 10:12.

Our Passover Lamb—1 Corinthians 5:7.

Purchased church with blood—Acts 20:28.

Purchased our freedom— Revelation 5:9.

Ransomed many—Matthew 20:28; 1 Timothy 2:6.

Secured our salvation forever—Hebrews 9:12.

Took away our sins—Hebrews 9:28.

Took upon Himself the curse—Galatians 3:13.

Attitude

Attitude toward suffering—1 Peter 4:12-16.

Bad attitude—Genesis 4:3-7; Deuteronomy 20:8;
Ecclesiastes 2:17.

Be gentle—Philippians 4:5.

Be humble—Luke 7:6,7.

Be kind—Ephesians 4:32.

Be merciful—Luke 6:36.

Disregard people's faults—Proverbs 17:9.

Do everything with love—1 Corinthians 16:14; Colossians
3:14; 1 Timothy 1:5.

Fix thoughts on what is true, honorable, right—
Philippians 4:8.

Forgive those who sin against you—Matthew 6:14.

Happy heart—Proverbs 15:13.

Let heaven fill thoughts—Colossians 3:1,2.

Rejoice—Psalm 118:24; Philippians 1:18.

Response to discipline—Hebrews 12:5-11.

Stop judging others—Matthew 7:1.

Thoughts consistently and totally evil—Genesis 6:5.

Attorney

Come to terms quickly with enemy—Matthew 5:25.

Do not be in hurry to go to court—Proverbs 25:8.

Expert in religious law—Matthew 22:35; Luke 10:25; Luke 11:45.

Tertullus pressed charges against Paul—Acts 24:1,2.

Why file lawsuit against Christians?—1 Corinthians 6:1.

See Lawyer.

Authority

Accept all authority—1 Peter 2:13.

Authority of disciples over demons—Matthew 10:1; Mark 3:14,15.

Christ in authority over all—Matthew 11:27; Ephesians 1:22; Colossians 2:10.

Father gave Jesus authority—John 3:35; 1 Corinthians 15:27.

God sovereign above all authority—Ephesians 1:20-22.

Jesus has authority to forgive sins—Matthew 9:2,6; Mark 2:5,10; Luke 5:20,24.

Jesus spoke with authority—Luke 4:31-36.

Moses' authority—Exodus 7:1,2.

Pray for kings and others in authority—1 Timothy 2:1,2.

Wife should accept authority of husband—1 Peter 3:1.

Avarice

Accumulating wealth, meaningless—Ecclesiastes 4:8.

Love of money, root of evil—1 Timothy 6:10.

Never have enough money—Ecclesiastes 5:10,11.

See Greed.

Baal

Altars to—2 Chronicles 33:3.
Prophets killed—1 Kings 18:40.
Seven thousand in Israel never bowed to—1 Kings 19:18.
Worship of—2 Chronicles 28:2.

Backbiting

Backstabbers, haters of God—Romans 1:30.
Backstabbing wrong—2 Corinthians 12:20.
Gossiping tongue—Proverbs 25:23.

Backsliding

Avoid slipping, stay connected to Jesus—John
15:4-10.
God's Word helps you not slip—Psalm 37:31.
Persevere in commitment—2 Timothy 2:12,13.
Put hand to plow, do not look back—Luke 9:62.
Watch out for false gospels—Galatians 1:6.
Watch out for love of money—1 Timothy 6:10.
Watch yourself carefully—Deuteronomy 4:9.

Bad Example

Ahab influenced Jehoram—2 Chronicles 21:5,6.
Ahaziah followed evil example of Ahab's family—
2 Chronicles 22:2,3.
Concubines led Solomon astray—1 Kings 11:3,4.
Do not be influenced by bad example—3 John 11.
Do not be stumbling block—1 Corinthians 8:9,13.
Eve influenced Adam—Genesis 3:6.
Jezebel influenced Ahab—1 Kings 21:25.
Judah/Jerusalem influenced by Manasseh—
2 Chronicles 33:9.
Judaizers influenced Galatians—Galatians 3:1.
Parents influenced children for paganism—Jeremiah
17:2.

Pharisees influenced Jews—Luke 12:1.
See Attitude.

Baldness

Elisha bald—2 Kings 2:23.
Priests should never shave heads—Leviticus 21:5.
Shave heads in grief and mourning—Ezekiel 27:31;
  Jeremiah 48:37.
Shave heads in sorrow—Ezekiel 7:18; Amos 8:10;
  Micah 1:16.

Banishment, Examples of

Adam and Eve banished from garden—Genesis 3:23.
Cain banished—Genesis 4:11,14.
John banished to Patmos—Revelation 1:9.
Priscilla and Aquila banished from Italy—Acts 18:2.

Baptism

Baptism in name of Father, Son, Holy Spirit—Matthew
  28:19.
Baptized into Christ—Galatians 3:27,28.
Believe and be baptized—Mark 16:16.
Buried with Christ in baptism—Romans 6:4;
  Colossians 2:12.
One baptism—Ephesians 4:4-6.
Repent and be baptized—Acts 2:38.

Bargaining

Abraham bargains for the righteous—Genesis
  18:20-33.
Bad exchange—Jeremiah 2:11.
Don't bargain away soul—Matthew 16:26.
Esau bargained away birthright—Genesis 25:27-34.
Jesus gives great bargain, living water—John 4:10.
Judas's insidious bargain—Matthew 26:14-16.

Barren

B

Elizabeth barren—Luke 1:7.
Judgment coming, blessed are the barren—Luke 23:29.
Rachel barren—Genesis 29:31.
Sarah barren—Genesis 11:30.

Beauty

Beauty does not last—Proverbs 31:30.
Beauty of bride—Song of Solomon 4.
Do not be concerned about outward beauty—1 Peter 3:3.
Unfading beauty of a gentle and quiet spirit—1 Peter 3:4.

Behavior

Behave well among Gentiles—1 Peter 2:12.
Blameless—Psalm 15:2.
Clean, innocent—Romans 16:19; Philippians 2:15.
Clear conscience—2 Corinthians 1:12.
Exemplary behavior—Philippians 1:9,10; 1 Timothy 3:2;
  Titus 2:11,12.
Get rid of malicious behavior—Ephesians 4:31;
  Colossians 3:8; 1 Peter 2:1.
Good behavior in Christ—1 Peter 3:16.
Holy behavior—1 Peter 1 Peter 1:15.
Pure—Matthew 5:8; 1 John 3:3.
Wise show good behavior—James 3:13.

Beheading

Believers beheaded for testimony of Jesus—Revelation
  20:4.
John beheaded in prison—Matthew 14:9,10.

Believers

At death, go to be with Lord—Philippians 1:23;
  2 Corinthians 5:8.
Beheaded for testimony of Jesus—Revelation 20:4.
Belong to the Lamb—Revelation 13:8.
Father gave believers to Christ—John 6:37; 17:2,6.

Full of light—Ephesians 5:8.

Holy Spirit fills—Ephesians 5:18.

Holy Spirit indwells—1 Corinthians 6:19.

Holy Spirit produces fruit in—Galatians 5:22,23.

Holy Spirit seals for day of redemption—Ephesians 4:30.

Judged by Christ—1 Corinthians 3:10-15; 2 Corinthians 5:10.

Satan accuses and slanders—Job 1:9-11; Revelation 12:10.

Satan plants doubt in minds of—Genesis 3:1-5.

Satan tempts to immorality—1 Corinthians 7:5.

Will be resurrected—Job 19:25-27; Psalm 49:15; Daniel 12:2,3,13; John 6:39,40,44,54; 1 Corinthians 6:14; 1 Thessalonians 4:13-17; Revelation 20:4-6.

Will judge angels—1 Corinthians 6:3.

Will never perish—John 10:28.

Benediction

Grace, mercy, peace—2 John 3.

In book of Revelation—Revelation 1:4-6; 7:12; 15:3,4; 19:6-8; 22:21.

In name of Father, Son, and Spirit—2 Corinthians 13:14.

Old Testament examples—Leviticus 9:22; Numbers 6:23-26; Joshua 22:6.

Bereavement and Loss

Even if parents forsake you, God will not—Psalm 27:10.

God will not forsake you in time of need—Deuteronomy 31:8.

God's Word comforts us—Psalm 119:50.

God's Word sustains us—Psalm 119:92.

Knowing Jesus makes up for our loss—Philippians 3:8.

See Comfort; Death; Grief.

Bestiality

B

Death penalty for—Exodus 22:19; Leviticus 20:16.
Never have sexual relations with animals—Leviticus 18:23.

Bethlehem

Children killed in—Matthew 2:16.
Jesus born in—Micah 5:2; Matthew 2:1.

Betrayal

Best friends may betray—Psalm 41:9.
Family members may betray—Matthew 10:21; Mark 13:12; Luke 21:16.
Joseph betrayed by brothers—Genesis 37:21-28; 50:20.
Judas Iscariot's betrayal—Matthew 26:14-16; Mark 14:10,11; Luke 22:48; John 13:21.
Son of Man will be betrayed—Matthew 20:18.
Wicked betray friends—2 Timothy 3:2-4.

Bible

Feeds the soul—Deuteronomy 8:3; Job 23:12; Psalm 119:103; Jeremiah 15:16.
Gives hope—Romans 15:4.
Gives us light—Psalm 19:8; 119:105,130; Proverbs 6:23; 2 Peter 1:19.
Inspired by God—Jeremiah 36:1,2; 2 Timothy 3:16; 2 Peter 1:21; Revelation 14:13.
Loved by Christians—Psalm 119:47,72,81,97,140.
Powerful influence—Jeremiah 5:14; Romans 1:16; Ephesians 6:17; Hebrews 4:12.
Purifies us—Psalm 119:9; John 17:17; Ephesians 5:25,26; 1 Peter 1:22.
Sacred—Deuteronomy 4:2; Proverbs 30:6; Revelation 22:19.
Teaches us—Deuteronomy 4:10; 2 Chronicles 17:9.
Tells us about eternal life—1 John 5:13.
Trustworthy—Psalm 111:7.
We should not be ignorant of—Matthew 22:29; John 20:9; Acts 13:27.

We should study—Deuteronomy 17:19; Isaiah 34:16; Acts 17:11; Romans 15:4.

Will never pass away—Psalm 119:89; Isaiah 40:8; Matthew 5:18; 24:35.

Birds

Father knows when sparrow falls—Matthew 10:29.

God created—Genesis 1:20.

God feeds—Psalm 147:9.

Man rules over—Genesis 1:26.

Birth

Angels announced Jesus' birth—Luke 2:9-11.

Birth pangs—Mark 13:8.

Day of death better than day of birth—Ecclesiastes 7:1.

God controls in womb—Psalm 139:15,16; Jeremiah 1:5.

Intense pain and suffering—Genesis 3:16.

Israel gave birth to Messiah—Revelation 12:2,4,5,13.

Jeremiah set apart before birth—Jeremiah 1:5.

New birth—1 Peter 1:23.

Paul called before birth—Galatians 1:15.

Unclean, woman giving birth—Leviticus 12:2.

Virgin will give birth, Messiah—Isaiah 7:14.

We are sinful from moment of birth—Psalm 51:5.

Birthday

Herod's birthday—Matthew 14:6.

Job cursed day of birth—Job 3:1.

Pharaoh's birthday—Genesis 40:20.

Bitterness

Bitter about punishment—Jeremiah 4:18.

Bitter and captive to sin—Acts 8:23.

Bitter mouths—Romans 3:14.

Bitterness of spirit—Deuteronomy 32:32.

Do not harbor bitter envy—James 3:14.

B

Do not let bitter root grow—Hebrews 12:15.
Get rid of all bitterness—Ephesians 4:31.
See Jealousy; Resentment.

Blame

Adam and Eve passed the buck—Genesis 3:12,13.
Be without blame at Second Coming—1 Thessalonians 5:23.
Job did not blame God—Job 1:22.
Joseph's brothers realize blame—Genesis 42:21,22.
See Responsibility.

Blasphemy

Antichrist blasphemes—2 Thessalonians 2:4; Revelation 13:5,6.
Blasphemy against Holy Spirit not forgiven—Matthew 12:31,32; Luke 12:10.
Do not misuse name of Lord—Exodus 20:7; Deuteronomy 5:11.
Do not treat God's holy name as common—Leviticus 22:32.
Do not use God's name to swear a falsehood—Leviticus 19:12.

Blessing

Contingent on Obedience

Be careful to obey—Exodus 19:5; 23:22; Deuteronomy 4:40; 12:28; 15:5; 28:1.
Be faithful to the end—Hebrews 3:14.
Follow God's ways—Zechariah 3:7.
Keep God's laws—Leviticus 26:3; 1 Kings 2:3.
Listen carefully to God—Exodus 15:26.
Obey God's regulations—Deuteronomy 7:12.

Spiritual

God arms me with strength—Psalm 18:32; 144:1.
God gives rest in green meadows—Psalm 23:2.

B

God is a fortress in times of trouble—Psalm 37:39.

God is the strength of my heart—Psalm 73:26.

God offers strength to the weak—Isaiah 40:29.

God places Holy Spirit in our hearts—2 Corinthians 1:22.

God renews my strength—Psalm 23:3; 29:11.

God will not permit the godly to slip—Psalm 55:22.

God will uphold you—Isaiah 41:10.

God's hand supports me—Psalm 18:35; 63:8.

Lord takes care of the godly—Psalm 37:17.

Take refuge in God—Psalm 144:2.

Though we stumble, we will not fall—Psalm 37:24.

We will run and not grow weary—Isaiah 40:31.

Temporal

All will go well—Deuteronomy 12:28.

Avoid diseases—Exodus 15:26.

Bear many children—Deuteronomy 7:13.

Enjoy long life—Deuteronomy 4:40; 5:33.

Food and water provided—Exodus 23:25; Psalm 111:5; 145:16; Joel 2:26.

Never lack any good thing—Psalm 34:10.

No attacks on land—Exodus 34:24.

No miscarriages or infertility—Exodus 23:26.

No need to worry about everyday life—Luke 12:22.

Plenty of provisions—2 Corinthians 9:8; Philippians 4:19.

Prosper in everything—Deuteronomy 28:8.

Riches, wealth, honor—2 Chronicles 1:12.

Seasonal rains—Leviticus 26:4.

Springtime and harvest—Genesis 8:22.

Windows of heaven opened—Malachi 3:10.

Blindness

Angels blinded men of Sodom—Genesis 19:11.

Elisha prayed to make them blind—2 Kings 6:18.

B

Lord can strike one with blindness—Deuteronomy 28:28.
Messiah helps the blind see—Matthew 11:5.
Saul was blinded—Acts 9:8,9.
Two blind men healed by Jesus—Matthew 9:27-30.

Spiritual

Blind guides—Matthew 15:14; 23:16,26.
Blindness of Jesus' crucifiers—Luke 23:34.
Blindness of Pharaoh—Exodus 5:2.
Fools say there is no God—Psalm 14:1.
Minds full of darkness—Ephesians 4:18.
Open my eyes—Psalm 119:18.
Satan blinds minds—2 Corinthians 4:4.
Unbelievers blind to truth—1 Corinthians 2:14,15.

Blood

Blood smeared on doorposts—Exodus 12:7,13.
Crime leads to bloodshed—Genesis 9:6.
Do not eat blood—Genesis 9:4; Leviticus 17:10,11,14;
Deuteronomy 12:23; 15:23.
Moon will become red as blood—Joel 2:31; Acts 2:20;
Revelation 6:12.
Nile River turned to blood—Exodus 7:17-20.
Pilate, "I am innocent of this man's blood"—Matthew
27:24.
Wine represents blood—Luke 22:20.

Of Christ

Blood confirms New Covenant—1 Corinthians 11:25;
Hebrews 9:20.
Cleanses us from sin—1 John 1:7.
Evil consciences cleansed by Christ's blood—Hebrews
10:19,22.
Freed us from sin—Revelation 1:5.
Made us right with God—Romans 5:9.
Purchased church—Acts 20:28.
Purchased our freedom—Colossians 1:14,20.
Ransomed people from every tribe—Revelation 5:9.

Seals the covenant—Matthew 26:28; Mark 14:24.

Boasting

Better to be lowly in spirit—Proverbs 16:19.

Boast in God—Psalm 44:8.

Boast in the cross—Galatians 6:14.

Boast in the Lord—Psalm 34:2; 1 Corinthians 1:31;
2 Corinthians 10:17.

Boasting is evil—James 4:16.

Can ax boast over person who uses it?—Isaiah 10:15.

Do not be conceited—Romans 12:16.

Do not brag—James 3:13.

Evildoers boast—Psalm 94:4.

God humbles the proud—Isaiah 13:11; Daniel 4:37.

Let not wise man boast—Jeremiah 9:23.

Love is not proud—1 Corinthians 13:4.

No one can boast about saving oneself—Ephesians
2:8,9.

Pride goes before destruction—Proverbs 16:18; 18:12.

Body of Christ

Build up body of Christ—Ephesians 4:11-13.

Christ is head of church—Ephesians 5:23; Colossians
1:18.

Equality in body of Christ—Galatians 3:26-28.

Boils

Egyptian people and animals stricken—Exodus 9:9.

Job stricken—Job 2:7.

See Tumor.

Boldness of Believers

Be full of courage—1 John 2:28.

Boldly enter heaven's Most Holy Place—Hebrews
10:19.

Come boldly to throne of grace—Hebrews 4:16.

Come fearlessly into God's presence—Ephesians 3:12.

37

B

We can say with confidence the Lord is our helper—
Hebrews 13:6.

Bondage

Believers are delivered from—Romans 6:18,22.
Bondage to devil—1 Timothy 3:7.
Bondage to sin—Acts 8:23; Romans 6:16; Galatians
4:3-7.
Enslavement to sinful desires—1 Corinthians 3:3.
God controls bondage in prisons—Acts 12:7-11.
Gospel delivers us—John 8:32.
Jesus delivers us—John 8:36; Romans 7:24,25.

Book of Life

Christians' names in—Philippians 4:3.
God will never erase believers' names—Revelation 3:5.
Judgment and the Book of Life—Revelation 20:15.
Moses' request, "Blot me out"—Exodus 32:32.
Rejoice, names registered in heaven—Luke 10:20.

Born Again

Born again to living hope—1 Peter 1:3.
New birth—1 Peter 1:23.
You must be born again—John 3:5-7.
See Regeneration; Salvation.

Botany

Good tree cannot produce bad fruit—Luke 6:43.
Plant few seeds, get small crop—2 Corinthians 9:6.
Reap what you sow—Galatians 6:7.
Seed dies before growing—1 Corinthians 15:36.
Solomon not dressed as nice as lilies—Matthew 6:28,29.
Tree identified by kind of fruit produced—Luke 6:44.
See Agriculture.

Bowels

Intestinal disease—2 Chronicles 21:15.
Judas burst open—Acts 1:18.

Bragging

See Boasting.

Bravery

See Boldness of Believers.

Breastplate

Breastplate of faith and love—1 Thessalonians 5:8.
Breastplate of God's righteousness—Ephesians 6:14.
Priestly breastplate, most careful workmanship—
    Exodus 28:15.

Bribery

Corrupts the heart—Ecclesiastes 7:7.
Never accept—Exodus 23:8; Deuteronomy 16:19.
Those who hate bribes will live—Proverbs 15:27.
Wicked accept secret bribes—Proverbs 17:23.

Bride

Beauty of bride—Song of Solomon 4.
Bride of Christ—2 Corinthians 11:2; Revelation 19:7;
    21:2.
Good wife, favor from the Lord—Proverbs 18:22.
Kindness of wife—Proverbs 31:26.
Share your love only with wife—Proverbs 5:15,18.
See Marriage; Wife.

Brother

Brother will betray brother—Matthew 10:21.
Brothers living together in harmony—Psalm 133:1.
Build up brothers—Luke 22:32.
Do not cause brother to stumble—Romans 14:21.
Do not slander brother—Psalm 50:20.
Feed and give water to brothers—Matthew 25:37-40.
Friend closer than brother—Proverbs 18:24.
Help brothers in need—1 John 3:16-18.
If brother sins, show him fault—Matthew 18:15-17.

B

Joseph's brothers jealous—Genesis 37:4.
Love your Christian brothers—1 Peter 2:17.
Maintain brotherly kindness—2 Peter 1:5-7.
Never cheat Christian brother—1 Thessalonians 4:6.
Reconcile with brother—Matthew 5:23,24.
Restore fallen brothers—Galatians 6:1.
Unbelief of Jesus' brothers—John 7:5.

Burial

Burial spices—Mark 16:1.
Bury body same day—Deuteronomy 21:23.
Funeral procession—Luke 7:12.
See Cremation; Death; Funeral.

Business

See Commerce.

Business Ethics

Be diligent—Proverbs 10:4; 13:4; 22:29; 2 Peter 3:14.
Be fair—Leviticus 19:36; Deuteronomy 25:13; Ezekiel 45:10.
Be faithful—Genesis 39:6,8; 2 Kings 12:15; Daniel 6:4.
Be honest—Leviticus 19:35,36; Proverbs 11:1; Romans 12:17; 13:8.
Be industrious—Proverbs 6:6-8; 10:5; 12:11; 13:11; 20:13.
Maintain integrity—Psalm 41:12; Proverbs 11:3; 19:1; 20:7.
No extortion—Isaiah 10:12; Ezekiel 22:12; Amos 5:11; Matthew 23:25.
No slothfulness—Proverbs 18:9; 24:30,31; Ecclesiastes 10:18.
No unjust gain—Proverbs 16:8; 21:6; Jeremiah 17:11; Ezekiel 22:13; James 5:4.
Pay prompt wages—Deuteronomy 24:15.

C

Calamity

Catastrophic earthquake coming—Revelation 16:18.
Day of disaster—Psalm 18:18.
God creates—Isaiah 45:7.
Guarding the mouth averts—Proverbs 21:23.
Will overtake the wicked—Psalm 34:21.

Call of Apostles

Levi—Mark 2:14; Luke 5:27.
Matthew—Matthew 9:9.
Peter and Andrew—Matthew 4:18; Mark 1:16,17.
The twelve—Luke 6:13-16.
See Apostles.

Call to Service

Barnabas and Saul called—Acts 13:2.
Disciples invited—Matthew 9:9; Mark 1:16,17.
God gives servants to the church—Ephesians 4:11,12.
Isaiah called—Isaiah 6:8.
Jeremiah set apart before birth—Jeremiah 1:5.
Paul chosen to be apostle—Romans 1:1; 1 Corinthians
    1:1; Colossians 1:1.

Calvary

Golgotha—Matthew 27:33; Mark 15:22; Luke 23:33;
    John 19:17.
See Crucifixion.

Cannibalism

Flesh of sons and daughters eaten—Leviticus 26:29;
    Deuteronomy 28:53.
Parents ate children—2 Kings 6:28,29; Ezekiel 5:10.
See Abomination; Heathen.

C

Canon of Scripture

Do not take away or add to God's words—Revelation 22:18-20.

Luke's Gospel recognized as Scripture—1 Timothy 5:18.

Old Testament recognized as Scripture—Matthew 5:17; 23:35-37; 2 Timothy 3:15,16.

Paul's writings recognized as Scripture—2 Peter 3:16.

See Scripture, Inspiration of.

Capital Punishment

Deterrent to crime—Deuteronomy 17:12.

Do not put innocent to death—Exodus 23:7.

For adultery—John 8:3-11.

For idolatry—Exodus 22:20.

For kidnapping—Exodus 21:16.

For lying to Holy Spirit—Acts 5:1-10.

For mediums, psychics, sorcerers—Exodus 22:18; Leviticus 20:27.

For murder—Genesis 9:6; Leviticus 24:17; Numbers 35:16,30,31.

For violating Sabbath—Exodus 31:14.

Instituted by God—Genesis 9:6.

Captivity (Figurative)

Captive to desires—2 Timothy 3:2,6.

Captive to sin—Romans 7:23.

Captive to the devil—2 Timothy 2:26.

Christ led captives free—Ephesians 4:8.

Overcoming captivity to rebellious ideas—2 Corinthians 10:5.

Care, Worldly

Be free from concerns of life—1 Corinthians 7:32.

Busy rushing ends in nothing—Psalm 39:6.

Do not be tied up in affairs of life—2 Timothy 2:4.

Do not worry about anything—Matthew 6:25; Philippians 4:6.

God's message crowded out by cares—Matthew 13:22; Mark 4:19; Luke 8:14.

Carnality

Carousing—2 Peter 2:13-16.
Cravings of sin, lust of eyes, boasting—1 John 2:16.
Do not be attached to world—1 Corinthians 7:29-31.
Do not be conformed to world—Romans 12:2.
Fleshly living—1 Corinthians 3:3.
Indulging in sinful nature—Romans 8:5; Galatians 5:13.
Loving all the wrong things—2 Timothy 3:2-7.
Prisoner of sin—Romans 7:23.
Testing God—1 Corinthians 10:14-23.
Turned from first love—Revelation 2:4.
See Apostasy; Backsliding; Hedonism.

Carpentry

Idols made—Isaiah 41:7.
Noah made boat—Genesis 6:14,22.
Temple made—2 Kings 12:11.

Caution

Be careful how you live—Ephesians 5:15.
Be careful lest you fall—1 Corinthians 10:12.
Be careful to love Lord—Joshua 23:11.
Be careful to obey God—Exodus 19:5; 23:22; Deuteronomy 4:40; 12:28; 15:5; 28:1.
Caution in friendship—Proverbs 12:26.
Listen carefully to truth—Hebrews 2:1.
Prudent carefully consider their steps—Proverbs 14:8,15,16.
Watch yourself carefully—Deuteronomy 4:9.

Cavalry

Of Pharaoh—Exodus 14:23.
Of Philistines—1 Samuel 13:5.

Of Solomon—1 Kings 4:26; 2 Chronicles 9:25.

Celebration

C

Banquet for Jesus—Luke 5:29-35.
Celebration of death of two witnesses—Revelation 11:7-11.
Celebration of Passover—Ezekiel 45:21.
Celebration with prodigal son—Luke 15:22-24.
Jesus celebrated Lord's Supper—Matthew 26:26-28; Luke 22:19,20.

Celibacy

Better not to marry—Matthew 19:10.
Better to be free from concerns of life—1 Corinthians 7:32.
Celibate life is good—1 Corinthians 7:1.
Get along without marrying—1 Corinthians 7:7.
Remain just as you are—1 Corinthians 7:26,27.

Census

Census in Roman Empire—Luke 2:1.
Census of people of Israel—Exodus 30:12.
David's census—2 Samuel 24:1; 1 Chronicles 21:1.

Centurion

Paul challenged—Acts 22:25.
Pleaded with Jesus—Matthew 8:5.
Recognized innocence of Jesus—Luke 23:47.
Recognized Jesus was Son of God—Matthew 27:54; Mark 15:39.

Certainty

See Confidence.

Chains

Gold chain for Joseph—Genesis 41:42.
Paul in chains for Christ—Ephesians 6:20; Philippians 1:7,13,14,17.

44

Peter chained between soldiers, rescued by angel—
Acts 12:6,7.

Character

C

Firmness of

Continue as you were when God called you—1 Corinthians 7:20.
Endure to the end—Matthew 10:22.
Hold tightly to hope—Hebrews 10:23.
Stand firm—2 Thessalonians 2:15.

Of Saints

Blameless—Psalm 15:2.
Clean, innocent—Romans 16:19; Philippians 2:15.
Clear conscience—2 Corinthians 1:12.
Devout—Luke 2:25; Acts 10:2.
Generous—Isaiah 32:8; 2 Corinthians 9:13.
Gentle and lowly—Matthew 5:5.
Holy—Deuteronomy 7:6.
Honest—John 1:47; 2 Corinthians 6:4,8.
Humble and contrite—Isaiah 66:2; 1 Peter 5:5.
Led by Spirit—Romans 8:14.
Live by faith—Habakkuk 2:4.
Love each other—1 Thessalonians 4:9.
Merciful—Matthew 5:7; Colossians 3:12.
Obedient to God—Luke 1:6.
Pure—Matthew 5:8; 1 John 3:3.
Thirst for justice—Matthew 5:6.
Totally committed—Titus 2:14.

Of Wicked

Betray friends—2 Timothy 3:2-4.
Consult fortunetellers—2 Kings 17:17.
Corrupt—Deuteronomy 32:5; Romans 1:29.
Deny God—Psalm 14:1; Acts 7:51; Romans 3:11.
Depraved minds—2 Timothy 3:8.
Dishonest—Psalm 62:4; Micah 6:11.

45

C

Disobedient—Nehemiah 9:26.
Evil desires—Psalm 10:2-4; Isaiah 59:7.
Foolish—Titus 3:3.
Foul talk—Romans 3:13.
Hypocritical—Isaiah 29:13.
Love themselves and money—2 Timothy 3:2.
Lustful—Ephesians 4:22.
Minds full of darkness—Ephesians 4:18.
Murderers and deceivers—Psalm 5:6.
No faithfulness, no kindness—Hosea 4:1.
Plot evil—Isaiah 59:4.
Proud—Psalm 5:4,5; 10:4.
Rebel against right teaching—Titus 1:10.
Stubborn rebels—Isaiah 30:9.
Treacherous—Psalm 38:12.
Troublemakers—Proverbs 24:8.
Unconcerned about right and wrong—Ephesians 4:19.
Unloving and unforgiving—2 Timothy 3:3.
Unruly, stubborn—Exodus 33:5.
Violent—Proverbs 16:29.
Walk crooked path—Proverbs 21:8.

Charismatic Issues

God pours out Spirit on all people—Ezekiel 39:29; Joel 2:28,29.
Instructions about laying on of hands—Hebrews 6:1,2.
Lay hands and heal—Mark 16:18.
Speaking in tongues—Acts 2:7-11; 10:46; 19:6; 1 Corinthians 12:10; 14:2.
Tongues of fire—Acts 2:3.
See Holy Spirit.

Charitable Attitude

Accept Christians weak in faith—Romans 14:1.
Be clothed with love—Colossians 3:14.
Be compassionate—Luke 6:36.

Be filled with love—1 Timothy 1:5.
Be kind—Ephesians 4:32.
Disregard people's faults—Proverbs 17:9.
Do everything with love—1 Corinthians 16:14.
Do not repay evil for evil—1 Peter 3:9.
Forgive those who sin against you—Matthew 6:14.
Love covers multitude of sins—Proverbs 10:12; 1 Peter 4:8.
Make allowance for people's faults—Colossians 3:13.
Reconcile with brother—Matthew 5:23,24.
Stop judging others—Matthew 7:1.
See Alms (Good Deeds).

Chastisement from God
See Discipline from God.

Cheating
Dishonesty an abomination to God—Proverbs 20:23.
Do not cheat anyone—Leviticus 19:13.
Do not cheat employees of wages—Jeremiah 22:13; Malachi 3:5; James 5:4.
Do not cheat Lord—Malachi 3:8,9.
Do not get rich by extortion—Psalm 62:10.
Do not use dishonest standards—Leviticus 19:35.
Lord despises double standards—Proverbs 20:10.
Lord hates cheating—Proverbs 11:1.
Never cheat Christian brother—1 Thessalonians 4:6.
See Dishonesty.

Childlessness
Considered a disgrace in ancient times—Luke 1:24,25.
Rachel's childlessness—Genesis 30:1.
Sarai's childlessness—Genesis 16:1,2.
See Barren.

Children
Boy delivered of demon—Matthew 17:18.

C

Do not despise children—Matthew 18:10.
Gift from God—Psalm 127:3.
Herod killed infant boys—Matthew 2:16.
Jesus as a child—Luke 2:52.
Jesus' attitude toward children—Luke 18:16.
Lord killed firstborn sons in Egypt—Exodus 12:29.
Parents are the pride of their children—Proverbs 17:6.
Pharaoh ordered newborn boys killed—Exodus 1:22.
To such belong kingdom of God—Matthew 19:14; Mark 10:13-16.
See Daughter; Family; Parents; Son.

Commandments to Children

Honor father and mother—Exodus 20:12; Deuteronomy 5:16; Matthew 15:4; 19:19; Mark 10:19; Luke 18:20.
Listen to what parents teach—Proverbs 1:8; 6:20; 23:22.
Obey parents—Ephesians 6:1; Colossians 3:20.
Respect parents—Leviticus 19:3.

Discipline of

Discipline children—Proverbs 13:24; 19:18; 29:17.
Discipline drives away foolishness—Proverbs 22:15.
Discipline may save children from death—Proverbs 23:14.
Discipline produces wisdom—Proverbs 29:15.

Good

Are pleasing to the Lord—Colossians 3:20.
Bring joy to father—Proverbs 23:24.
Joseph was a good son—Genesis 46:29; 47:12.
Will live long—Ephesians 6:2,3.

Instruction of

Teach children about God—Deuteronomy 11:19.
Teach children God's laws—Deuteronomy 4:10.
Teach children right path—Proverbs 22:6.
Teach children what Lord has done—Deuteronomy 4:9.

Wicked

Curse parents—Exodus 21:17; Proverbs 20:20; 30:11.

C

Despise and defy parents—Deuteronomy 27:16; Micah 7:6.

Disobedient—Romans 1:30; 2 Timothy 3:2.

Foolish—Proverbs 10:1; 15:5,20; 17:25.

Mistreat parents—Exodus 21:15; Proverbs 19:26.

Mock—Proverbs 13:1.

Rebel—Deuteronomy 21:18; Proverbs 17:21; Mark 13:12.

Rob parents—Proverbs 28:24.

Shameful—Proverbs 17:2.

Choice

Choose for or against Jesus—John 3:36.

Choose good, not evil—Amos 5:15.

Choose life—Deuteronomy 30:19.

Choose Lord—Genesis 28:21; Psalm 16:2; 140:6.

Choose way of truth—Psalm 119:30.

Choose whom you will follow—Joshua 24:15.

Choosing right over wrong—1 Kings 3:9.

Moses' wise choice—Hebrews 11:24,25.

See Decisions, Guiding Principles of.

Christian

First called Christians in Antioch—Acts 11:26.

No shame to suffer as a Christian—1 Peter 4:16.

See Believers; Disciples and Discipleship.

Christmas

Child is born to us—Isaiah 9:6; Luke 1:35.

Jesus born in Bethlehem—Micah 5:2; Matthew 2:4,5.

Jesus born of a woman—Genesis 3:15; Galatians 4:4.

Jesus born of virgin—Isaiah 7:14; Matthew 1:23.

Jesus came to earth in real body—2 John 7.

Church

A "new man"—Ephesians 2:15.

All are equal in body of Christ—Galatians 3:26-28.

49

C

Body of Christ—Colossians 1:18.
Bride of Christ—Revelation 21:2.
Church will reign with Christ—Revelation 20:4,6.
Distinct from Israel—1 Corinthians 10:32.
God's household—1 Timothy 3:14,15.
God's temple—1 Corinthians 3:16.
Jesus builds church—Matthew 16:18.
Jesus purchased church—Acts 20:28.
Members of God's household—Ephesians 2:19,20.
One body, many members—Romans 12:4,5;
    1 Corinthians 12:12.
Spiritual house—1 Peter 2:4,5.

Christ in Authority over
Christ is cornerstone—Ephesians 2:20; 1 Peter 2:7.
Christ is in authority over all—Colossians 2:10;
    Ephesians 1:22.
Christ is the foundation—1 Corinthians 3:11.
Christ is the head—Colossians 1:18; 2:19; Ephesians
    4:15; 5:23.

Discipline in
After discipline, restoration—2 Corinthians 2:6-8.
Correct when necessary—Titus 2:15.
Discipline for offense against Paul—2 Corinthians
    2:6-11.
Excommunication sometimes necessary—
    2 Thessalonians 3:14.
Jesus commends church for discipline—Revelation 2:2.
Jesus rebukes church that did not discipline—
    Revelation 2:14-16.
No harmony between light and darkness—2 Corinthians
    6:14,15.
Proper protocol for discipline—Matthew 18:15-17.
Rebuke when necessary—Titus 1:13.
Restore one who has fallen with gentleness—Galatians
    6:1.

C

Seek to save erring sinner—James 5:19,20.
Sexual immorality calls for discipline—1 Corinthians 5:1-11.

Government of

Appointment of deacons—Acts 6:1-6.
Appointment of elders—Acts 14:23; Titus 1:5.
Church discipline—Matthew 18:15-18; 1 Corinthians 5:1-5.
Feed and shepherd God's flock—Acts 20:28.
Instructions to elders—Acts 20:17,28; 1 Peter 5:1-4.
Qualifications for elders and deacons—1 Timothy 3:1-13; Titus 1:6-9.

Membership Growing

Large numbers of Gentiles believed—Acts 11:20,21.
Many believed in the Lord—Acts 9:42.
Many were brought to the Lord—Acts 5:14.
One body, many members—1 Corinthians 12:12; Ephesians 5:29,30.
Those who believed were added—Acts 2:41,47.

Mission of

Be Christ's witnesses—Luke 24:45-49; Acts 1:7,8.
Build up body of Christ—Ephesians 4:11-13.
Do good to all people—Galatians 6:10; Titus 3:14.
Exercise spiritual gifts—Romans 12:6-8.
Financially support God's work—1 Corinthians 16:1-3.
Help brothers in need—1 John 3:16-18.
Love each other—Hebrews 13:1-3,16.
Make disciples—Matthew 28:19,20.
Offer hospitality to each other—1 Peter 4:9-11.
Preach the Word—Mark 16:15,16; 1 Timothy 4:6,13.
Take care of orphans and widows—1 Timothy 5:3,4,16; James 1:27.
Take care of the sick—James 5:14,15.

C

Unity of
Jesus' prayer for unity—John 17:21.
One flock with one shepherd—John 10:16.
Peace between Jews and Gentiles—Ephesians 2:14,21.
United—John 17:11.
We are one body—1 Corinthians 10:17; 12:12; Ephesians 4:4,12,13,16,25.

Circumcision
Boy must be circumcised—Genesis 17:12-14; Leviticus 12:3.
Makes no difference—1 Corinthians 7:19.
Not required of New Testament believers—Acts 15:1-10.
Spiritual circumcision—Colossians 2:11.

Cities of Refuge
For people to flee to—Exodus 21:13; Numbers 35:11.
Three cities of refuge—Deuteronomy 4:41,42; 19:2.

Citizens
Duties of
Accept all authority—1 Peter 2:13.
Do not exalt yourself—Proverbs 25:6.
Fear the Lord and the king—Proverbs 24:21.
Jesus on paying taxes—Matthew 17:24-27.
Obey the government—Romans 13:1,5; Titus 3:1.
Patience can persuade a prince—Proverbs 25:15.
Pray for kings and others in authority—1 Timothy 2:1,2.
The wise appease anger of king—Proverbs 16:14.

Rights of
Citizenship in heaven—Philippians 3:20.
Rights of citizens—Nehemiah 5:4-13.
Violation of Roman citizenship—Acts 16:37; 22:25; 23:27.

Civil Service, Corruption in
Anxious to please crowd—Mark 15:15.

Bribes accepted by government officials—Acts 24:26.
Corrupt government—Psalm 12:8; 94:20; Daniel 6:4-15.
Lay heavy burdens on people—Nehemiah 5:15.

Cleanliness

Burn unclean things—Leviticus 7:19.
Clean hands—Job 17:9.
Cleansing ceremony—Leviticus 14:8,9.
Hearts sprinkled clean—Hebrews 10:22.
Purification, shave and wash—Numbers 8:7.
Purify and change clothes—Genesis 35:2.
Unclean person pronounced clean again—Leviticus 13:6.
Wash and perfume—Ruth 3:3.
Wash face—Matthew 6:17.
See Purity of Heart; Sanitation, Disinfection.

Clergy

God gives servants to the church—Ephesians 4:11.
Pray over the sick—James 5:14,15.
Preach the Word—Mark 16:15; 1 Timothy 4:6,13.
Sent out to preach—Mark 3:14.
Should be paid well—1 Timothy 5:17,18.

Cloud, Pillar of

Cloud of glory—Isaiah 6:1-5.
Cloud upon Mount Sinai—Exodus 16:10; 19:16; 24:16.
Lord appeared in pillar of cloud—Deuteronomy 31:15.
Lord guided Israelites by pillar of cloud—Exodus 13:21,22; 40:36; Psalm 78:14.
Voice from cloud—Matthew 17:5; Luke 9:35.
See God, Glory of.

Color

Black cloud—Job 3:5.

C

Blue cloth—Exodus 28:28,31; Numbers 4:7.

Blue, purple, scarlet material—Exodus 26:1.

Blue, purple, and scarlet yarn—Exodus 26:31; 28:15; 35:23; 39:1.

Blue sapphire—Ezekiel 1:26.

Clothed in white—Revelation 4:4; 7:9.

Pavement of brilliant sapphire—Exodus 24:10.

Purple cloth—Numbers 4:13.

Purple robes—Daniel 5:7,16,29.

Red as crimson, white as wool—Isaiah 1:18.

Scarlet cloth—Leviticus 14:4,49,51; Numbers 4:8.

Scarlet robe—Matthew 27:28.

Tanned ram skins dyed red—Exodus 26:14; 36:19.

White robe—Revelation 6:11.

Comfort

Christ gives us rest—Matthew 11:28-30.

Comforter is with you—John 14:16-18.

Fear not, God is with you—Psalm 23:4.

God consoles us—2 Thessalonians 2:16,17.

God of all comfort is with you—2 Corinthians 1:3,4.

God's compassions never fail—Lamentations 3:22,23.

Scripture comforts us—Romans 15:4.

Those who mourn will be comforted—Matthew 5:4.

Commendation

David commended—1 Samuel 29:6-9.

Great faith commended—Matthew 15:28; Luke 7:9.

Honoring Christ commended—Mark 14:6.

John the Baptist commended—Luke 7:28.

Poor widow's donation commended—Luke 21:3,4.

Timothy commended by Paul—Philippians 2:19-23.

Commerce

Cinnamon, spice, incense, myrrh, frankincense—Revelation 18:13.

Egyptian chariots—1 Kings 10:29.

Gold, silver, ivory, apes, and peacocks—1 Kings 10:22; 2 Chronicles 9:21.

Jewelry, linen, and other fine goods—Revelation 18:12.

C

Joseph sold as slave—Genesis 37:27,28.

Purchase of field—Genesis 23:13.

Solomon's horses—1 Kings 10:28.

Turquoise, purple dyes, embroidery, fine linen, and jewelry—Ezekiel 27:16.

Wheat, barley, olive oil, and wine—2 Chronicles 2:15.

Wrought iron, cassia, and calamus—Ezekiel 27:19.

Commitment

Abraham tested—Genesis 22:1-14.

Count the cost—Matthew 8:19,20.

Do not look back—Luke 9:62.

Keep vow to God—Psalm 65:1; Ecclesiastes 5:4,5.

Living sacrifice—Romans 12:1.

Love shows our commitment to Christ—1 John 2:9-11; 3:10,11,16-18.

Partial commitment—1 Kings 3:3; 22:43.

Persevere in commitment—2 Timothy 2:12,13.

Totally committed—Joshua 24:14; Titus 2:13,14.

Communion

Of Saints

Brothers living together in harmony—Psalm 133:1.

Build each other up—Luke 22:32; 1 Thessalonians 5:11.

Comfort and encourage each other—1 Thessalonians 4:18; Hebrews 10:24,25.

Good fellowship—Psalm 55:13,14.

Jonathan and David—1 Samuel 23:16.

Maintain unity—John 17:21.

Pray for each other—James 5:16.

Warn each other every day—Hebrews 3:13.

C

With God

Comforter never leaves us—John 14:16.

Father and Jesus live with us—John 14:23.

Lord guides us—Psalm 16:7.

Our fellowship is with Father and Son—1 John 1:3.

Share meal as friends—Revelation 3:20.

Spirit in our hearts—Galatians 4:6.

We are temple of Holy Spirit—2 Corinthians 6:16.

See Fellowship, with God.

Companionship

Can two walk together without agreeing?—Amos 3:3.

Companionship among disciples—Galatians 2:9.

Companionship with Father and Jesus—1 John 1:3.

Companionship with righteous people—Psalm 119:63.

Companionship with unrighteous people—Psalm 1:1; Proverbs 24:1.

Two by two—Luke 10:1.

See Friendship.

Company, Evil

Bad company corrupts good character—1 Corinthians 15:33.

Do not act like Egyptians—Leviticus 18:3.

Do not carouse with drunkards—Proverbs 23:20.

Do not eat with stingy people—Proverbs 23:6.

Do not join crowd that intends evil—Genesis 49:5,6; Exodus 23:2,32,33.

Do not participate in sins of others—1 Timothy 5:22.

Do not spend time with liars—Psalm 26:4.

Do not team up with unbelievers—2 Corinthians 6:14,15,17.

Evil is like yeast—Galatians 5:7-9.

Keep away from angry people—Proverbs 22:24.

Stay away from evil people—Proverbs 1:10,15.

Stay away from fools—Proverbs 13:20; 14:7.

C

Compassion

Be a Good Samaritan—Luke 10:30-37.

Be compassionate and humble—1 Peter 3:8.

Be compassionate to the poor—Proverbs 19:17.

Be compassionate to the weak—Psalm 41:1; Galatians 6:2.

Be compassionate toward enemies—Psalm 35:13.

Be compassionate toward the afflicted—Job 6:14.

Do not just pretend to love others—Romans 12:9,10.

God's compassions never fail—Lamentations 3:22,23.

Jesus felt compassion for people without shepherd—Mark 6:34.

Jesus understands our weaknesses—Hebrews 4:15.

Love your neighbor as yourself—Leviticus 19:18; James 2:8.

Competition

See Athletics.

Complain

Avoid complaining and arguing—Philippians 2:14.

Complaining wife—Proverbs 21:19.

Complaints about manna—Numbers 11:6.

Complaints against God—Psalm 44:9-26.

Complaints to God—Psalm 142:2.

Do not grumble—John 6:43.

God hears all complaints—Numbers 14:27.

Israelites complain about Moses—Exodus 15:24; 16:2.

Notable examples—Genesis 4:13,14; Exodus 5:22,23; 2 Samuel 6:8; 1 Kings 19:4,10; Psalm 73:3; 116:10,11.

Compliment

See Commendation.

C

Compromise

Believers cannot marry unbelievers—1 Corinthians 7:16.
Cannot serve two masters—Matthew 6:24.
Do compromise before litigation—Proverbs 25:8-10; Luke 12:58.
Do not assist in evil—2 Chronicles 19:2.
Do not blur good and evil—Isaiah 5:20.
Do not compromise in righteousness—Psalm 119:3.
Partial obedience unacceptable—2 Kings 14:3,4; 15:3-5,34,35.
Seek to please God, not men—1 Thessalonians 2:3,4.
Solomon's wrongful compromise—1 Kings 3:3.
See Apostasy; Backsliding.

Conceit

Do not be impressed with your own wisdom—Proverbs 3:7.
Do not try to act important—Romans 12:16.
Fools think they need no advice—Proverbs 12:15.
Hypocritical Pharisees—Luke 18:11.
Let not the wise man boast in his wisdom—Jeremiah 9:23.
Trusting oneself is foolish—Proverbs 28:26.

Condemnation

Adam's sin brought—Romans 5:18-21.
God disciplines us so we can avoid—1 Corinthians 11:32.
Hypocrisy leads to—Matthew 23:14.
Jewish leaders condemned—Matthew 23:33.
No condemnation in Christ—Romans 8:1.
Pride leads to—1 Timothy 3:6.
Unbelief leads to—Mark 16:16; John 3:18.
Unbelievers remain under—John 3:18,36.

Conduct, Proper

Abstain from evil—1 Thessalonians 5:22.
Behave in manner worthy of gospel—Philippians 1:27.

Do not be rude or self-seeking—1 Corinthians 13:5.

Do work of the Lord—1 Corinthians 15:58.

Follow Golden Rule—Matthew 7:12; Luke 6:31.

Forgive—Romans 12:19,20.

Free from accusation—Colossians 1:22.

Generous—Romans 12:13.

Live blamelessly—Philippians 1:10; 2:15; 1 Thessalonians 3:13.

Live good life—James 3:13; 1 Peter 2:12; 2 Peter 3:11.

Live soberly—Titus 2:12.

Put away sin—Hebrews 12:1.

Self-controlled—1 Corinthians 9:27; 1 Timothy 3:2.

Set example—1 Timothy 4:12.

Subdue temper—Ephesians 4:26.

Sympathetic—Galatians 6:2.

Walk honestly—1 Thessalonians 4:11,12.

Walk worthy of the Lord—Colossians 1:10.

Confession

Confess Jesus is Lord—Romans 10:9.

Confess sins, God forgives—Exodus 10:17-19; Proverbs 28:13; 1 John 1:9.

Confess sins to each other—James 5:16.

Fasting and confession of sin—1 Samuel 7:6.

Notable confessions—Matthew 16:16; John 1:49; 4:29; 6:69; 11:27; 20:28.

Personal sins confessed—Joshua 7:20; 1 Samuel 15:24; Mark 1:5; Luke 5:8; 15:18.

Confidence

Boldness and confidence—Ephesians 3:10-12.

Can do all things through Christ—Philippians 4:13.

Do not cast away your confidence—Hebrews 10:35.

Fear not, God is with you—Psalm 27:3,4.

Fear of the Lord is strong confidence—Proverbs 14:26.

Lord is your confidence—Proverbs 3:26.

Quietness and confidence—Isaiah 30:15.

C

False

Confidence in leader—1 Corinthians 3:21.

Confidence in prosperity—Psalm 30:6; 49:6; Proverbs 18:11; Jeremiah 48:7.

Confidence in strong army—Psalm 20:7; 33:16,17.

"Everything is peaceful and secure"—1 Thessalonians 5:3.

Overconfidence in self—Luke 22:33,34.

Trust in mere humans—Jeremiah 17:5.

Trusting oneself is foolish—Proverbs 28:26.

Conscience

Conscience can be seared—1 Timothy 4:2.

Conscience can become corrupted—Titus 1:15.

Conscience can confirm—Romans 9:1.

Evil conscience cleansed by Christ's blood—Hebrews 10:22.

God's law on human hearts—Romans 2:14,15.

Keep a clear conscience—2 Corinthians 1:12; 1 Timothy 1:5,19; Hebrews 13:18.

Not bothered by evil—Proverbs 30:20.

Paul, a good conscience—Acts 23:1.

Weak consciences easily violated—1 Corinthians 8:7,12.

Guilty

Be cleansed of guilty conscience—Hebrews 10:22.

David sought purification—Psalm 51:7.

Judas filled with remorse—Matthew 27:3.

See Conviction of Sin.

Consciousness Following Death

Absent from body, at home with Lord—2 Corinthians 5:8.

Paul desired to depart and be with Christ—Philippians 1:23.

Rich man and Lazarus—Luke 16:19-31.
Souls under God's altar—Revelation 6:9.
Thief with Christ in paradise—Luke 23:43.
See Death, Intermediate State.

Consecration

Be slaves of righteousness—Romans 6:19.
Give your bodies to God—Romans 12:1.
Give yourselves completely to God—Romans 6:13.
See Commitment.

Consistency

Cannot eat at Lord's Table and table of demons—
   1 Corinthians 10:21.
Do not blur good and evil—Isaiah 5:20.
Do not compromise in righteousness—Psalm 119:3.
Do not waver back and forth—1 Kings 18:21; James
   1:8.
No one can serve two masters—Matthew 6:24; Luke
   16:13.
See Dependability.

Constellations

Bear, Orion, the Pleiades—Job 9:9.
Pleiades and Orion—Amos 5:8.
Spirit made the heavens beautiful—Job 26:13.
See Astronomy.

Consultation

Do not consult fortunetellers—2 Kings 17:17.
Do not consult mediums and psychics—Leviticus
   19:31; Isaiah 8:19.
Fools think they need no advice—Proverbs 12:15.
Listening makes one wise—Proverbs 19:20.
Obtain guidance—Proverbs 20:18.
Plans fail for lack of counsel—Proverbs 15:22.

C

Contentment

Accept situation Lord has put you in—1 Corinthians 7:17.

Be content with your pay—Luke 3:14.

Be satisfied with what you have—Hebrews 13:5.

Better to be godly and have little—Psalm 37:16; Proverbs 16:8.

Cheerful heart is good medicine—Proverbs 17:22.

Content with little or a lot—Philippians 4:11,12.

Enjoy life—Ecclesiastes 3:12,13.

Gift of God—Ecclesiastes 5:18,19.

Glad heart makes happy face—Proverbs 15:13.

God is our satisfaction—Psalm 90:14.

God satisfies the thirsty—Psalm 107:9.

Godliness with contentment is great gain—1 Timothy 6:6,8.

Just enough to satisfy needs—Proverbs 30:8.

Love of money robs contentment—Ecclesiastes 5:10.

Those who fear Lord have contentment—Proverbs 19:23.

Contrite

Broken and repentant heart—Psalm 34:18; 51:17.

God heals the brokenhearted—Psalm 147:3.

Humble and contrite—Isaiah 66:2; 1 Peter 5:5.

See Repentance.

Conversation

Do not use foul or abusive language—Ephesians 4:29.

Good words come from good heart—Matthew 12:35.

Let your conversation be gracious—Colossians 4:6.

Let your yes be yes—Matthew 5:37; James 5:12.

No dirty language—Colossians 3:8.

See Criticism; Flattery; Gossip.

Conviction of Sin

Awareness of need for salvation—Acts 16:30.

Conscience accuses—Romans 2:15.
Convicted of sin—1 Corinthians 14:24.
Holy Spirit convicts people—John 16:8-11.
See Conscience, Guilty.

Correction

Correct in love—Hebrews 12:6.
Correct when necessary in the church—Titus 2:15.
Do not fail to correct children—Proverbs 23:13.
Government corrects us—1 Peter 2:13,14.
Happy are those God corrects—Job 5:17; Psalm 94:12;
   Jeremiah 10:23,24.
Patiently correct, rebuke, and encourage—2 Timothy
   4:2.
Scripture corrects us—2 Timothy 3:16,17.
Whoever hates correction will die—Proverbs 15:10.

Cosmetics

Brighten eyes with mascara—Jeremiah 4:30.
Painted eyelids—2 Kings 9:30; Ezekiel 23:40.

Counsel

Heartfelt counsel of a friend—Proverbs 27:9.
Many counselors bring success—Proverbs 15:22.
The wise listen to others—Proverbs 12:15.
Victory depends on many counselors—Proverbs 24:6.
With many counselors, there is safety—Proverbs
   11:14.
See Advice; Guidance.

Countenance

Broken heart crushes the spirit—Proverbs 15:13.
Cain, angry and dejected—Genesis 4:5.
Glad heart makes happy face—Proverbs 15:13.
Gossiping tongue causes anger—Proverbs 25:23.

Guilty faces—Isaiah 3:9.
Let the smile of your face shine on us—Psalm 4:6.
Why so sad?—Psalm 42:11; 43:5.

Courage

Be people of courage—1 Corinthians 16:13.
Be strong and courageous—Deuteronomy 31:7,8,23;
　　1 Chronicles 22:13.
Boldness of disciples—Acts 4:13.
Do not be afraid or discouraged—1 Chronicles 28:20.
Encourage the timid—1 Thessalonians 5:14.
God did not give us spirit of timidity, but of power—
　　2 Timothy 1:7.
God gives us boldness—Psalm 138:3.
Holy Spirit gives boldness—Acts 4:29,31.
Speak boldly for the Lord—Acts 14:3.

Courtesy

Always be kind—1 Thessalonians 5:15.
Be considerate—Romans 15:1-5.
Be courteous to everyone—Galatians 6:10; Titus 3:2;
　　1 Peter 2:17.
Be courteous to strangers—Ruth 2:14-18.
Be kind and compassionate—Ephesians 4:32.
Do good to enemies—Luke 6:35.
Love is patient and kind—1 Corinthians 13:4.

Covenants

Abrahamic Covenant—Genesis 12:1-3.
Davidic Covenant—2 Samuel 7:5-17.
Mosaic Covenant—Exodus 19:3-6; 20–40.
New Covenant—Jeremiah 31:31-34.
Palestinian Covenant—Deuteronomy 30.

Covetousness

Always greedy for more—Proverbs 21:26.
Coveting leads to fighting—James 4:2.

Coveting violates law of love—Romans 13:9.

Do not be greedy for what you do not have—Luke 12:15.

Do not be lover of money—1 Timothy 3:3; Hebrews 13:5.

Do not covet neighbor's house or wife—Exodus 20:17; Deuteronomy 5:21.

Do not store treasures on earth—Matthew 6:19.

Hard for rich person to get into heaven—Matthew 19:23.

Lure of wealth—Matthew 13:22.

Money lovers never have enough—Ecclesiastes 5:10.

No one can serve two masters—Matthew 6:24.

Selfish greed—Jeremiah 22:17.

Cowardice

Abraham, an example—Genesis 12:11-19.

Before the Philistines—1 Samuel 13:6,7.

Contagious—Deuteronomy 20:8.

Cowardly Christians desert Paul—2 Timothy 4:16.

David, an example—2 Samuel 15:13-17.

Disciples, an example—Matthew 8:25,26.

Fear of man—Proverbs 29:25; Galatians 2:12.

Nicodemus, an example—John 3:1,2.

Peter, an example—Matthew 26:69-74.

Creation

All things created by Christ—John 1:3; Colossians 1:16; Hebrews 1:2.

Creation took place by God's great power—Jeremiah 32:17.

Creation was in six days—Exodus 20:11.

Earth was created according to wisdom—Proverbs 3:19.

Father is source; Son is agent—1 Corinthians 8:6; Hebrews 1:2.

God alone is Creator—Isaiah 44:24.

God existed before creation—Psalm 90:2.
God spoke and it was done—Psalm 33:6,9.

C

In the beginning God created—Genesis 1:1; Nehemiah 9:6.
We know there was creation by faith—Hebrews 11:3.

Cremation

Achan and family cremated—Joshua 7:25.
Saul and sons cremated—1 Samuel 31:12.
See Burial; Funeral.

Crime

Crime leads to bloodshed—Genesis 9:6.
Crime not worth it—Acts 1:18.
Crimes emerge in the heart—Matthew 15:19,20.
Criminals are crafty—Proverbs 1:11,15,18.
Criminals will not inherit kingdom—1 Corinthians 6:10.
Perfect crime—Psalm 64:6.
When crime not punished, people do wrong—Ecclesiastes 8:11.
Worldwide crime—Genesis 6:11.

Criticism

Do not ignore constructive criticism—Proverbs 13:18.
Gentle words bring life and health—Proverbs 15:4.
Harsh words stir up anger—Proverbs 15:1; Ephesians 4:31.
Listen to constructive criticism—Proverbs 15:31.
Notable examples of criticism—Genesis 4:13,14; Exodus 17:7; Matthew 16:8-11.
Reckless words pierce soul—Proverbs 12:18.
Rejecting constructive criticism harms yourself—Proverbs 15:32.
Take log out of own eye first—Luke 6:41,42.
Tongue can cut like sharp razor—Psalm 52:2.
Tongue can do enormous damage—James 3:5.

Tongue can sting like a snake—Psalm 140:3.

Tongue is a flame of fire—James 3:6.

Valid criticism is treasured—Proverbs 25:12.

Wound of friend, better than kiss of enemy—Proverbs 27:6.

Cross

Christ obedient to the cross—Philippians 2:8.

Cross was in God's plan—Acts 2:23.

Jesus carried cross—John 19:17.

Crown of Thorns

Jesus wore—Matthew 27:29; Mark 15:17; John 19:5.

Crucifixion

Blindness of crucifiers—Luke 23:34.

Crucified with Christ—Galatians 2:20.

Crucifixion prophesied—Zechariah 12:10; Matthew 26:2; Mark 8:31.

Darkness fell across land—Matthew 27:45; Luke 23:44.

Jesus betrayed and crucified—Matthew 26:2.

Preach Christ crucified—1 Corinthians 1:23.

Prediction, Christ's disciples scatter—Zechariah 13:7.

Seven sayings from cross—Matthew 27:46; Luke 23:34,43,46; John 19:26-28,30.

With criminals—Matthew 27:38.

See Atonement, Made by Jesus.

Cults

Blinded by Satan—2 Corinthians 4:4.

Deceived by Satan—2 Corinthians 11:14.

Departure from sound doctrine—2 Timothy 4:3,4.

Doctrines of demons—1 Timothy 4:1-3.

False Christs—Matthew 24:4,5,11,24.

False gods—1 John 5:21.

False gospel—Galatians 1:6-8.

False prophets, false teachers—2 Peter 2:1-3.
Scripture twisting—Jeremiah 7:8.

Strange teachings—Hebrews 13:9.
Wandering away from truth—2 Timothy 2:17,18.

D

Dancing

A time to dance—Ecclesiastes 3:4.
David danced before Lord—2 Samuel 6:14.
Herodias' daughter danced—Matthew 14:6.
Miriam led women in dance—Exodus 15:20.
Mourning turns into joyful dancing—Psalm 30:11.
Praise God with dancing—Psalm 149:3; 150:4.

Danger, Protection from

Angel of the Lord encamps around us—Psalm 34:7.
Dwell in secret place of Most High—Psalm 91:1.
Fear no evil—Psalm 23:4.
God is our hiding place—Psalm 32:7.
God's angels watch over us—Psalm 91:11.
Lord delivers us out of trouble—Psalm 34:17-19;
    121:8.
When pass through waters, God will be there—Isaiah
    43:2.

Darkness

Darkness descends on Egypt—Exodus 10:21.
Earth, a formless mass cloaked in darkness—Genesis
    1:2.
God called darkness "night"—Genesis 1:5.
Lord makes the darkness—Isaiah 45:7.
Minds full of darkness—Ephesians 4:18.
No harmony between light and darkness—
    2 Corinthians 6:14,15.
Our hearts were once full of darkness—Ephesians 5:8.

Daughter

Daughters of Jerusalem weep—Luke 23:28.
Do not let daughter become prostitute—Leviticus
    19:29.

Flesh of sons and daughters eaten—Leviticus 26:29; Deuteronomy 28:53.

Given in marriage by parents—1 Samuel 17:25; 18:20,21.

Herodias' daughter performed dance—Matthew 14:6.

Pharaoh's daughter got baby in basket—Exodus 2:5,6.

Sacrifice of sons and daughters—Psalm 106:37.

Sold as concubine—Exodus 21:7-10.

Day

God called the light "day"—Genesis 1:5.

Like a thousand years to the Lord—2 Peter 3:8.

Six days work—Exodus 20:9.

Twelve hours of daylight every day—John 11:9.

Days, Forty

Embalming process for Jacob took 40 days—Genesis 50:3.

Flood prevailed 40 days—Genesis 7:17.

Forty days and Nineveh will be destroyed—Jonah 3:4.

Jesus fasted 40 days—Matthew 4:2.

Moses stayed on mountain 40 days—Exodus 24:18.

Deacon

Oversee temporal affairs of church—Acts 6:3-6.

See Church, Government of; Clergy.

Deaconess

Our sister Phoebe—Romans 16:1.

Dead People

Believers go to be with Lord—Luke 23:43; Philippians 1:23; 2 Corinthians 5:8.

Unbelievers go to a place of suffering—Luke 16:19-31.

Deafness

Lord makes one hear or not hear—Exodus 4:11.

Messiah enables deaf to hear—Matthew 11:2-5.

Spirit of deafness ousted—Mark 9:25.

Treat the deaf with respect—Leviticus 19:14.

Death

After death comes judgment—Hebrews 9:27.

All people die—Job 30:23; Ecclesiastes 7:2.

Breath ceases—Genesis 49:33.

Death of saints precious to Lord—Psalm 116:15.

Death promised for disobedience—Genesis 2:16,17.

Death resulted from sin—Romans 5:12.

Fear not walking through valley of death—Psalm 23:4.

Foolish people do not plan for death—Luke 12:20.

God takes no pleasure in death of wicked—Ezekiel
    18:23; 33:11.

God will do away with death—Isaiah 25:8.

Jesus destroyed death—2 Timothy 1:9,10.

Jesus holds keys of death and Hades—Revelation
    1:18.

Joining one's ancestors—Deuteronomy 31:16.

King of terrors—Job 18:14.

Last enemy to be destroyed—1 Corinthians 15:26.

No more death—Revelation 21:3,4.

No man has power over day of death—Ecclesiastes
    8:8.

Resurrection will defeat death—1 Corinthians
    15:54-56.

Return to the ground—Genesis 3:19.

Some ways seem right but lead to death—Proverbs
    14:12.

Sting of death—1 Corinthians 15:56.

Time to die—Ecclesiastes 3:1,2.

To live is Christ; to die is gain—Philippians 1:21.

Wages of sin is death—Romans 6:23.

We quickly disappear—Job 14:2.

Whether we live or die, we are the Lord's—Romans
    14:8.

D

As Judgment
Ananias and Sapphira—Acts 5:1-10.
Human race—Genesis 6:7.
Saul—1 Chronicles 10:13.
Sodom and Gomorrah—Genesis 19:1-29.

Desired
Growing weary in present bodies—2 Corinthians 5:2.
Job disgusted with life—Job 7:15,16; 10:1.
Jonah yearns for death—Jonah 4:3,8.
Paul would rather be with the Lord—2 Corinthians 5:8;
   Philippians 1:23.
People will long for death during Tribulation—Revelation
   9:6.
Simeon seeks to die in peace—Luke 2:29.

Exemption from
Christians will be raptured—1 Corinthians 15:51;
   1 Thessalonians 4:17.
Elijah taken to heaven—2 Kings 2:1.
Enoch taken to heaven—Genesis 5:24; Hebrews 11:5.
See Rapture.

Intermediate State
Abraham's bosom—Luke 16:19-31.
Away from body; at home with Lord—2 Corinthians 5:8.
Better to depart and be with Christ—Philippians
   1:21,23,24.
In paradise—Luke 23:43.
Souls under God's altar—Revelation 6:9,10.
See Consciousness Following Death.

Of Christ
Appeased God's wrath—1 John 2:2.
Brought reconciliation—2 Corinthians 5:18-21.
Brought redemption—Galatians 3:13.
Paid a ransom for us—1 Timothy 2:6.
See Atonement, Made by Jesus.

D

Of Righteous

Beggar died, carried by angels to Abraham—Luke 16:22.

Better to be away from body—2 Corinthians 5:8.

Blessed are those who die in the Lord—Revelation 14:13.

Dying is better—Philippians 1:21-23.

Entrusting spirit into God's hand—Psalm 31:5.

Falling asleep—John 11:11.

God will snatch us from power of death—Psalm 49:15.

Godly have a refuge when they die—Proverbs 14:32.

Godly often die before their time—Isaiah 57:1.

Godly who die will rest in peace—Isaiah 57:2.

Not all of us will die— 1 Corinthians 15:51.

Our death is precious to God—Psalm 116:15.

Paul knew time of death was near—2 Timothy 4:6.

Peter knew time of death was near—2 Peter 1:14.

Stephen commits spirit to Jesus—Acts 7:59.

When we die, we go to be with the Lord—Romans 14:8.

Will receive an eternal body—2 Corinthians 5:1.

Will rise again—Daniel 12:13.

Wonderful future lies before—Psalm 37:37.

Of Wicked

Disaster strikes like a cyclone—Proverbs 10:25.

Egyptians killed by plague—Psalm 78:50.

God cuts off the godless—Job 27:8.

Ground opened up and swallowed sinners—Numbers 16:30.

Rich man died—Luke 16:22.

Wicked do not anticipate death—Luke 12:20.

Wicked will be destroyed—Proverbs 2:22; Psalm 37:9,10.

Years of the wicked are cut short—Proverbs 10:27.

Preparation for

Be mindful of how brief time is on earth—Psalm 39:4.

D

In life and death, we belong to Lord—Romans 14:8.
Living is for Christ, dying is even better—Philippians
1:21.
Make the most of your time on earth—Psalm 90:12.
Set your affairs in order—2 Kings 20:1.
We look forward to city in heaven—Hebrews 13:14.

Spiritual

Dead in sin—Colossians 2:13.
Once we too were dead—Ephesians 2:1,2.
Sin entered human race through Adam—Romans
5:12,15.

Debt

Creditor seizes all—Psalm 109:11.
Debt canceled—Deuteronomy 15:2; Matthew
18:23-27.
Every seventh year, cancel debts—Deuteronomy 15:1.
No excessive interest—Exodus 22:25.
Pay debts—Deuteronomy 24:14,15; Romans 13:8.
Refusal to go into debt—Genesis 14:22-24.

Decalogue

Tablets of stone with God's commands—Exodus 24:12;
31:18; 32:16.
Ten Commandments—Exodus 34:28; Deuteronomy 4:13.

Deceit/Deception

Ananias and Sapphira tried to deceive—Acts 5:1-10.
Antichrist uses wicked deception—2 Thessalonians 2:10.
Do not be deceived—Colossians 2:4.
Eve was deceived—2 Corinthians 11:3.
False apostles deceive—2 Corinthians 11:13.
False witness is a traitor—Proverbs 14:25.
False witness tells lies—Proverbs 12:17.
Human heart is most deceitful—Jeremiah 17:9.
Joseph deceived brothers—Genesis 42–44.
Keep lips from telling lies—1 Peter 3:10.

74

Lord detests deceivers—Psalm 5:6.
Many deceivers in the world—2 John 1:7.
Pharisees try to deceive—Matthew 22:16.
Satan deceives—Genesis 3:4.

D

Decisions, Guiding Principles of

Ask for God's wisdom—1 Samuel 14:36-41; James 1:5.
Do all for God's glory—1 Corinthians 10:31.
Do all in name of Jesus—Colossians 3:17.
Do not follow worthless pursuits—Proverbs 28:19.
Many counselors bring success—Proverbs 15:22.
Read Word of God—Psalm 119:105.
With many counselors, there is safety—Proverbs 11:14; 12:15.
Work as if serving Lord—Colossians 3:23.

Defense, Spiritual

See Armor, Spiritual.

Deity

See Holy Spirit, Deity of.
See Jesus Christ, Deity of.

Demons

Authority of disciples over—Matthew 10:1.
Believers cast out—Mark 16:17.
Can inflict physical pain—2 Corinthians 12:7.
Destiny is Lake of Fire—Matthew 25:41.
Doctrines of—1 Timothy 4:1-3.
Evil spirits—Luke 10:19,20.
Fallen angels—Matthew 12:24-28.
Fled when Jesus commanded—Matthew 8:16.
In blind and mute man—Matthew 9:32,33; 12:22; Luke 11:14.
In land of the Gadarenes—Matthew 8:28.
In mute boy—Mark 9:17,18.

D

Jesus casts out—Matthew 4:24.

Lying spirits—1 Timothy 4:1.

Many can be present in one person—Luke 8:30.

Sacrifices to—Deuteronomy 32:17; Psalm 106:37;
1 Corinthians 10:20.

Scream as they leave victims—Acts 8:7.

Some are presently confined—2 Peter 2:4.

Some committed unnatural sin—Genesis 6:2-4.

Some did not keep their first estate—Jude 6.

Tormenting spirit—1 Samuel 16:14; 18:10; 19:9.

Worship of—Revelation 9:20.

See Exorcism; Satan.

Dentistry

See Teeth.

Dependability

Faithful in small matters—Luke 16:10.

Faithful to the end—Hebrews 3:14.

Remain faithful—2 Timothy 3:14.

Stand true to what you believe—1 Corinthians 16:13.

Stay true to the Lord—Philippians 1:27.

See Faithful, Choose to Remain; Integrity.

Depravity of Man

All have sinned—Romans 3:23.

Born a sinner—Psalm 51:5.

Earth became corrupt—Genesis 6:11.

From human heart comes evil—Mark 7:21.

Hearts full of darkness—Ephesians 5:8.

Human heart is most deceitful—Jeremiah 17:9.

Lord observes people's wickedness—Genesis 6:5.

Not a single person who never sins—Ecclesiastes 7:20.

Sinful nature loves to do evil—Galatians 5:17.

See Sin.

Depression

Broken heart—Psalm 34:18; Proverbs 17:22.
Can result from failure to confess—Psalm 32:3,4.
Can result from guilt—Genesis 4:6,7.
God is with you through deep waters—2 Samuel 22:17; Isaiah 43:2.
God of all comfort helps us—2 Corinthians 1:3,7.
Take courage—James 5:8.
Trust God in times of trouble—Psalm 50:15.
We are pressed, but not crushed—2 Corinthians 4:8.

Desire

Avoid shameful desires—Colossians 3:5; 1 Peter 2:8,10,11.
Captive to desires—2 Timothy 3:6.
Desire for God—Psalm 73:25; Isaiah 26:9.
Desire for things of world—1 John 2:15,16.
Desires are known to God—Psalm 38:9.
Do not chase evil desires—1 Peter 4:2,3.
God fulfills desires of those who fear Him—Psalm 145:10.
Paul desired to depart and be with Christ—Philippians 1:23.
Stubbornly follow evil desires—Jeremiah 16:12.
Thirst for God—Psalm 42:1,2; 63:1; 143:6; Amos 8:11.

Despondency

Hope deferred makes heart sick—Proverbs 13:12.
People will beg mountains to fall on them—Luke 23:30.
People will seek death but not find it—Revelation 9:6.
We are as good as dead—Numbers 17:12.
See Anxiety; Discouragement, Overcoming.

Devil

See Satan.

D

Devotions

All-night prayer—1 Samuel 15:11; Psalm 55:17; 119:62; Luke 6:12.

David's devotions—Psalm 57:8.

Hezekiah's devotions—2 Chronicles 29:20.

Jesus' devotions—Mark 1:35.

Job's devotions—Job 1:5.

New strength every morning—Isaiah 33:2.

Pray day and night—Luke 2:37; 1 Thessalonians 3:10.

Pray privately—Matthew 6:5,6.

Prayer in the morning—Psalm 5:3; 119:147.

Samuel's parents—1 Samuel 1:19.

Devout

Blameless—Job 1:1.

Do all for glory of God—1 Corinthians 10:31.

Do not look back—Luke 9:62.

Honor God with body—1 Corinthians 6:20.

Live and die to the Lord—Romans 14:8; Philippians 1:20.

Live to please God—1 Thessalonians 4:1.

Live worthy of God—1 Thessalonians 2:12.

Living sacrifice—Romans 12:1.

Love Lord with whole heart—Luke 10:27.

No halfhearted commitment—Matthew 6:24.

Offer yourselves to God—Romans 6:13.

Sacrifice everything—Luke 14:33.

Serve God in holiness—Luke 1:74,75.

Treasure God's words—Job 23:12.

Dichotomy View of Man

See Man, Dichotomy View of.

Diet

Body is temple of Holy Spirit—1 Corinthians 6:19.

Do not eat blood—Deuteronomy 12:16; 15:23.

78

Do not eat unclean animals—Leviticus 11:26,27,29;
Deuteronomy 14:3.
Do not make stomach a god—Philippians 3:19.
Eat, drink, and be merry—Ecclesiastes 5:18;
1 Corinthians 15:32.
Fish for food—Genesis 9:3; Leviticus 11:9;
Deuteronomy 14:9.
Grasses and other green plants—Genesis 1:30.
Locusts—Matthew 3:4.
Meat for food—Genesis 9:3.
Never eat fat—Leviticus 7:23.
Restraint in eating—Proverbs 23:2,20,21; 25:16;
Philippians 3:19.
Seed-bearing plants—Genesis 1:29.
Subdue the body—1 Corinthians 9:27.
Vegetarian and nonvegetarian—Romans 14:2.

Difficulties, Enduring

See Endurance.

Diligence

Be persistent in preaching—2 Timothy 4:2.
Be strong and steady—1 Corinthians 15:58.
Diligently obey commands of Lord—Deuteronomy
6:17; 11:13.
Do not tire of doing good—Galatians 6:9.
Guard your heart, for it affects everything—Proverbs
4:23.
Never forget what Lord has done for you—
Deuteronomy 4:9.
Strain to reach end of race—Philippians 3:14.
Whatever you do, do well—Ecclesiastes 9:10.

Diplomacy

David sends Hushai to Absalom's court—2 Samuel
15:32-37.
Diplomatic witness—1 Corinthians 9:20.

Paul's circumcision of Timothy—Acts 16:3.
Solomon's alliance with Hiram—1 Kings 5:1-12;
9:10-14.

D Disagreement

Avoid disputes—Proverbs 17:14.
Settle disputes—1 Corinthians 6:1-7.
Stay away from arguing—Philippians 2:14.
Stay free from controversy—1 Timothy 2:8.
Stop arguing—1 Corinthians 1:10.

Disappointment

Cast burdens on Lord—Psalm 55:22.
Hope in God—Psalm 43:5.
Let not your heart be troubled—John 14:27.
We are troubled but not distressed—2 Corinthians 4:8,9.
See Discouragement, Overcoming.

Discernment

Discerning of spirits—1 John 4:1-6; Revelation 2:2.
Importance of discernment—Job 12:11.
Lack of discernment—Psalm 82:5; 92:6; Romans 3:11;
Hebrews 5:11.
Messiah has discernment—Isaiah 11:3,4.
Prayer for discerning heart—1 Kings 3:9; Psalm 119:125.
Spiritual man discerns—1 Corinthians 2:14-16.
Word of God helps us discern—Acts 17:11; Hebrews 5:14.

Disciples and Discipleship

Be servant of everyone—1 Corinthians 9:19.
Bear fruit—John 15:8.
Disciples invited—Matthew 9:9; Mark 1:16,17.
Do not lose race—Philippians 2:16.
Influence world as salt—Matthew 5:13.
Jesus must be above family—Luke 14:26.
Leave all for Jesus—Luke 14:33.
Listen to Jesus—John 10:27.

Love God with whole heart—Deuteronomy 6:5; Mark 12:30.

Make disciples—Matthew 28:18-20.

Potential disciple's excuse—Matthew 8:21; Luke 9:59.

Resist devil—James 4:7.

Run so that you will win—1 Corinthians 9:24.

Self-denial—Matthew 16:24.

Steadfast in commitment—John 8:31.

D

Discipline from God

Blessed are those God corrects—Job 5:17; Psalm 94:12.

Do not ignore it when Lord disciplines you—Proverbs 3:11,12; Hebrews 12:5.

God disciplines people with sickness and pain—Job 33:19.

God disciplines those He loves—Proverbs 3:12; Revelation 3:19.

Lord can discipline severely—Psalm 118:18; Jeremiah 31:18.

Lord disciplines because we need it—Psalm 119:75.

See Children, Discipline of; Self-Control.

Discouragement, Overcoming

Be of good cheer, Christ has overcome world—John 16:33.

Be of good courage—Joshua 1:9.

Go boldly to throne of grace—Hebrews 4:16.

Have confidence in prayer requests—1 John 5:14.

Let not your heart be troubled—John 14:27.

Wait on the Lord—Psalm 27:14.

Disease

Bleeding—Matthew 9:20.

Blindness—Matthew 9:27.

Caused by evil spirit—Luke 13:10-16.

Caused by Satan—Job 2:6,7.

Caused by sin—Leviticus 26:14-16; John 5:14.

Deafness—Mark 7:32.

Disobedience brings fever and disease—Deuteronomy 28:21,22.

Divine discipline—Psalm 51:8.

Dumbness (mute)—Matthew 9:32.

Epaphroditus was sick near death—Philippians 2:25-27.

Famine and disease—Jeremiah 29:17; Ezekiel 5:17.

Fever—Matthew 8:14.

God can prevent—Exodus 15:26.

God heals our diseases—Psalm 103:3.

Hope deferred makes heart sick—Proverbs 13:12.

Intestinal disease—2 Chronicles 21:15.

Invalid—John 5:3-9.

Jesus heals—Matthew 4:23,24; 14:14; Luke 4:40.

Job's bones burn with fever—Job 30:30.

Leprosy—Leviticus 13:2.

Peter's mother-in-law—Matthew 8:14.

Plagues that destroy—Leviticus 26:25.

Prayer of faith shall save the sick—James 5:15,16.

Sick people need a doctor—Matthew 9:12; Mark 2:17.

Suffering illness has some value—James 1:2-4,12; 1 Peter 1:6,7.

Wasting diseases—Leviticus 26:16.

See Health; Medicine.

Disgrace

See Shame.

Dishonesty

Do not cheat anyone—Leviticus 19:13.

Do not use dishonest standards—Leviticus 19:35.

Lord despises double standards—Proverbs 20:10.

Lord hates cheating—Proverbs 11:1.

Never cheat Christian brother—1 Thessalonians 4:6.

Wicked borrow and never repay—Psalm 37:21.

See Falsehood; Honesty; Liars/Lies; Perjury.

Dishonor
See Disrespect.

Disloyal
See Unfaithfulness.

Disobedience
Adam and Eve warned—Genesis 2:17.
Brings fever and disease—Deuteronomy 28:22.
Brings punishment—Isaiah 42:24,25.
Death promised—Genesis 2:16,17.
Disobey, be least in kingdom—Matthew 5:19.
Disobey, God withholds blessing—Deuteronomy
    11:17; 1 Kings 8:35,36.
God angry at—1 Samuel 28:18; Ephesians 5:6.
Unintentional disobedience—Numbers 15:22.
Warnings against—Deuteronomy 28:15-68; 1 Samuel
    12:15; Jeremiah 12:17.
See Apostasy; Backsliding; Obedience; Rebellion.

Disrespect
For age—Job 30:1.
For God—Malachi 1:6.
For other people—Luke 18:2.
For parents—Proverbs 30:17.
See Respect.

Divination
See Occultism.

Divorce
Bound together until death separates—Romans 7:1-3.
God hates divorce—Malachi 2:16.
God permitted because of men's hard hearts—
    Matthew 19:7,8.
Marital unfaithfulness and divorce—Matthew 5:31,32.
Mosaic law, bill of divorcement—Deuteronomy 24:1-4.

Paul's instruction on divorce—1 Corinthians 7:10-13.
Reconciliation the better way—Romans 12:18.
See Marriage.

D Doctor

See Physician.

Doctrine

Be nourished by—1 Timothy 4:6.
Bereans tested Paul's teaching from Scripture—Acts 17:11.
Beware deceptive philosophy—Colossians 2:8.
Correctly explain the Word—2 Timothy 2:15.
Do not be carried away by strange teachings—Hebrews 13:9.
Do not distort Word of God—2 Corinthians 4:2.
Do not forsake teaching—Proverbs 4:2.
Do not tolerate false teachers—2 John 10.
Doctrinal disagreement—1 Corinthians 1:10-17.
Doctrine of Pharisees—Matthew 16:11; Luke 6:1-11.
Doctrines of demons—1 Timothy 4:1-3.
Encourage by sound doctrine; refute opposers—Titus 1:9.
False teachers deceive—Matthew 24:5.
Hold steadfastly—2 Timothy 1:13.
Preach the Word—Mark 16:15,16; 1 Timothy 4:2,13.
Spiritual milk (basic doctrine)—1 Corinthians 3:2; Hebrews 5:12.
Teach doctrine—1 Timothy 4:6.
Teach sound doctrine—Titus 2:1.

False

Another gospel—Galatians 1:6-8.
Different Jesus, different Spirit, different gospel—2 Corinthians 11:4.
Do not be attracted by strange ideas—Hebrews 13:9.
Do not be deceived—Colossians 2:4.
Do not be led astray—Colossians 2:8.

84

Doctrines of demons—1 Timothy 4:1.
Eve was deceived—2 Corinthians 11:3.
False prophets—2 Peter 2:1.
False teachers—1 Timothy 6:3.
Guard what God has entrusted to you—1 Timothy
6:20.
Many deceivers in the world—2 John 7.
Some have wandered from the faith—1 Timothy 6:21.
Spirit of the Antichrist—1 John 4:3.
Turned away from the truth—Titus 3:10,11.
See Heresy.

Doer of the Word

Be doer, not just a hearer—James 1:22.
Blessed are those who hear and obey—Matthew 12:50.
Not all who sound religious are godly—Matthew 7:21.

Dominion of Man

See Man, Dominion of.

Doubt

Doubting Thomas—John 20:25-29.
Even small faith brings big miracles—Matthew 17:20.
O you of little faith—Matthew 6:30; 8:25,26; 14:31;
16:8.
When in doubt, gain strength from God—Psalm 42:5;
Isaiah 40:27-31.
See Unbelief.

Dove

Be harmless as doves—Matthew 10:16.
Selling doves in temple—Matthew 21:12.
Spirit descended on Jesus as dove—Matthew 3:16;
Luke 3:22; John 1:32.

Dress

Adam and Eve ashamed at nakedness—Genesis 3:7.

D

Do not be concerned about outward beauty—1 Peter 3:3.
God made clothing from animal skins—Genesis 3:21.
Man must not wear women's clothing—Deuteronomy 22:5.
Woman must not wear men's clothing—Deuteronomy 22:5.

Drunkenness

See Intoxication.

Duties of Christian Servants

Announce Kingdom of Heaven—Matthew 10:7.
Avoid love of money—1 Timothy 6:10.
Be a servant—Mark 10:43.
Be an example to believers—1 Timothy 4:12.
Be Christ's ambassadors—2 Corinthians 5:20.
Be shrewd as snakes and innocent as doves—Matthew 10:16.
Equip God's people—Ephesians 4:11,12.
Fan into a flame your spiritual gift—2 Timothy 1:6.
Go and make disciples—Matthew 28:19,20.
Keep your conscience clear—1 Timothy 1:19.
Please God, not people—1 Thessalonians 2:4.
Pray, preach, and teach—Acts 6:4; Ephesians 6:20; 2 Timothy 4:2.
Take God's message everywhere—Acts 22:15.
Train yourself for spiritual fitness—1 Timothy 4:7.

Duty of Man to God

Fear God, do His will, worship Him—Deuteronomy 10:12.
Love God completely—Deuteronomy 6:5.
Obey God's commands—Joshua 22:5.
Walk humbly with God—Micah 6:8.
See Consecration.

E

Early Riser

See Rising, Early.

Earnest

Holy Spirit as guarantee of future— 2 Corinthians
1:22; 5:5; Ephesians 1:13,14.

Earth

Earth is the Lord's—1 Samuel 2:8.
God created heavens and earth—Isaiah 45:18.
God gave earth to man—Psalm 115:16.
God placed world on its foundation—Psalm 104:5.
God's footstool—Isaiah 66:1.
Ground of earth cursed—Genesis 3:17.
New heavens and a new earth—Isaiah 65:17;
Revelation 21:1.

Destruction of

Earth and sky fled from God's presence—Revelation
20:11.
Earth staggers like a drunkard—Isaiah 24:20.
Earth will wear out like piece of clothing—Isaiah 51:6.
End of the world—Matthew 24:3,14.
Heaven and earth will disappear—Matthew 24:35;
Revelation 21:1.

Earthquakes

Earthquake, prisoners freed—Acts 16:26.
Earthquake, stone rolled away from Christ's tomb—
Matthew 28:2.
Earthquakes in many parts of the world—Matthew
24:7; Mark 13:8.
Greatest earthquake in human history—Revelation
16:18.
Mount of Olives will split apart—Zechariah 14:4.
Mount Sinai—Exodus 19:18; Hebrews 12:26.
Sixth seal judgment—Revelation 6:12.

E

Easter

Christ's resurrection, part of gospel—1 Corinthians 15:1-3.

Father raised Jesus—Acts 13:30.

First to rise from the dead—Colossians 1:18; Revelation 1:5.

Flesh and bones body—Luke 24:39.

He is risen—Matthew 28:6,7; Mark 16:6; Luke 24:1-12.

If Christ not raised, our faith is in vain—1 Corinthians 15:17,20.

Jesus raised Himself—John 2:19-22.

See Resurrection.

Eclipse

Darkness will cover you—Micah 3:6.

Heavens veiled, stars darkened—Ezekiel 32:7,8.

No light from stars or sun or moon—Isaiah 13:10; Joel 2:10; 3:15.

Sun will be darkened—Joel 2:31; Matthew 24:29; Mark 13:24; Acts 2:20.

Ecological Concerns

Adam and Eve cultivated Garden of Eden—Genesis 2:8,15; 3:23.

Barren land—Deuteronomy 29:23.

Bitter water—Exodus 15:23-25.

Do not destroy trees—Deuteronomy 20:19,20.

Earth defiled—Isaiah 24:5.

Earth will wear out—Isaiah 51:6.

Fields ruined—2 Kings 3:19.

Forest destroyed—Isaiah 10:18; James 3:5.

God has given earth to man—Psalm 115:16.

Land cries out—Job 31:38.

Muddied spring, polluted well—Proverbs 25:26.

New heavens and a new earth—Isaiah 65:17;
Revelation 21:1.
See Earth; Nature, World of.

Eden

Cherubim guards—Genesis 3:24.
Garden in Eden—Genesis 2:8.
God banished Adam and Eve from—Genesis 3:23.
Lucifer was in Eden—Ezekiel 28:12,13.

E

Education

Holy Spirit is our teacher—John 14:26.
Knowledge can make one prideful—1 Corinthians 8:1.
Knowledge is better than wealth—Ecclesiastes 7:12.
Learn from personal experience—Psalm 78:1-8.
Learn from the ants—Proverbs 6:6.
Listen to what parents teach—Proverbs 1:8; 6:20;
23:22.
Paul educated under Gamaliel—Acts 22:3.
Pray for God to give wisdom—James 1:5.
Teach children about God—Deuteronomy 4:10; 11:19.
See Teaching.

Ego

See Pride.

Elders of Church

See Church, Government of; Clergy.

Election

Chosen in Christ—Ephesians 1:4.
Elect are still responsible to believe—Acts 13:48;
Romans 10:12-14; Ephesians 2:8,9.
Encompasses past through future—Romans 8:29,30.
Father draws people to Christ—John 6:44.
Father gave believers to Christ—John 6:37; 17:2,6.
Glorifies God—Ephesians 1:12.

God chose you—Deuteronomy 7:6; 2 Thessalonians 2:13.
God's plan stands firm—Isaiah 14:26,27.
Is from all eternity—Ephesians 1:4; 2 Timothy 1:9.
Jeremiah called before birth—Jeremiah 1:5.
Originates in free choice of God—Ephesians 1:5,6.
Paul called before birth—Galatians 1:15; Acts 9:15.

E

Eloquence

Apollos possessed—Acts 18:24,25.
Lord guides speech—Matthew 10:19,20.
Moses lacked—Exodus 4:10.
Paul lacked—2 Corinthians 10:10.

Embalming

Burial spices purchased for Jesus—Mark 16:1.
Jacob embalmed—Genesis 50:2,3.
Jesus' body wrapped in cloth—Mark 15:46.
Joseph embalmed—Genesis 50:26.
See Burial; Funeral.

Embarrassment

See Shame.

Embezzlement

Be honest in financial dealings—Deuteronomy
    25:13-16; 1 Timothy 3:8.
Danger of greed—1 Peter 5:2,3.
Dishonest manager—Luke 16:1-15.
Dishonest money dwindles away—Proverbs 13:11.
Gold a snare—Judges 8:24-27.
See Dishonesty; Falsehood.

Emotion

Angels have emotions—Luke 2:13.
Anger causes quarrels—Proverbs 30:33.
Anger is the friend of fools—Ecclesiastes 7:9.
Avoid angry people—Proverbs 22:24,25.

Be content in any circumstance—Philippians 4:11,12.
Cheerful look brings joy—Proverbs 15:30.
Devil instigates jealousy—James 3:14-16.
Do not bear grudge—Leviticus 19:18.
Do not hate for no reason—Psalm 38:19; 69:4.
God anoints with oil of joy—Psalm 45:7.
Happy are those who fear the Lord—Psalm 112:1.
Happy heart makes face cheerful—Proverbs 15:13.
Holy Spirit has emotion—Ephesians 4:30.
Jealousy is destructive—Proverbs 27:4.
Jealousy kills—Job 5:2.
Love is not easily angered—1 Corinthians 13:5.
Quarreling, jealousy, outbursts of anger—
    2 Corinthians 12:20.
Restrain anger—Proverbs 19:11.
Satan has emotions—Revelation 12:17.
Turn from rage and envy—Psalm 37:8.
Watch out for jealousy—James 4:2.

Empathy

See Compassion.

Employee

Hard workers get rich—Proverbs 10:4.
Parable of the workers in the vineyard—Matthew
    20:1-16.
Those who work deserve their pay—Luke 10:7;
    Romans 4:4; 1 Timothy 5:18.
Those who work deserve to be fed—Matthew 10:10.
Trustworthy employees—Titus 2:9,10.
Work hard and become a leader—Proverbs 12:24.
Work six days—Exodus 23:12; Deuteronomy 5:13.
See Labor.

Employer

Be fair—Job 31:13,14.

Do not cheat employees of wages—Jeremiah 22:13; Malachi 3:5; James 5:4.

Never take advantage of poor laborers—Deuteronomy 24:14,15.

Pay workers promptly—Leviticus 19:13.

Treat employees well—Leviticus 25:43.

E

Encouragement

Angels give encouragement—Acts 27:23,24.

Christians encourage each other—1 Thessalonians 4:18; Hebrews 10:24,25.

Comfort from Jesus—Matthew 14:27.

Encourage prisoners—Hebrews 13:3.

Encourage the timid—1 Thessalonians 5:14.

Encourage young men to live wisely—Titus 2:6.

Exhortation to encourage each other—Philippians 2:1,2; 1 Thessalonians 4:18.

God encourages us—2 Corinthians 7:6.

God's Word encourages us—Psalm 119:28.

Kind words cheer people up—Proverbs 12:25.

Patiently correct, rebuke, and encourage—2 Timothy 4:2.

Speak encouraging words—Ephesians 4:29.

Endurance

Adversity builds endurance—Romans 5:3,4; James 1:3.

Endurance is rewarded—2 Timothy 3:11; James 1:12.

Endure God's chastening—Hebrews 12:7; Revelation 3:19.

Endure suffering—2 Timothy 2:3.

Endure to the end—Matthew 10:22.

God gives rest to the weary—Jeremiah 31:25.

Hope gives endurance—1 Thessalonians 1:3.

Patient endurance—2 Corinthians 1:6; 2 Peter 1:6; Revelation 1:9.

Patiently endure testing—James 1:12.

Patiently endure unfair treatment—1 Peter 2:19.

Run with endurance—Hebrews 12:1.

Enemies

Do not rejoice when enemy falls—Proverbs 24:17,18.
Fall into their own traps—Psalm 57:6.
Feed hungry enemies—Proverbs 25:21,22; Romans 12:20.
Love your enemies—Luke 6:27.
Pray for those who persecute you—Romans 12:14.
See Opposition.

E

Envy

Do not envy evil people—Psalm 37:1; Proverbs 23:17; 24:1.
Do not envy violent people—Proverbs 3:31.
Envy emerges in heart—Mark 7:20-22.
Envy leads to evil—James 3:14-16.
Envy of neighbors harmful—Ecclesiastes 4:4.
Envy rooted in sinful nature—Galatians 5:19-21.
Envy rots bones—Proverbs 14:30.
Love does not envy—1 Corinthians 13:4.
Rid yourself of envy—1 Peter 2:1.
See Jealousy.

Eternal Life

Believers will never perish—John 10:28.
Comes through faith in Christ—John 3:14-16,36; 5:24.
Eternal glory awaits us—2 Corinthians 4:17,18; 5:1.
Eternal life and knowing God—John 17:3.
Eternal life in the Son—1 John 5:11-13,20.
Gift of God—Romans 6:23.
Living water wells up to eternal life—John 4:14.
See Salvation.

Eternal State

Better things await us in eternity—Hebrews 10:34.
Creation eagerly awaits redemption—Romans 8:19-21.
Eternal glory awaits us—2 Corinthians 4:17,18.

In my Father's house are many rooms—John 14:2,3.
Inheritance awaits us—1 Peter 1:3,4.
New heaven and new earth—Revelation 21:1,4.
No more curse, no more night—Revelation 22:3-5.
Our resurrection body lives forever—2 Corinthians 5:1.
We will shine—Daniel 12:3.
See Heaven.

E

Eternality of God

See God, Eternality of.

Eternality of Jesus Christ

See Jesus Christ, Eternality of.

Eternity

Election is from all eternity—Ephesians 1:4; 2 Timothy
1:9.
God inhabits eternity—Isaiah 57:15.
God is from eternity to eternity—Isaiah 43:13.
God put eternity in human heart—Ecclesiastes 3:11.
God's plan is from all eternity—Ephesians 3:11.
Jesus is from eternity past—Micah 5:2.

Ethics

See Morality.

Ethnicity

See Race, Ethnic.

Evangelism

Commanded of Christ's followers—Matthew 28:19,20;
2 Timothy 4:5.
Fishers of men—Luke 5:10.
God gives evangelists to church—Ephesians 4:11.
Gospel message—1 Corinthians 15:1-5.
Lord does not want anyone to perish—2 Peter 3:9.
One lost sheep worthy of finding—Matthew 18:12-14.

One plants, another waters—1 Corinthians 3:6-9.
Pray for harvesters—Luke 10:2.
We are Christ's witnesses—Luke 24:45-49; Acts 1:8.
See Gospel; Missionary Work; Witnesses.

Evil

Avoid Appearance of

Avoid every kind of evil—1 Thessalonians 5:22.
Do not violate another's conscience—Romans 14:1;
1 Corinthians 8:7; 10:28.
Live quiet life—1 Thessalonians 4:11.
Live so others respect you—1 Thessalonians 4:12.

For Good

Betraying a friend—Psalm 7:4.
Repay evil for good—Psalm 35:12; 109:5; Proverbs
17:13.
Seeking to stone Jesus for His miracles—John 10:32.
See Betrayal.

Evolution

Contradicts creation account—Genesis 1–2.
Creation proves a Creator—Psalm 19:1-4; Hebrews
3:4.
Creation was in six days—Exodus 20:11.
Design of universe proves Designer—Romans 1:18-20.
Human morality proves Moral Source—Romans
2:14-16.
Human personhood proves Divine Person—Acts 17:29.
Species distinct—Genesis 1:24,25.
See Creation; Proofs of God's Existence.

Exaltation of Jesus Christ

See Jesus Christ, Exaltation of.

Example

Bad

See Bad Example.

E

Christ Is Our

    Eternal perspective—Hebrews 12:2.

    Forgiving—Colossians 3:13.

    Humility—Philippians 2:5-11.

    Loving—John 13:34; Ephesians 5:2.

    Sacrifice for others—1 John 3:16.

    Self-giving—2 Corinthians 8:9.

    Servanthood—Matthew 20:28; Mark 10:43-45; Luke 22:27.

    Suffering—1 Peter 2:21.

Good

    Be example by doing good deeds—Titus 2:7.

    Be example to all believers—1 Timothy 4:12.

    Imitate apostles and Lord—1 Thessalonians 1:6,7.

    Leaders lead by good example—1 Peter 5:3.

    Prophets, examples of patience—James 5:10.

    See Model.

Heavenly Father Is Our

    Compassion—Luke 6:36.

    Holy—Leviticus 11:44; 19:2.

    Perfect—Matthew 5:48.

Paul as

    Follow Paul's example—1 Corinthians 4:16; 11:1; Philippians 3:17.

Excuses

    A potential disciple's excuse—Matthew 8:21; Luke 9:59.

    Adam's excuse—Genesis 3:12.

    Eve's excuse—Genesis 3:13.

    Moses' excuse—Exodus 4:1,10.

    People are without excuse—Romans 1:20.

Existence of God

    See God, Existence of.

Exorcism

Apostles have authority to cast out demons—Mark 3:14,15.

Believers cast out demons—Mark 16:17.

Demons cast out by Spirit of God—Matthew 12:28.

Jesus cast out demons—Matthew 4:24; Mark 1:34.

See Demons; Satan.

E

Exports

Egyptian chariots—1 Kings 10:29; 2 Chronicles 1:17.

Gold, silver, ivory, wood, and precious jewels—1 Kings 10:11,22.

Grain—Genesis 42:1,2.

Horses—1 Kings 10:28.

Solomon's horses—2 Chronicles 1:16.

Spices, balm, and myrrh—Genesis 37:25.

See Merchant.

Extent of the Atonement

See Atonement, Extent of.

Extortion

Swindlers—1 Corinthians 5:10,11; 6:10.

Tax collector—Luke 18:11.

Fable

Clever stories—2 Peter 1:16.
Myths—1 Timothy 1:4; 2 Timothy 4:4; Titus 1:14.
Old wives' tales—1 Timothy 4:7.

Face

Jesus' face shone like sun—Matthew 17:2; Luke 9:29.
Make your face shine down on us—Psalm 80:3.
Moses' face glowed—Exodus 34:29.
Seraphim's face—Isaiah 6:2.
Wash face—Matthew 6:17.
When fasting—Matthew 6:16.

Failure

Christ's strength made perfect in weakness—
    2 Corinthians 12:9.
Disciples failed to cast out demon—Matthew 17:14-21.
God helps us through failures—Psalm 34:19,20.
New mercies every morning—Lamentations 3:22,23.
Peter sank in the water—Matthew 14:28-31.
Total life failure—1 Corinthians 3:15.

Faith

Blessed are those who trust—Jeremiah 17:7.
Cling tightly to your faith—1 Timothy 1:19.
Do not throw away trust—Hebrews 10:35.
Faith and healing—Matthew 9:22.
Faith brings answered prayer—Matthew 15:28; 21:22.
Faith grows from hearing God's Word—Romans 10:17.
Faith is certainty of what we do not see—Hebrews 11:1.
Faith without works dead—James 2:17,18.
Joy in trusting God—Psalm 40:4.
Justification by faith—Romans 3:28; 5:1,2; Galatians
    2:16.
Live by faith, not sight—2 Corinthians 5:7.

Miracles through faith—Matthew 21:21.

Righteous live by faith—Romans 1:17; Hebrews 10:38.

Small faith yields big results—Luke 17:5,6.

Tests of faith—1 Peter 1:7.

Trust in Lord with whole heart—Proverbs 3:5.

Trust in Lord, not man—Psalm 118:8.

Trusting Lord leads to prosperity—Proverbs 28:25.

Without faith, impossible to please God—Hebrews 11:6.

F

Enjoined

Be strong and courageous—Deuteronomy 31:6; Joshua 10:25; Psalm 27:14.

Do not be afraid, for God is with you—Isaiah 41:10.

Do not worry about everyday life—Matthew 6:25; Luke 12:22.

Faith as small as mustard seed brings results—Luke 17:6.

Give burdens to Lord—Psalm 55:22.

God will be with you—Isaiah 43:2.

Trust God, He will help you—Psalm 37:5.

Trust in God at all times—Psalm 62:8.

Trust in Lord with all your heart—Proverbs 3:5.

Trial of

Faith tested—Psalm 81:7; 1 Peter 1:7.

Patiently endure testing—James 1:12.

When faith is tested, endurance grows—James 1:3.

Faithful, Choose to Remain

Always be faithful—Proverbs 3:3.

Be a faithful servant—Matthew 25:23.

Be faithful in prayer—Romans 12:12.

Choose today whom you will serve—Joshua 24:15.

Faithful in small matters—Luke 16:10.

Fruit of the spirit and faithfulness—Galatians 5:22.

God preserves the faithful—Psalm 31:23.

Hold tightly to hope—Hebrews 10:23.

Keep grip on everything taught you—2 Thessalonians 2:15.

Let us cling to Him—Hebrews 4:14.

Listen carefully to the truth we have heard—Hebrews 2:1.

Lord does not forsake the faithful—Psalm 37:28.

Lord guards the faithful—Psalm 97:10.

Remain faithful even in face of death—Revelation 2:10.

Stand true to what you believe—1 Corinthians 16:13.

Stay true to the Lord—Philippians 1:27.

You must remain faithful—2 Timothy 3:14.

F

Faithfulness, God's

See God, Faithfulness of.

Fall of Man

Adam and Eve warned not to disobey—Genesis 2:17.

Adam's sin brought condemnation—Romans 5:18-21.

Each of us has gone astray—Isaiah 53:6.

Each turned to follow downward path—Ecclesiastes 7:29.

Eve deceived—2 Corinthians 11:3.

In Adam all die—1 Corinthians 15:22.

Sin entered entire human race—Romans 5:12.

False Apostles

See Apostles, False.

False Christs

Many will arise—Matthew 24:5-26; Mark 13:6-22; Luke 21:8.

See Apostles, False.

False Confidence

Confidence in powerful people—Psalm 146:3.

Do not trust in bow—Psalm 44:6.

Do not trust own understanding—Proverbs 3:5.

Nations boast of their armies—Psalm 20:7; Isaiah 31:1.

Peter's self-confidence—Matthew 26:35.

Trust in mere humans—Isaiah 2:22; Jeremiah 17:5; Psalm 118:8.

Trust in oneself—Proverbs 28:26.

Trust in wealth—Psalm 49:5,6; Proverbs 11:28; Jeremiah 48:7.

False Witness

F

Corrupt witness—Proverbs 19:28.

Do not lie—Leviticus 19:11.

Do not pass along false reports—Exodus 23:1.

Do not testify falsely—Exodus 20:16; Deuteronomy 5:20.

From the heart comes lying—Matthew 15:19.

Speaks lies—Proverbs 14:5.

Will not go unpunished—Proverbs 19:9; 21:28.

Falsehood

Abhor falsehood—Psalm 119:163.

Constant liars—Proverbs 6:12-14.

Corrupt speech—Proverbs 2:12.

Evil words—Proverbs 11:9.

Expert at telling lies—Psalm 52:2; Proverbs 12:17.

Father of lies is devil—John 8:44.

Keep lips from telling lies—Psalm 34:13; Colossians 3:9.

Lord hates liars—Proverbs 12:22.

Lying tongue hates its victims—Proverbs 26:28.

Mouths full of lies—Psalm 50:19; 144:8,11.

Put away all falsehood—Ephesians 4:25.

See Liars/Lies.

Family

Adopted into God's family—Romans 8:15.

Family instituted—Genesis 2:23,24.

Family may betray you—Matthew 10:21; Mark 13:12; Luke 21:16,17.

Family quarrels—Genesis 21:10; Proverbs 18:19; 19:13; 21:9; 27:15.

Jesus must be above family—Luke 14:26.

Jesus' true family—Matthew 12:48,49; Luke 8:21.

Provide for family—1 Timothy 5:8.

See Daughter; Father; Husband; Parents; Son; Wife.

F

Famine

Barns and granaries empty—Joel 1:16,17.

Death by famine—Jeremiah 14:15.

Famine and disease—Ezekiel 5:17; Luke 21:11.

Famines and earthquakes—Matthew 24:7.

God rescues in times of famine—Psalm 33:18,19.

Plant a lot, but harvest little—Deuteronomy 28:38.

War, famine, and disease—Jeremiah 29:17.

See Hunger; Thirst.

Farming

See Agriculture.

Fasting

David's fast—2 Samuel 3:35.

Do not make a show of it—Matthew 6:16.

Fasting and confession of sin—1 Samuel 7:6.

Jesus fasted, then tempted—Matthew 4:2,3.

Moses fasted 40 days—Exodus 34:28.

See Self-Denial.

Fat (Overweight)

Gluttony—Proverbs 23:2.

Gorging—Proverbs 23:20,21.

Overeating—Proverbs 25:16.

Stomach is a god—Philippians 3:19.

Take care of body—1 Corinthians 6:19,20.

See Gluttony.

Father

Authority of father—Numbers 30:3-5.

Do not address anyone on earth as father—Matthew 23:9.

Even if father forsakes you, God will not—Psalm 27:10.

Exemplary fathers—Genesis 17:18,20; 35:1-5; 2 Samuel 12:15,16; 1 Chronicles 29:19.

Fatherly discipline—Proverbs 3:11,12.

Father-son rivalry—2 Samuel 15.

Good children bring joy to father—Proverbs 23:24.

Honor father, live long—Exodus 20:12.

Influence of good father—Proverbs 20:7.

Pagan father sacrifices son in fire—2 Kings 16:3.

Son listen to father—Proverbs 1:8; 13:1.

Striking father—Exodus 21:15.

See Daughter; Parents; Son.

Heavenly

Author of divine plan (decree)—Psalm 2:7-9.

Author of election—Ephesians 1:5,6.

Cares for the redeemed—Matthew 7:11.

Disciplines Christians who do not repent—Hebrews 12:9,10.

Gave us the Holy Spirit as a gift—John 14:16.

Has a set purpose—Acts 2:23.

Is the Father of all people—Acts 17:29.

Is the Father of believers—Galatians 4:6.

Is the Father of Jesus—Matthew 3:17.

Keeps us secure in salvation—John 10:29.

Sent Jesus into the world—John 5:36.

Relation to Jesus Christ

See Jesus Christ, Relation to Father.

Fatherhood of God

See God, Fatherhood of.

F

Favoritism, Examples of

Asher, favored son—Deuteronomy 33:24.
Elkanah's partiality—1 Samuel 1:4,5.
Israel (Jacob) loved Joseph more—Genesis 37:3,4.
Joseph's partiality—Genesis 43:34.

Fear

Do not be afraid of sudden fear—Proverbs 3:25.
God has not given us spirit of fear—2 Timothy 1:7.
If God is for us, who can be against us?—Romans 8:31.
In God I trust—Psalm 56:11.
Let not your heart be troubled—John 14:27.
There is no fear in love—1 John 4:18.
Whom shall I fear?—Psalm 27:1.
See Anxiety; Worry.

Of the Lord

Always act in the fear of the Lord—2 Chronicles 19:9.
Angel of the Lord guards all who fear him—Psalm 34:7.
Be sure to fear the Lord—1 Samuel 12:24.
Beginning of knowledge—Psalm 111:10; Proverbs 1:7; 9:10.
Do not fear anything except Lord—Isaiah 8:13.
Fear Lord alone—Deuteronomy 13:4.
Fear Lord and obey commands—Deuteronomy 5:29; Ecclesiastes 12:13.
Fear Lord and serve Him—Deuteronomy 6:13.
Fear Lord as long as you live—Deuteronomy 6:2.
Fear the Lord and turn back on evil—Proverbs 3:7; 16:6.
Gives life, security, and protection—Proverbs 19:23.
God accepts those who fear Him—Acts 10:34,35.
God blesses those who fear Him—Psalm 115:13.
God fulfills desires of those who fear Him—Psalm 145:19.
God's mercy goes out to those who fear Him—Luke 1:50.
Happy are those who fear the Lord—Psalm 112:1.
Is true wisdom—Job 28:28; Proverbs 15:33.

Leads to riches, honor, and long life—Proverbs 10:27; 22:4.

Feelings

See Emotion.

Fellowship

Holy Spirit

Fellowship with Holy Spirit—2 Corinthians 13:14.
Holy Spirit (Comforter) helps us—John 14:16-18.
Holy Spirit our advocate—John 14:16.
Joy from the Holy Spirit—Romans 14:17; 1 Thessalonians 1:6.
Necessity of relationship with Holy Spirit—Galatians 5:22,23.
Spirit of God lives in you—Romans 8:9; 1 Corinthians 3:16; 2 Timothy 1:14.
See Holy Spirit.

Of Righteous

Agree wholeheartedly—Philippians 2:2.
Be knit together by ties of love—Colossians 2:2.
Be of one mind—1 Corinthians 1:10; 1 Peter 3:8.
Build up brothers—Luke 22:32.
Can two walk together without agreeing?—Amos 3:3.
Confess sins to each other—James 5:16.
Encourage each other—1 Thessalonians 4:18; 5:11; Hebrews 10:24.
Fellowship with those who fear Lord—Psalm 119:63.
Love each other—John 13:34; Hebrews 13:1; 1 John 4:7.
Meet together constantly—Acts 2:44.
Warn each other—Hebrews 3:13.

With Christ

Christ is among you—2 Corinthians 13:5.
Christ is the true vine—John 15:1.
Christ lives in you—Romans 8:10; Colossians 1:27.

F

Christ welcomes those who welcome children—Mark 9:37.

Fellowship with Son—1 Corinthians 1:9; 1 John 2:24,28; 2 John 1:9.

Jesus' true family—Matthew 12:48,49; Luke 8:21.

Joined to the Lord—1 Corinthians 6:17.

We are Christ's body—Romans 12:5; 1 Corinthians 12:27; Ephesians 5:30.

Where two or three gather together—Matthew 18:20.

With God

Enoch, close fellowship with God—Genesis 5:22,24.

God's home will be among His people—Revelation 21:3.

Noah, close relationship with God—Genesis 6:9.

Requires obedience to God's commands—1 John 3:24.

Those who love Jesus are loved by Father—John 14:23.

With Wicked

Avoid divisive people—Romans 16:17.

Bad company corrupts good character—1 Corinthians 15:33.

Do not assist a thief—Proverbs 29:24.

Do not associate with those who indulge in sexual sin—1 Corinthians 5:9.

Do not be trapped by bad example—Deuteronomy 12:30.

Do not do as the wicked do—Proverbs 4:14,15.

Do not fellowship with sinners—1 Corinthians 5:11.

Do not spend time with liars—Psalm 26:4.

Do not team up with unbelievers—2 Corinthians 6:14.

Evil people will be a snare for you—Joshua 23:13.

God hates gatherings of those who do evil—Psalm 26:5.

Make no treaties with evil people—Deuteronomy 7:2.

Separate from pagans—Ezra 10:11.

Stay away from evil people—Numbers 16:26; Proverbs 1:10.

Stay away from fools—Proverbs 14:7.

Stay away from idle—2 Thessalonians 3:6.

See Company, Evil.

F

Fever

Disobedience brings fever and disease—Leviticus 26:15,16; Deuteronomy 28:22.

Job's bones burn with fever—Job 30:30.

Peter's mother-in-law—Matthew 8:14.

See Disease.

Fight of Faith

Fight the good fight—1 Timothy 6:12.

Paul fought good fight—2 Timothy 4:7.

See Faith, Enjoined.

Finance

Bad financial planning—Luke 12:16-21; 14:28-30; 19:20,21.

Be honest in financial dealings—Deuteronomy 25:13-16; Proverbs 11:1.

Do not build up treasure on earth—Matthew 6:19-21.

Do not owe anyone anything—Romans 13:8.

Generosity brings blessing—Proverbs 22:9; Malachi 3:10; 2 Corinthians 9:7-10.

Give money to the poor—Matthew 19:21; 1 John 3:17.

Good financial planning—Genesis 41:34-36; Ecclesiastes 11:2; Luke 19:23; 1 Corinthians 16:2; 2 Corinthians 9:4,5.

Paul earned a living—1 Thessalonians 2:9; 2 Thessalonians 3:6-10.

Provide for family—1 Timothy 5:8.

Share money generously—Romans 12:8.

Tithing—Malachi 3:8-10.

Trust God, not money—1 Timothy 6:17.

Trust in money and down you go—Proverbs 11:28.

Use money for good—1 Timothy 6:18.

Watch out for love of money—1 Timothy 6:10.

We are stewards of what God gives us—Luke 16:1-13.

Fire

Baptism of fire—Matthew 3:11.
Burning bush—Exodus 3:2.
Eternal fire prepared for devil—Matthew 25:41.
Fire from heaven—Revelation 20:9.
God is a devouring fire—Deuteronomy 4:24.
God's word burns in Jeremiah's heart like fire—Jeremiah 20:9.
Human sacrifice in fire—2 Kings 16:3; 17:17.
Lake of fire—Revelation 21:8.
Lord descended on Mount Sinai in fire—Exodus 19:18.
Pillar of fire—Exodus 13:21,22.
Tongues of fire—Acts 2:3.

Firstborn

Christ as firstborn—Colossians 1:15.
Dedicate firstborn to God—Exodus 13:2,12,13,15; 34:19; Numbers 8:17.
Firstborn from the dead—Revelation 1:5.
Firstborn sons in Egypt will die—Exodus 11:5; 12:12,29.
Redemption of firstborn—Exodus 22:29,30.

Fish

Coin in fish's mouth—Matthew 17:27.
For food—Genesis 9:3; Leviticus 11:9; Deuteronomy 14:9.
God created fish—Genesis 1:20.
Jesus' miracle of a big catch—Luke 5:4-6.
Jonah and great fish—Matthew 12:40.
Man rules over fish—Genesis 9:2.
Two fish feed thousands—Matthew 14:19.

Fishermen

Become fishers of men—Matthew 4:19.
Disciples fishing—John 21:3.

Flattery

Enticed by flattery—Proverbs 7:21.

Flattering lips—Psalm 12:2.
Flattery causes ruin—Proverbs 26:28.
Flattery for favor—Jude 16.
Flattery lays a trap—Proverbs 29:5.
Flattery of an adulterous woman—Proverbs 7:5.
Frankness better than flattery—Proverbs 28:23.
Wicked speech filled with flattery—Psalm 5:9.

Flood

Destroyed all living creatures—Genesis 6:13,17.
God said no more floods—Isaiah 54:9.
Noah told to go into boat—Genesis 7:1.
See Ark, Noah's.

Food

Breakfast—Judges 19:5.
Butter—Deuteronomy 32:14.
Cheese—1 Samuel 17:18.
Do not let stomach become a god—Philippians 3:19.
Do not overeat—Proverbs 23:1-3.
Dried fruit—1 Samuel 25:18.
Evening meal—Genesis 24:25,33.
Feeding 5,000—Matthew 14:15-21.
Fish—Genesis 9:3; Leviticus 11:9; Deuteronomy 14:9;
    Matthew 7:10.
Food eaten by angels—Genesis 19:1-3.
Fruit—Amos 8:2.
Honey—Genesis 43:11.
Locusts—Matthew 3:4.
Manna—Psalm 78:25.
Meat—Genesis 9:3; 1 Kings 4:22,23.
Noon meal—Genesis 43:16; John 4:6,31.
Quail—Numbers 11:32.
Share food with the hungry—Isaiah 58:7,10.
Sweat to produce food—Genesis 3:19.
Thanks given before partaking—Mark 8:6.

Vegetables—Numbers 11:5.

From God

Feast—Psalm 23:5.
For every living thing—Psalm 136:25.
For today—Matthew 6:11.
From God—Genesis 1:29; Job 36:31; Psalm 104:14; 136:25; Matthew 6:26.
From the earth—Psalm 104:14.
Grasses and other green plants—Genesis 1:30.
Seed-bearing plants—Genesis 1:29.

Fool

Constant quarrels—Proverbs 18:6.
Despises wisdom and discipline—Proverbs 1:7.
Does not save money—Proverbs 21:20.
Enjoys doing wrong—Proverbs 10:23.
Gives full vent to anger—Proverbs 29:11.
Ignores Christ's teaching—Matthew 7:26.
Invites trouble—Proverbs 10:14.
Is put to shame—Proverbs 3:35.
Is simple-minded—Proverbs 1:22.
Misuses mouth—Proverbs 18:7.
Quick-tempered—Ecclesiastes 7:9.
Refuses to work—Ecclesiastes 4:5.
Says there is no God—Psalm 14:1; 53:1.
Slanders—Proverbs 10:18.

Foreigners

Be fair to—Deuteronomy 1:16; 27:19; Jeremiah 22:3.
Do not detest—Deuteronomy 23:7.
Do not exploit—Leviticus 19:33.
Do not oppress—Exodus 22:21; 23:9.
Show love—Deuteronomy 10:19.
Treat nicely for Christ's sake—Matthew 25:35.
You were once foreigners yourselves—Leviticus 19:34.

Foreknowledge of God

See God, Foreknowledge of.

Forgetting God

Be careful not to forget Lord—Deuteronomy 6:12.

Do not forget covenant—2 Kings 17:38.

Do not forget God's commands—Psalm 119:16,93,153,176.

Never forget good things God has done—Psalm 103:2.

People forgot about God's power—Psalm 78:42.

People forgot God—Psalm 106:13.

People forgot what God had done—Psalm 78:11.

See Apostasy; Backsliding.

Forgive Others

Forgive and be forgiven—Luke 6:37.

Forgive as you have been forgiven—Ephesians 4:32.

Forgive one another—Matthew 6:12,14; Ephesians 4:32; Colossians 3:13.

Forgive without measure—Matthew 18:21,22.

Forgiveness and prayer—Mark 11:25.

Forgiveness

Of Enemies

Do not repay evil for evil—Romans 12:17,19; 1 Peter 3:9.

If enemy hungry, feed—Proverbs 25:21.

Love your enemy—Matthew 5:43,44; Luke 6:27.

Turn the other cheek—Matthew 5:39.

See Enemies.

Of Sins

Acknowledge your sins to God—Psalm 32:5.

Blessedness of forgiveness—Psalm 32:1.

Confess your sins, God forgives—1 John 1:9.

Forgiveness in Jesus—Ephesians 1:7.

God forgives our iniquities—Psalm 103:3.

God pardons abundantly—Isaiah 55:7.

111

Jesus forgives—Matthew 9:2-6.

Those who confess sins find mercy—Proverbs 28:13.

Though sins as scarlet, shall be white as snow—Isaiah 1:18.

Formalism

Broken spirit much preferred—Psalm 51:17.

Do not honor God with mere lip service—Isaiah 29:13; Matthew 15:8,9.

God does not want sacrifices—Isaiah 1:11; Jeremiah 6:20; Hosea 6:6.

God hates pretense—Amos 5:21.

God will not accept offerings—Malachi 1:10.

Obedience is better than sacrifice—1 Samuel 15:22; 1 Corinthians 7:19.

See Legalism.

Fortunetelling

Do not listen to fortunetellers—Jeremiah 27:9.

Do not practice fortunetelling—Leviticus 19:26; Deuteronomy 18:10,11.

No more fortunetellers—Micah 5:12.

Friendship

Avoid friendship with easily angered people—Proverbs 22:24.

Avoid friendship with world—James 4:4.

Best friends can betray—Psalm 41:9.

Can two walk together if not agreed?—Amos 3:3.

Caution in friendship—Proverbs 12:26.

David and Jonathan, good friends—1 Samuel 20:42.

Do not forsake friend—Proverbs 27:10.

Earnest counsel from friend—Proverbs 27:9.

Friend closer than brother—Proverbs 18:24.

Friend loves at all times—Proverbs 17:17.

Gossip separates friends—Proverbs 16:28.

Jesus, friend of tax collectors—Matthew 11:19.

Lay down life for friends—John 15:13.
Love your neighbor—Matthew 22:39; John 13:35.
The rich have many friends—Proverbs 14:20.
Wounds from a friend—Proverbs 27:6.
You are Christ's friend if you obey—John 15:14.

Funeral

Embalming—Genesis 50:2,3.
Funeral procession—Genesis 50:7-9; Luke 7:12.
Mourning—1 Samuel 25:1.
Music—Matthew 9:23,24.
See Bereavement and Loss; Burial; Cremation.

F

G

Gambling

Destructive lifestyle—1 Timothy 6:9.
Rooted in covetousness—Luke 12:15; Philippians 2:3,4;
1 Timothy 6:10.
Throwing dice—Joshua 14:1,2.

Games, Spiritual

Boxer—1 Corinthians 9:26.
Do not lose race—Philippians 2:16.
Fight a good fight—2 Timothy 4:7.
In race everyone runs, one gets prize—1 Corinthians
9:24.
Run with endurance—Hebrews 12:1.

Garden

Adam and Eve banished from garden—Genesis 3:23.
Adam and Eve placed in garden to work—Genesis 2:15.
Eden had every tree good for food—Genesis 2:9.
Romantic garden—Song of Solomon 5:1.
Vegetable garden—1 Kings 21:2.

Generosity

All goes well for the generous—Psalm 112:5.
Blessings of—Psalm 41:1; Proverbs 22:9; Acts 20:35.
Characteristic of believers—Psalm 112:9; Isaiah 32:8.
Christ sets example—2 Corinthians 8:9.
Exhortations to—1 Corinthians 16:1; 1 Timothy 6:17,18.
Generous man is happy—Proverbs 22:9.
Give generously to others in need—Ephesians 4:28.
Godly give generous loans—Psalm 37:26.
Secret generosity—Matthew 6:1-4.
Share money generously—Romans 12:8.

Gentiles, Conversion of

Gentiles received Word of God—Acts 11:1.

114

God has blessed the Gentiles—Galatians 3:14.
Good news for the Gentiles—Acts 13:46; Romans 11:11; Galatians 1:16; 2:2.
Holy Spirit poured out on Gentiles—Acts 10:45.

Geology

Catastrophic earthquake coming—Revelation 16:18.
Christ laid foundation of the earth—Hebrews 1:10.
Earth, formless mass cloaked in darkness—Genesis 1:2.
Foundation of the earth—2 Samuel 22:16; Psalm 18:15; 24:2; Jeremiah 31:37.
God placed world on its foundation—Psalm 104:5.
Ground of earth cursed—Genesis 3:17.
Ground opened up and swallowed sinners—Numbers 16:30-32.
Mighty shaking in the land—Ezekiel 38:19.

Gifts from God

Spiritual

Bread from heaven—John 6:32.
Eternal life—Acts 11:18.
Gift of God's Son—John 3:16.
Living water—John 4:10.

Temporal

Food, drink, and clothes—Psalm 136:25; 145:15; Matthew 6:11,25.
Plenty of dew—Genesis 27:28.
Rain—Leviticus 26:4; Isaiah 30:23; Zechariah 10:1.
Riches, wealth, and honor—2 Chronicles 1:12.

Giving, Advice on

Do not do publicly—Matthew 6:1.
Give money to the poor—Deuteronomy 15:7,8; Matthew 19:21; Galatians 2:10.
Give to those in need—Luke 11:41; 12:33; Hebrews 13:16.

G

115

Give to those who ask—Matthew 5:42.
Give what you are able—2 Corinthians 8:12.
Help others with money—1 John 3:17.
Share food with the hungry—Isaiah 58:7.

Gleaning

Leave grain at edge of field—Leviticus 19:9,10; 23:22.

Glorifying God

Glorify God in death—John 21:19.
Glorify God through gifts—2 Corinthians 9:13.
Glorify God's name forever—Psalm 86:12.
God is worthy—Revelation 4:11.

Glory of God

See God, Glory of.

Glossolalia

See Charismatic Issues.

Gluttony

Command against—Romans 13:13,14.
Consequence of—Proverbs 23:21.
Danger of—Luke 12:45,46.
Do not let stomach be a god—Philippians 3:19.
Eat, drink, be merry—Luke 12:19,20.
Folly of—Luke 12:19-46.
Leads to poverty—Proverbs 23:21.
Warning against—Proverbs 23:2,3.
See Fat (Overweight).

God

Access to

Approach with confidence—Hebrews 4:16.
Close to all who call on Him—Psalm 145:18.
Come boldly—Hebrews 4:16; 10:19.
Draw near—James 4:8.

God is near—Deuteronomy 4:7.

Hears our cries—Psalm 145:19.

Through Jesus—John 14:6; Romans 5:2; Ephesians 2:13; 3:12; Colossians 1:22.

Creator

By faith we understand about creation—Hebrews 11:3.

Created all things—Psalm 89:11; Isaiah 44:24; Ephesians 3:9; Revelation 4:11.

Created heaven and earth—Genesis 1:1,21; Psalm 102:25; 146:6; Isaiah 40:28; 42:5; 48:13; 66:2; Jeremiah 33:2; Acts 4:24; 7:50; 14:15; Revelation 10:6.

Created male and female—Genesis 5:1,2.

Father created all through Son—1 Corinthians 8:6; Hebrews 1:2.

God spoke world into existence—Psalm 33:9; 148:5.

Six days, Lord made everything—Exodus 20:11.

Eternality of

Alpha and Omega—Revelation 1:8.

Everlasting—Deuteronomy 33:27.

Everlasting King—Jeremiah 10:10.

First and the Last—Isaiah 44:6; 48:12.

From eternity to eternity—Isaiah 43:13.

From everlasting to everlasting—Psalm 90:2.

King Eternal—1 Timothy 1:17.

Lives forever from eternal ages past—Psalm 41:13; 102:12,27; Isaiah 57:15.

Existence of

Existence of world proves God's existence—Romans 1:18-20.

Fool says there is no God—Psalm 14:1.

God's law in human heart proves His existence—Romans 1:19.

God's provisions testify to His existence—Acts 14:17.

G

117

Heavens declare glory of God—Psalm 19:1.

Faithfulness of

Even when we are not faithful—2 Timothy 2:13.

Every promise fulfilled—Joshua 23:14.

Everything God does is worthy of trust—Psalm 33:4.

Faithful in every way—Psalm 89:1,2,8.

Faithfulness continues to each generation—Psalm 100:5; 119:90.

Faithfulness endures forever—Psalm 117:2.

God who promises is faithful—Hebrews 10:23.

Great is God's faithfulness—Lamentations 3:22,23.

Keeps every promise—Psalm 146:6.

Keeps His covenant—Deuteronomy 7:9.

Promises prove true—Psalm 18:30.

Unfailing faithfulness—Psalm 25:10.

Fatherhood of

Father created—1 Corinthians 8:6.

Father disciplines us as children—Hebrews 12:9,10.

Father to the fatherless—Psalm 68:5.

Kingdom will be turned over to Father—1 Corinthians 15:24.

Pray to the Father—Matthew 6:9.

Source of every mercy—2 Corinthians 1:3.

Foreknowledge of

Foreknew His people—Romans 8:29.

Foretells future, unlike false gods—Isaiah 42:9; 44:7.

Only God knows future—Isaiah 46:9,10.

Glory of

Dwells in unapproachable light—1 Timothy 6:16.

Glorious in holiness—Exodus 15:11.

Glory filled tabernacle—Exodus 40:34.

Glory on mountaintop—Exodus 24:17.

God will not give glory to another—Isaiah 42:8.

Heavens tell of glory of God—Psalm 19:1.

Illuminates eternal city—Revelation 21:23.

118

King of glory—Psalm 24:8.

Moses' face glowed from God's glory—Exodus 34:29.

Moses requested to see glory—Exodus 33:18-23.

Son reflects God's own glory—Hebrews 1:3.

Stephen saw glory of God—Acts 7:55.

Train of God's glorious robe filled temple—Isaiah 6:1.

Whole earth is filled with God's glory—Isaiah 6:3.

Goodness of

Give thanks, for God is good—1 Chronicles 16:34; Psalm 118:29; 136:1.

God is good—Psalm 25:8; 86:5; 100:5; 106:1; 119:68.

Good to all people—Psalm 145:8,9.

Good to those who hope in Him—Lamentations 3:25.

Only God is good—Matthew 19:17; Mark 10:18; Luke 18:19.

Taste and see—Psalm 34:8.

Grace of

Abounds for every need—2 Corinthians 9:8.

By grace we are saved—Ephesians 2:8,9; Titus 2:11.

Do not miss out on God's grace—Hebrews 12:15.

Empowers us for service—1 Corinthians 3:10.

Finding grace at God's throne—Hebrews 4:16.

Given by Christ—1 Corinthians 1:4.

Given to each of us—Ephesians 4:7.

Gives grace to humble—Proverbs 3:34; 1 Peter 5:5.

God of all grace—1 Peter 5:10.

Grace and truth from Jesus Christ—John 1:14-17.

Justification by grace—Romans 3:24.

Not to be abused—Romans 3:8; Romans 6:1,15.

Sufficiency of God's grace—1 Corinthians 15:10; 2 Corinthians 12:9.

Unmerited favor—Romans 4:16; Romans 9:16; Titus 3:5.

Where sin increased, grace increased—Romans 5:20,21.

119

G

Holiness of

Be holy because God is holy—Leviticus 11:44; 19:2; 20:26; 21:8; 1 Peter 1:15.

Cannot be tempted by evil—James 1:13.

God alone is holy—1 Samuel 6:20; Psalm 99:9; Revelation 15:4.

God is light, no darkness—1 John 1:5.

God shows Himself holy—Isaiah 5:16.

God's name is holy—Psalm 99:3; Isaiah 57:15.

Holy, holy, holy—Isaiah 6:3; Revelation 4:8.

Holy One—Psalm 22:3; Hosea 11:9.

Majestic in holiness—Exodus 15:11.

Moses stood on holy ground—Exodus 3:5.

No one is holy like Lord—1 Samuel 2:2.

Immutability of

God does not change—Malachi 3:6.

God does not change mind—Numbers 23:19; 1 Samuel 15:29; Isaiah 31:2.

God endures—Psalm 102:25-27.

God's purpose will stand—Psalm 33:11; Isaiah 46:10; Hebrews 6:17.

No variation in God—James 1:17.

Impartiality of

Does not despise anyone—Job 36:5.

Has no favorites—Romans 2:11; Colossians 3:25; 1 Peter 1:17.

Shows no partiality—Deuteronomy 10:17; Acts 10:34.

Incomprehensible

God's thoughts higher than our thoughts—Isaiah 55:8,9.

Vast thoughts—Psalm 139:17.

Who can know what Lord is thinking?—1 Corinthians 2:16.

Independent

Needs no counsel—Romans 11:34,35.

Needs no help—Isaiah 44:24; Acts 17:25.

Infinite
High above all nations—Psalm 113:4-6.
Highest heavens cannot contain Him—1 Kings 8:27;
2 Chronicles 6:18.
His greatness is unsearchable—Psalm 145:3.
His understanding is beyond comprehension—Psalm
147:5.

Invisible
Invisible—Colossians 1:15; Hebrews 11:27.
No one has seen Him—John 1:18; 1 Timothy 6:16;
1 John 4:12.
Unseen one who never dies—1 Timothy 1:17.

Jealous
Do not worship other gods—Exodus 20:5; 34:14;
Deuteronomy 5:9.
God is a devouring fire, a jealous God—Deuteronomy
4:24.

Judge
Almighty Judge—Job 34:17.
Day has been set for judging world—Acts 17:31.
Judge in righteousness—Psalm 7:11.
Judge of all the earth—Genesis 18:25.
Judges with equity—Psalm 96:10.
Only one lawgiver and judge—James 4:12.
Will judge men's secrets—Romans 2:16.

Just
Deals with earth justly—Genesis 18:25.
Justice is foundation of His throne—Psalm 89:14.
No injustice in God—Deuteronomy 32:4.
Will not pervert justice—Job 34:12.

Kindness of
Everlasting kindness—Isaiah 54:8.
Exercises kindness—Jeremiah 9:24.
Full of lovingkindness—Jeremiah 31:3.

Kindness in Jesus Christ—Ephesians 2:6,7.
Rich in kindness—Romans 2:4.
Shows kindness by His provisions—Acts 14:17.

Knowledge of

Carefully watches—Job 34:21; Proverbs 15:3; Psalm 11:4.
Examines deepest thoughts—Jeremiah 11:20; 20:12.
Examines secret motives—Proverbs 16:2; Jeremiah 17:10.
Knows all hearts—Proverbs 21:2; 24:12; Romans 8:27.
Knows all secrets—Matthew 6:4,18.
Knows what you need before asking—Matthew 6:8.
Sees everything—Job 31:4.
Tells the future—Isaiah 42:9.

Love of

Abounds in love—Psalm 86:5.
Demonstrated love in sending Jesus—John 3:16; Romans 5:8.
Earth full of His unfailing love—Psalm 33:5.
Everlasting love—Jeremiah 31:3.
God is love—1 John 4:8,16.
God loved us first—1 John 4:19.
God of love—2 Corinthians 13:11.
God's love endures forever—1 Chronicles 16:34; Psalm 106:1.
Great love moved God to save us—Ephesians 2:4,5.
Loves people of the world—John 3:16.
Mercy and love—Psalm 25:6,7.
Nothing can separate us from God's love—Romans 8:38,39.
Unfailing love—Psalm 130:7; Isaiah 54:10.

Mercy of

Father of mercies—2 Corinthians 1:3.
Merciful and compassionate—Deuteronomy 4:31; Psalm 116:5.

G

Merciful and forgiving—Daniel 9:9.

New mercies every morning—Lamentations 3:22-24.

Rich in mercy—Ephesians 2:4,5.

Salvation depends on God's mercy—Romans 9:16.

Omnipotence of

Abundant in strength—Psalm 147:5.

Great power and might—2 Chronicles 20:6; Ephesians 1:19-21.

Incomparably great power—Ephesians 1:19,20.

No one can hold back God's hand—Daniel 4:35.

No one can reverse God—Isaiah 43:13.

No one can thwart God—Isaiah 14:27.

Nothing is impossible with God—Matthew 19:26; Mark 10:27; Luke 1:37.

Nothing too difficult for God—Genesis 18:14; Jeremiah 32:17,27.

The Almighty reigns—Revelation 19:6.

Omnipresence of

God is everywhere—Psalm 139:2-12.

Highest heaven cannot contain Him—1 Kings 8:27; 2 Chronicles 2:6.

In heaven and earth—Psalm 113:4-6; Isaiah 66:1; Jeremiah 23:23,24.

In Him we live and move and exist—Acts 17:27,28.

Omniscience of

Counts and names all stars—Psalm 147:4,5.

Declares end from beginning—Isaiah 46:9,10.

Eyes penetrate all things—Hebrews 4:13.

Knows all about us—Psalm 139:1-4.

Knows all outcomes—Matthew 11:21.

Knows all things—1 John 3:20.

Knows secrets of the heart—Psalm 44:21.

No one teaches Him—Isaiah 40:13,14.

Understands every intent of the thoughts—1 Chronicles 28:9.

Unlimited understanding—Isaiah 40:28.
Unsearchable in judgments—Romans 11:33.

Patience of

Does not want any to perish—2 Peter 3:9.
Forbearance—Romans 2:4.
Slow to anger—Exodus 34:6; Numbers 14:18; Psalm 86:15; 103:8; Nahum 1:3.
Waits patiently for people to be saved—2 Peter 3:15.

G

Perfection of

Father is perfect—Matthew 5:48.
His way is perfect—2 Samuel 22:31.
His work is perfect—Deuteronomy 32:4.
Whatever is perfect comes from God—James 1:17.

Power of

Everything is possible with God—Mark 10:27; Luke 1:37.
God of miracles—Job 9:10; Psalm 77:14.
Has power to do as He pleases—Psalm 135:6; Daniel 4:35.
His power is absolute—Psalm 147:5.
His power is great—Nahum 1:3.
His power is not diminished in the least—Habakkuk 3:6.
Nothing is too hard for God—Jeremiah 32:17,27.

Presence of

God lives with the humble—Isaiah 57:15.
In God we live and move and exist—Acts 17:28.
No one can escape from God's spirit—Psalm 139:7.

Righteousness of

Commands are righteous—Psalm 119:172.
Does no wrong—Deuteronomy 32:4.
Judges world in righteousness—Acts 17:31.
Judgments are righteous—Psalm 72:2; 98:9.
Righteous altogether—Psalm 19:9.
Righteous in all His ways—Psalm 145:17.

Savior

God is a God who saves—Psalm 68:20.

Lord alone is Savior—Isaiah 43:11.

Our God and Savior—Psalm 27:9; 38:22; 42:11.

Rock and Savior—2 Samuel 22:47.

Self-Existent

Has life within Himself—John 5:26.

"I Am"—God's name—Exodus 3:14.

Sovereign

Above all rule and authority—Ephesians 1:20-22.

Can do all things—Job 42:2.

Enthroned over all—Isaiah 40:21-26.

Eternal dominion—Daniel 4:34,35.

Every knee will bow before God—Romans 14:11.

God Almighty reigns—Psalm 93:1; Revelation 19:6.

His plans alone stand—Psalm 33:8-11; Isaiah 46:10.

His sovereignty rules over all—Psalm 103:19.

King over the earth—Psalm 47:2.

Lord does whatever pleases Him—Psalm 135:6.

Lord is enthroned as King forever—Psalm 29:10.

Lord is God in heaven above and earth below—
Deuteronomy 4:39; Acts 17:24.

Most High over all the earth—Psalm 83:18.

No one delivers from God's power—Deuteronomy
32:39.

Potter rules over clay—Isaiah 45:9,10.

Rules all nations—2 Chronicles 20:6.

Rules forever—Exodus 15:18; Psalm 9:7; Revelation
1:6.

Rules over all things—Deuteronomy 10:14;
1 Chronicles 29:12.

Who can stop God?—Job 9:12.

Who resists God's will? Romans 9:19.

Spirit

Cannot be represented by an idol—Exodus 20:4; Acts 17:29.

God is invisible—1 Timothy 1:17.

God is Spirit—John 4:24.

No one has seen or can see God—1 Timothy 6:15,16.

Trinity

Baptism in name of Father, Son, and Spirit—Matthew 28:19.

Benediction mentions Jesus, God, and Spirit—2 Corinthians 13:14.

Father, Messiah, and Spirit mentioned—Isaiah 48:16.

Father, Son, and Spirit involved in salvation—1 Peter 1:1,2.

God is one—James 2:19.

God said, "Let *us* go down and confuse their language"—Genesis 11:7.

God said, "Man has now become like one of *us*"—Genesis 3:22.

God said, "Who will go for *us*"?—Isaiah 6:8.

Holy, holy, holy is the Lord—Isaiah 6:3; Revelation 4:8.

Jesus baptized, Father speaks, Spirit descends—Matthew 3:16,17.

Jesus, Spirit, and God mentioned—Romans 15:15,16,30.

Lord is one—Deuteronomy 6:4.

Man made in God's ("our") image—Genesis 1:26.

One Spirit, one Lord, one Father—Ephesians 4:4-6.

Only one God—Deuteronomy 4:35; Isaiah 46:9.

Upper Room Discourse mentions Father, Son, and Spirit—John 14:16-23; 15:26.

True

All God's words are true—Psalm 33:4; 119:160.

Cannot lie—Numbers 23:19; Titus 1:2.

Commands are true—Psalm 119:151.

God is true—1 John 5:20.

God's truth is everlasting—Psalm 117:2.

Let God be found true—Romans 3:4.
Living and true God—1 Thessalonians 1:9.
True God—Jeremiah 10:10; John 17:3.

Uniqueness
He alone is God—Deuteronomy 4:35,39.
No other God—1 Kings 8:60; Mark 12:32;
    1 Corinthians 8:6; 1 Timothy 2:5.
Only true God—John 17:3.

Unity
God is one—James 2:19.
Lord is one—Deuteronomy 6:4.
Lord our God is one Lord—Mark 12:29.
No God but one—1 Corinthians 8:4.

Wise
Deep in wisdom and knowledge—Romans 11:33.
Full of wisdom and understanding—Proverbs 3:19;
    James 3:17.
In wisdom God created—Psalm 104:24.
Possesses full understanding—Job 12:13.
The only wise God—Romans 16:27.

Works of
Everything God does is worthy of trust—Psalm 33:4.
His work is perfect—Deuteronomy 32:4.
How amazing are the deeds of the Lord—Psalm
    111:2,4.
How awesome are God's deeds—Psalm 66:3.
Many miracles—Psalm 40:5.
Whatever God does is final—Ecclesiastes 3:14.

Godlessness
All have turned away from God—Psalm 14:3.
Minds full of darkness—Romans 1:21; Ephesians 4:18.
No fear of God—Romans 3:18.
Refusal to acknowledge God—Romans 1:28.
Too proud to seek God—Psalm 10:4.

God's Ministry of Preservation

In Him all things hold together—Colossians 1:17.
In Him we live and move and exist—Acts 17:28.
Upholds all things by His word—Hebrews 1:3.

God's Providential Control

Controls bondage in prisons—Acts 12:7-11.
Controls fish—Jonah 1:17.
Controls governments—Romans 13:1.
Controls kings—Proverbs 21:1.
Controls nations—Psalm 22:28.
Controls one before birth—Psalm 139:15,16; Jeremiah 1:5.
Makes all things work for good for believers—Romans 8:28.
Protects us against overwhelming temptation—1 Corinthians 10:13.
Provides for animals—Matthew 6:26.

God's Sovereign Decree (Plan)

Declares end from beginning—Isaiah 46:10.
Plan includes building the church—Matthew 16:18.
Plan includes God's final victory—1 Corinthians 15:23-28.
Plan includes Jesus' death on cross—Acts 2:23.
Plan of salvation formed before foundation of world—1 Peter 1:20.
Sovereign plan for Israel—Romans 9–11.
Works out His sovereign purpose—Ephesians 1:11.

Golden Rule

Do for others as you would like them to do for you—Matthew 7:12; Luke 6:31.
Love your neighbor as yourself—Leviticus 19:18; Romans 13:9; Galatians 5:14.
See Behavior; Conduct, Proper.

G

Good Reputation

See Reputation, Good.

Gospel

Good News about Christ—Romans 1:16.

Good News about God's wonderful kindness—Acts 20:24.

Gospel defined—1 Corinthians 15:1-3.

Satan blinds people to the gospel—2 Corinthians 4:4.

G

Gossip

Do not spread slanderous gossip—Leviticus 19:16.

Gossiper betrays confidence—Proverbs 11:13.

Gossiper separates close friends—Proverbs 16:28.

Gossiper tells secrets—Proverbs 20:19.

Gossiping tongue causes anger—Proverbs 25:23.

Gossiping busybodies—1 Timothy 5:13.

Government

Bribes accepted by government officials—Acts 24:26.

Corrupt government—Psalm 94:20.

David a good leader—1 Chronicles 18:14.

God controls governments—Romans 13:1.

Government will rest on Messiah's shoulders—Isaiah 9:6.

Obey God *over* government—Acts 5:29.

Obey the government—Romans 13:1,5; Titus 3:1; 1 Peter 2:13.

Righteous government—Proverbs 14:34.

Solomon a good leader—1 Kings 4:20,21,25.

World government coming—Revelation 13:7.

See Leadership; Politics; Rulers, Wicked.

Grace Before Meals

Give thanks for food—1 Corinthians 10:30,31.

Give thanks to God before eating—Romans 14:6.

129

Jesus as our example—Matthew 14:19; 15:36; 26:26; Mark 6:41; 8:6; John 6:11.

Grace of God

See God, Grace of.

Grandchildren/Grandparents

Blessing of being grandparent—Psalm 128:5,6.
Influence of grandmother's faith—2 Timothy 1:5.
Inheritance for grandchildren—Proverbs 13:22.
Jacob sees grandchildren—Genesis 48:11.
Job sees grandchildren—Job 42:16.
Lots of grandchildren promised to Rebekah—Genesis 24:60.

Gratitude

See Appreciation.

Grave

See Burial.

Greed

Always greedy for more—Proverbs 21:26.
Do not be greedy for money—1 Peter 5:2.
Do not be greedy for what you do not have—Luke 12:15.
God angry at greed—Isaiah 57:17.
Greed harms others—Psalm 52:7.
Greedy dogs—Isaiah 56:11.
Greedy person tries to get rich quick—Proverbs 28:22.
Judas' greed, not worth it—Matthew 26:14-16,47-50.
Selfish greed—Jeremiah 22:17.

Grief

Christ a man of grief—Isaiah 53:3-10.
Don't grieve Holy Spirit—Ephesians 4:30.
Foolish child brings grief to mother—Proverbs 10:1.
Grief of unbelievers—1 Thessalonians 4:13.

130

Shave heads in grief—Ezekiel 27:31.
*See Bereavement and Loss; Mourning, Examples of;
     Tears.*

Growing Spiritually

Be rooted in Christ—Ephesians 3:17-19.
Grow in grace—2 Peter 3:18.
Grow on milk of God's Word—1 Peter 2:2.
Let Word of Christ dwell in you—Colossians 3:16.
Meditate on things of God—1 Timothy 4:15.
Pray for one another—Colossians 1:9-11.
Rightly divide word of truth—2 Timothy 2:15.
Spiritual growth described—2 Peter 1:5-8.
See Disciples and Discipleship.

Guidance

God guides our feet—Luke 1:79.
God will direct your path—Isaiah 30:21.
God will show the way to go—Psalm 32:8.
God's Spirit guides us—John 16:13.
God's Word a lamp—Psalm 119:105.
Lord will guide continually—Isaiah 58:11.

Guilt

Be cleansed of guilty conscience—Hebrews 10:22.
Confession cleanses guilt away—Psalm 51:2.
David seeks purification—Psalm 51:7.
Guilt removed—Psalm 32:5.
Guilty faces—Isaiah 3:9.
Judas filled with remorse—Matthew 27:3.
See Confession; Conscience.

H

Habit

Habitual cursing—Psalm 109:17-19.

Habitual disobedience—Jeremiah 22:21.

Habitual hospitality—Romans 12:13.

Habitual iniquity—Micah 2:1.

Habitual sin—1 John 3:7-9.

Hair

Disgraceful for man to have long hair—1 Corinthians 11:14.

Do not be concerned about fancy hairstyles—1 Peter 3:3.

Hairs on your head are numbered—Luke 12:7.

Long hair is woman's pride and joy—1 Corinthians 11:15.

Women should have head covered—1 Corinthians 11:5,6.

Women should have modest appearance—1 Timothy 2:9.

Hallelujah

Hallelujah—Revelation 19:1.

Praise the Lord—Psalm 106:1; 111:1; 112:1; 113:1; 117:1; 135:1; 146:1,10; 148:1.

See Praise; Worship.

Handicap

See Lameness.

Hands

Church laid hands on Timothy—1 Timothy 4:14.

Instructions about laying on of hands—Hebrews 6:2.

Jesus laid hands—Mark 6:5; 7:32; Luke 4:40.

Jesus lifted hands to heaven—Luke 24:50.

Lay hands and heal—Mark 16:18.

Lay hands on animal—Exodus 29:15,19; Leviticus 3:2,8,13; 4:15,24.

Paul laid hands—Acts 19:6; 2 Timothy 1:6.

Happiness

Be happy and do good—Ecclesiastes 3:12.

Be happy when times are good—Ecclesiastes 7:14.

Forgiveness makes happy—Psalm 32:1,2.

Generous man is happy—Proverbs 22:9.

Happy are those who avoid counsel of wicked—Psalm 1:1.

Happy are those who take refuge in God—Psalm 34:8.

Happy heart makes face cheerful—Proverbs 15:13.

Jesus' formula for happiness (Beatitudes)—Matthew 5:3-12.

Righteous are glad—Psalm 68:3.

Those who trust Lord are happy—Psalm 84:12.

Of the Righteous

In doing God's will—Psalm 40:8.

In fearing the Lord—Psalm 128:1.

In finding wisdom—Proverbs 3:13.

In helping the poor—Proverbs 14:21.

In knowing the Lord—Psalm 144:15.

In looking forward to future glory—Romans 5:2.

In obeying God's law—Proverbs 29:18.

In trusting the Lord—Proverbs 16:20.

Of the Wicked? No!

Anguish—Luke 16:25.

Destruction—Hosea 8:4.

Filled with sorrow—Psalm 16:4.

Humiliated and disgraced—Isaiah 45:16.

Many sorrows—Psalm 32:10; Luke 6:25.

Hardness

Apathy—Luke 18:1-5.

Do not harden your hearts—Hebrews 3:8.

God permitted divorce, men's hearts hard—Matthew 19:7,8.

133

Hard hearts do not believe—Ezekiel 2:4; Mark 6:52;
Ephesians 4:18.
Warnings against—Psalm 95:8-11; Proverbs 21:9;
Revelation 9:20-21.

Harlot

Do not bring offering from earnings of prostitute—
Deuteronomy 23:17,18.
Do not let daughter become prostitute—Leviticus 19:29.
Do not let your heart stray toward her—Proverbs 7:25,26.
Rahab the prostitute—Joshua 6:17-23,25.
Wisdom will save you from immoral woman—Proverbs
2:16.

Harmony

Can two walk together without agreeing?—Amos 3:3.
Keep unity of the Spirit—Ephesians 4:3.
Live in harmony and peace—Psalm 133:1; Romans 12:16;
14:19; 15:5,6.
Maintain unity—John 17:21.
No harmony between light and darkness—2 Corinthians
6:14,15.
Peace between Jews and Gentiles—Ephesians 2:14,21.
We are one body—Romans 12:5; Ephesians
4:4,12,13,16,25.

Harp

David played harp for Saul—1 Samuel 16:23.
Harps in heaven—Revelation 5:8; 14:2.
Praise God with harp—Psalm 43:4; 71:22; 98:5; 144:9;
147:7; 149:3; 150:3,4.
Prayer accompanied by harp—Habakkuk 3:19.
Psalm accompanied by harp—Psalm 4:1; 6:1; 55:1; 61:1;
67:1; 76:1.
See Music and Musical Instruments.

Haste

Do not hastily go to court—Proverbs 25:8.

Hasten to deliver message—Matthew 28:7.

Hasten to Jesus—Mark 5:2-6.

Hasten to pray—Zechariah 8:21.

Hatred

See Malice.

Of Bad Things

Abhor all falsehood—Psalm 119:104,128,163.

Hate all who do evil—Psalm 5:5.

Hate divorce—Malachi 2:16.

Hate evil—Psalm 45:7; 97:10.

Healing, God Does Not Always Grant

Epaphroditus was sick near death—Philippians 2:25-27.

Paul had "thorn in the flesh"—2 Corinthians 12:7-9.

Timothy had perpetual stomach problem—1 Timothy 5:23.

See Disease; Medicine.

Health

Gentle words bring life and health—Proverbs 15:4.

Jesus healed blind, lame, lepers, and deaf—Matthew 15:30; Luke 7:21,22.

Obedience brings health—Exodus 15:26; Deuteronomy 7:15; Proverbs 4:22.

Physical health connected to spiritual health— 1 Corinthians 11:30; 3 John 1:2.

Prayer for health—Isaiah 38:16.

Restored health for Job—Job 33:25.

Satan assaulted Job's health—Job 2:3-6.

Timothy took wine for the stomach—1 Timothy 5:23.

Hearing

See Deafness.

Heart

Affections of

Avoid lustful desires—2 Peter 2:10.

Burning hearts for Jesus—Luke 24:32.

Desire for God—Psalm 73:25.

Heart longs for God—Psalm 42:1.

Let heaven fill thoughts—Colossians 3:1,2.

Love each other—Romans 12:9,10.

Love God more than parents—Matthew 10:37.

Love God with whole heart—Deuteronomy 6:5; Mark 12:30.

Love God's decrees—Psalm 119:97,103,167.

Return to your first love—Revelation 2:4.

Known to God

Examines motives—Proverbs 16:2; Jeremiah 17:10.

Knows every heart—1 Kings 8:39; Jeremiah 12:3; Acts 1:24; 15:8; Romans 8:27.

Knows every plan and thought—1 Chronicles 28:9; Psalm 94:11; Isaiah 66:18.

Knows everything about us—Psalm 139:1.

Knows evil hearts—Luke 16:15.

Knows secrets of every heart—Psalm 44:21.

Knows thoughts of the wise—1 Corinthians 3:20.

Looks at thoughts and intentions—1 Samuel 16:7; Revelation 2:23.

See God, Omniscience of.

Of Unregenerate People

Crooked heart will not prosper—Proverbs 17:20.

Fickle hearts—Hosea 10:2.

Hard hearts that do not believe—Ezekiel 2:4; Mark 6:52; Ephesians 4:18.

Heart deceitful and desperately wicked—Jeremiah 17:9.

Heart of pride—Daniel 5:20.

Heart that plots evil—Psalm 140:2; Proverbs 6:14,18.

Heart that turns away from God—Hebrews 3:10.

136

Satan fills heart—Acts 5:3.
Sly of heart—Proverbs 7:10.
Stubborn and rebellious hearts—Jeremiah 5:23.
Twisted hearts—Proverbs 11:20.
Unfaithful hearts and lustful eyes—Ezekiel 6:9.

Renewed

Christ can make heart strong—1 Thessalonians 3:13.
God can create a clean heart—Psalm 51:10.
God can give a new heart—Ezekiel 36:26.
God can give singleness of heart—Ezekiel 11:19.
Lord can cleanse heart—Deuteronomy 30:6.
Spiritual renewal—Ephesians 4:23.
See Born Again; Regeneration.

Heathen

Babble to false gods—Matthew 6:7.
Conspire against God—Psalm 2:1.
Danger of mingling with—Psalm 106:35.
Detestable—Leviticus 18:24-30.
Do not imitate their ways—Jeremiah 10:2.
Evil practices—2 Kings 17:8.
Gospel should be preached to—Matthew 24:14; 28:19;
    Romans 16:26.
Idolatrous—Psalm 135:15.
Punished by God—Psalm 44:2; Joel 3:11-13.
Reap judgment—Psalm 9:15.
Sacrifice son in fire—2 Kings 16:3.
Scoff at believers—Psalm 79:10.
Unclean practices—Ezra 6:21.
Without Christ—Ephesians 2:12.
See Idol; Pagans.

Heaven

Blessing of heaven—Revelation 22:1-5.
City of glory—Revelation 21:23.
God's throne—Isaiah 66:1; Acts 7:49.

H

Heavenly homeland—Hebrews 11:16.

Holy city—Revelation 21:1,2.

Home of righteousness—2 Peter 3:13.

Inconceivably wonderful—1 Corinthians 2:9.

Jesus ascended to—Mark 16:19.

Jesus preparing place for us—John 14:1-3.

Kingdom of light—Colossians 1:12.

New heaven and new earth—2 Peter 3:13.

Paradise of God—2 Corinthians 12:2-4.

People from all races saved in heaven—Revelation 7:9.

H

Hedonism

Constant partying—Isaiah 5:11,12.

Godless living—1 Peter 4:3.

God's message crowded out by pleasures—Luke 8:14.

Love pleasure rather than God—2 Timothy 3:4; 2 Peter 2:13.

Pleasure is meaningless—Ecclesiastes 2:1.

Sin nature craves lustful pleasures—Galatians 5:19-21.

Slaves to evil pleasures—Titus 3:3.

Those who love pleasure become poor—Proverbs 21:17.

Turn from sinful pleasures—Titus 2:12.

Unfaithful hearts and lustful eyes—Ezekiel 6:9.

Hell

Better to lose one part of body than go to hell—Matthew 5:29,30; 18:9.

Curse someone, in danger of hell—Matthew 5:22.

Eternal punishment—Matthew 25:46.

How will Jewish leaders escape?—Matthew 23:33.

Lake of Fire—Revelation 20:13-15.

Place of fire—Matthew 25:41.

Place of gloomy dungeons—2 Peter 2:4.

Place of torment—Luke 16:23.

Help from God

Angel of Lord encamps around those who fear Him—Psalm 34:7.

Cast all anxiety on God—1 Peter 5:7.

Cast burdens on Lord—Psalm 55:22.

Go boldly to throne of grace—Hebrews 4:16.

God will be our shield—Psalm 91:4.

God will never forsake you—Hebrews 13:5,6.

Lord helps those who follow Him—2 Chronicles 16:9.

Lord upholds us—Psalm 37:24.

No weapon formed against you will prosper—Isaiah 54:17.

Trust God, He will be with you—Psalm 37:5.

H

Heredity

Born blind because of parents?—John 9:2.

Descendants of Abraham—Matthew 3:9.

Everything reproduces after its kind—Genesis 1:21,25.

Flesh gives birth to flesh—John 3:6.

Seth was the very image of his father—Genesis 5:3.

Sin inherited from Adam—Romans 5:12.

Heresy

Destructive heresies—2 Peter 2:1.

Different Jesus, different Spirit—2 Corinthians 11:4.

False gospel—Galatians 1:6-8.

Paul accused of heresy—Acts 18:13.

Upsetting teachings—Acts 15:24.

See Cults; Doctrine, False.

Holiness

See God, Holiness of.

See Jesus Christ, Holiness of.

Personal

Be blameless—Deuteronomy 18:13; Philippians 2:14,15.

139

Be holy because God is holy—Leviticus 11:45; 19:2.
Be holy in all you do—Leviticus 20:7; Ephesians 1:4; 1 Peter 1:15,16.
Do not let sin reign in body—Romans 6:12-14.
Follow God's example—Ephesians 5:1.
Fruit of the spirit—Galatians 5:22,23.
Get rid of all the filth—James 1:21.
God blesses those whose hearts are pure—Matthew 5:8.
Keep yourself pure—1 Timothy 5:22; 1 John 3:3.
Put to death sinful things lurking in you—Colossians 3:5.
Seek to live clean life—Hebrews 12:14.
Turn from evil, do good—Psalm 37:27.
Walk in God's ways—Psalm 119:1-3.
Without holiness one cannot see God—Hebrews 12:14.

Holy Spirit

Begot Jesus in Mary's womb—Matthew 1:18; Luke 1:35.
Blasphemy against Spirit—Matthew 12:32.
Body is temple of Holy Spirit—1 Corinthians 6:19.
"By my Spirit," says the Lord—Zechariah 4:6.
Comforter—John 14:16; 15:26; 16:7.
Day of Pentecost—Acts 2.
Descended on Jesus like dove—Matthew 3:16; Mark 1:10; Luke 3:22; John 1:32.
Do not grieve Holy Spirit—Ephesians 4:30.
Do not quench Holy Spirit—1 Thessalonians 5:19.
Father gives Holy Spirit to those who ask—Luke 11:13.
Father sent Holy Spirit—John 14:26.
Filled with joy and with the Holy Spirit—Acts 13:52.
Fruit of the Spirit—Galatians 5:22,23.
God has given us His Spirit—1 John 4:13.
God pours out Spirit on all people—Ezekiel 39:29; Joel 2:28,29.
Guarantee of things to come—2 Corinthians 1:22; 5:5.
Holy Spirit lives in us—2 Timothy 1:14.
Jesus baptizes with Spirit—Matthew 3:11.

Jesus resurrected by Holy Spirit—Romans 1:4.

Jesus was filled with the Spirit—Luke 4:1,18.

Joy from the Holy Spirit—Romans 14:17;
1 Thessalonians 1:6.

Living water—John 7:37-39.

Participated in creation—Genesis 1:2; Psalm 104:30.

Power of the Holy Spirit—Romans 15:13.

Promise of baptism—Acts 1:5.

Promise of power from Spirit—Acts 1:8.

Receive the Holy Spirit—John 20:22.

Renewed by the Holy Spirit—Titus 3:5.

Spirit reminds us of Jesus' teachings—John 14:26.

Walk in dependence on Spirit—Galatians 6:8.

Activities of

Baptizes believers—1 Corinthians 12:13.

Convicts of sin—John 16:8-11.

Fills believers—Ephesians 5:18.

Gives spiritual gifts—Romans 12:6-8; 1 Corinthians 12:7-10,28-30.

Illumines God's Word for us—1 Corinthians 2:9–3:2.

Indwells believers—1 Corinthians 6:19.

Inspired Scripture—2 Peter 1:21.

Prays for us—Romans 8:26.

Produces fruit in us—Galatians 5:22,23.

Regenerates believers—Titus 3:5.

Restrains sin—Genesis 6:3.

Seals believers unto day of redemption—Ephesians 4:30.

Teaches believers—John 16:12-15.

Testifies of Christ—John 15:26.

Deity of

Begat humanity of Christ—Luke 1:35.

Blasphemy against Holy Spirit—Matthew 12:22-32.

Holy Spirit is eternal—Hebrews 9:14.

H

Human body is temple of God/Holy Spirit—1 Corinthians 6:19.

Inspired Scripture—2 Peter 1:21.

Is called the Spirit of God—1 Corinthians 6:11.

Is one person in the divine Trinity—Matthew 28:19; 2 Corinthians 13:14.

Lying to Holy Spirit is lying to God—Acts 5:3,4.

Omnipresent—Psalm 139:7-10.

Omniscient—1 Corinthians 2:11.

Participated in the creation—Genesis 1:2; Job 26:13; Psalm 104:30.

H

Personhood of

Can be lied to like a person—Acts 5:3.

Can be obeyed like a person—Acts 10:19-21.

Can be outraged like a person—Hebrews 10:29.

Commands like a person—Acts 13:2.

Has emotion—Ephesians 4:30.

Has intelligence—1 Corinthians 2:10,11.

Personal pronouns used of Him—John 15:26; John 16:7,8,13,14.

Prays like a person—Romans 8:26.

Teaches like a person—Luke 12:11,12; John 14:26.

Testifies like a person—John 15:26.

Procession from Father and Son

Father sent the Spirit—John 14:26.

Jesus sent the Spirit from the Father—John 15:26.

Homicide

Accidental

Cities of refuge, flee to—Exodus 21:13; Numbers 35:11; Deuteronomy 4:41,42.

Unintentional killing—Deuteronomy 19:4-7.

Murder

Commandment not to murder—Exodus 20:13; Deuteronomy 5:17.

From the heart comes murder—Matthew 15:19; Mark 7:21.

Lord detests murderers—Psalm 5:6.

Murder is forbidden—Genesis 9:5.

Murderers do not have eternal life—1 John 3:15.

Punishment of

Murderers must be executed—Genesis 9:6; Leviticus 24:17.

Homosexual

Do not practice homosexuality—Genesis 19:5-7; Leviticus 18:22.

Homosexuals have no share in Kingdom— 1 Corinthians 6:9.

Male and boy prostitutes—Deuteronomy 23:17; Job 36:14; Joel 3:3.

Penalty for homosexual acts—Leviticus 20:13.

Practiced at Sodom—Genesis 19:4,5.

Honesty

Avoid dishonest standards—Leviticus 19:35,36.

Be honorable before Lord—2 Corinthians 8:21.

Dishonest money dwindles away—Proverbs 13:11.

Do not punish innocent man—Proverbs 17:26.

God likes integrity—1 Chronicles 29:17.

Golden Rule—Matthew 7:12; Luke 6:31.

Honest answers are appreciated—Proverbs 24:26.

Kings take pleasure in honest lips—Proverbs 16:13.

Lord delights in honesty—Proverbs 11:1.

Lord demands fairness—Proverbs 16:11.

Lord despises double standards—Proverbs 20:10,23.

Man of integrity walks securely—Proverbs 10:9.

Show your honesty—Luke 3:13.

Trustworthy people are given more responsibility— Luke 16:10.

H

Truthful witness gives honest testimony—Proverbs 12:17.

Use accurate scales—Deuteronomy 25:13; Ezekiel 45:10.

See Dishonesty; Integrity; Truth.

Honor

Do not honor God with mere lip service—Isaiah 29:13; Matthew 15:8,9.

Fear of Lord brings wealth, honor, and life—Proverbs 22:4.

God blesses with riches, wealth, honor—2 Chronicles 1:12.

Honor father and mother—Exodus 20:12; Deuteronomy 5:16; Matthew 15:4.

Honor God with thanksgiving—Psalm 69:30.

Honor Lord with best produce—Proverbs 3:9,10.

Humble will be honored—Proverbs 15:33; 18:12; 29:23; Luke 14:11; 18:14.

Husbands give honor to wives—1 Peter 3:7.

Jesus given highest place of honor—Hebrews 7:26.

Refused by Paul and Barnabas—Acts 14:11-18.

Refused by Peter—Acts 10:26.

Wicked are brought to dishonor—Proverbs 12:8; 24:24; Isaiah 66:24; Daniel 12:2.

Wisdom and virtue lead to honor—Proverbs 3:16; 13:18; 21:21; Romans 2:10.

Hope

Be ready to explain your hope to others—1 Peter 3:15.

Be strong and take courage—Psalm 31:24.

Confident assurance—Hebrews 11:1.

Everlasting comfort and good hope—2 Thessalonians 2:16.

Faith and hope in God—1 Peter 1:21.

God's plans involve hope—Jeremiah 29:11.

Hope deferred makes heart sick—Proverbs 13:12.

Hope gives endurance—1 Thessalonians 1:3.

Hope in God—Psalm 39:7; 43:5; 71:5; Lamentations 3:24; Acts 24:15.

144

Hope in God's unfailing love—Psalm 33:18,20,22.

Hope in God's Word—Psalm 119:74,81; 130:5;
Romans 15:4.

Hope in Lord, will not be disappointed—Isaiah 49:23.

Hopes of the godly result in happiness—Proverbs
10:28.

Live in eager expectation and hope—Philippians 1:20.

Look forward to joys of heaven—Colossians 1:5.

Those who hope in Lord renew strength—Isaiah 40:31.

Three things endure: faith, hope, love—1 Corinthians
13:13.

We have a living hope—1 Peter 1:3.

Of the Wicked, No!

Hope of the godless comes to nothing—Job 8:13.

What hope do the godless have?—Job 27:8.

Wicked are without hope—Ephesians 2:12.

Wicked will lose hope—Job 11:20.

Hosanna

Bless the one who comes in name of Lord—Mark
11:9,10; John 12:13.

Praise God for the Son of David—Matthew 21:9-15.

See Praise; Worship.

Hospitality

Feed and give water to brothers—Matthew 25:31-46.

Golden Rule—Matthew 7:12; Luke 6:31.

Leave some of crop for the poor—Leviticus 19:10.

Show hospitality to strangers—Hebrews 13:2.

Human Beings, Equality of

From one man God created all the nations—Acts
17:26.

Never think of anyone as impure—Acts 10:28.

No Jew/Gentile, slave/free, male/female in Christ—
Galatians 3:28.

Human Body

See Anatomy.

Human Sacrifices

Children burned—2 Kings 17:31.
Detestable to Lord—Deuteronomy 12:31.
Do not offer children to Molech—Leviticus 18:21.
Incredible evil—Jeremiah 32:35.
Penalty for child sacrifice: death—Leviticus 20:2.
Sacrifice of sons and daughters—Psalm 106:37-39.

Humanity of Jesus Christ

See Jesus Christ, Humanity of in the Incarnation.

Humiliation

See Shame.

Humility

Be clothed with humility—Colossians 3:12; 1 Peter 5:5,6.
Be compassionate and humble—1 Peter 3:8.
Be humble and gentle—Ephesians 4:2.
Consider others as better—Philippians 2:3.
Do not praise yourself; let others do it—Proverbs 27:2.
God gives grace to the humble—Proverbs 3:34; James 4:6.
God guides the humble—Psalm 25:9.
God humbles the prideful—Isaiah 13:11; Daniel 4:37.
God prospers the humble—Job 5:11.
God saves the humble—2 Samuel 22:28.
Humble will be exalted—Matthew 23:12.
Humble will be filled with fresh joy—Isaiah 29:19.
Humble will be honored—Proverbs 15:33; 18:12; 29:23;
    Luke 14:11; 18:14.
Humble yourselves before Lord—James 4:10.
Humility brings healing—2 Chronicles 7:14.
Humility brings wisdom—Proverbs 11:2.
Lord supports the humble—Psalm 147:6.
Seek humility—Zephaniah 2:3.

Show humility toward all men—Titus 3:1,2.
Walk humbly with your God—Micah 6:8.

Hunger

Feed brothers—Matthew 25:31-46.
Feed hungry enemies—Romans 12:20.
Hunger for righteousness—Matthew 5:6.
Jesus fasted 40 days—Matthew 4:2; Luke 4:2.
Jesus fed hungry thousands—Mark 6:30-44.
Jesus hungered—Matthew 21:18; Mark 11:12.
No more hunger in heaven—Revelation 7:16.
Paul knew hunger—1 Corinthians 4:11.
Workers' appetite—Proverbs 16:26.

Hurry

See Haste.

Husband

Do not deprive wife sexually—1 Corinthians 7:3-5.
Give honor to wives—1 Peter 3:7.
Live happily with woman you love—Ecclesiastes 9:9.
Love your wives—Colossians 3:19.
Share your love only with your wife—Proverbs 5:15.
Two become one flesh—Matthew 19:5; Mark 10:7.
Wives should submit to—Ephesians 5:22; Colossians 3:18.
See Family; Marriage; Wife.

Hypocrisy

Be done with hypocrisy—1 Peter 2:1.
Do not fast like hypocrites do—Matthew 6:16.
Do not pray like hypocrites do—Matthew 6:5.
Get rid of log from your own eye—Matthew 7:5.
Hypocrites call on Lord but will not obey—Luke 6:46.
Hypocrites clean on outside, filthy on inside—Luke 11:39; 16:15.
Purify your hearts, hypocrites—James 4:8.

I Am that I Am

"I am that I am"—Exodus 3:14.
Jesus is "I am"—John 8:58.
See Names of God.

Idleness

Be lazy and become slave—Proverbs 12:24.
Full of excuses—Proverbs 22:13; 26:13.
Hands refuse to work—Proverbs 21:25; Ecclesiastes 4:5.
Idle lives—2 Thessalonians 3:11.
Lazy people a pain to their employer—Proverbs 10:26.
Lazy people soon poor—Proverbs 10:4; 14:23.
Lazy people want much but get little—Proverbs 13:4.
Lazy person goes hungry—Proverbs 19:15.
Lazy person has trouble all through life—Proverbs 15:19.
Love of sleep—Proverbs 20:13.
On the road to poverty—Proverbs 23:21.
Take a lesson from the ants—Proverbs 6:6.
Whoever does not work should not eat—2 Thessalonians 3:10.
See Laziness.

Idol

Destroy idols—Genesis 35:2.
Do not corrupt yourselves with idols—Deuteronomy 4:25.
Do not make idols—Exodus 20:4; Leviticus 26:1.
Do not turn to idols—Leviticus 19:4.
Do not worship other gods—Deuteronomy 5:7.
Flee from worship of idols—1 Corinthians 10:14.
Golden calf—Exodus 32:4.
How foolish are those who make idols—Isaiah 44:9.
Idol worshipers not in kingdom—1 Corinthians 6:9.
Idols detestable to the Lord—Deuteronomy 27:15.
Let nothing take God's place in your heart—1 John 5:21.
Make no gods for yourselves—Exodus 34:17; Psalm 81:9.
Never pray to other gods—Exodus 23:13.

Those who worship idols are disgraced—Psalm 97:7.
Worship of creation instead of Creator—Romans 1:25.
See Heathen; Pagans.

Idolatry, Wicked Practices of

Child sacrifices—Leviticus 18:21; 20:2; 2 Kings 3:27; 17:17; Psalm 106:37,38.
Detestable acts—Deuteronomy 12:31.
Pagan revelry—1 Corinthians 10:7.
Shrine prostitutes—1 Kings 14:24; 15:12.
Sorcery and divination—2 Kings 21:6.

Ignorance

Can you solve mysteries of God?—Job 11:7.
Ignorance of true God—Acts 17:23.
Lean not on own understanding, trust Lord—Proverbs 3:5,6.
Now we see imperfectly—1 Corinthians 13:9,12.
Simpleton goes blindly on—Proverbs 22:3; 27:12.
Zeal without knowledge is not good—Proverbs 19:2.
See Blindness, Spiritual.

Sins of

Eating sacred offerings without realizing it—Leviticus 22:14.
Forgive them, for they know not what they do—Luke 23:34.
Ignorant are punished less—Luke 12:48.
Jews acted in ignorance toward Jesus—Acts 3:17.
Paul persecuted Christians in ignorance—Galatians 1:13.
Unintentional disobedience—Numbers 15:22.

Illness

See Disease.

Imagination

Consistently evil thoughts—Genesis 6:5.

149

Fix thoughts on what is true, honorable, right—
Philippians 4:8.
Foolish ideas—Romans 1:21.
Imagining idols—Ezekiel 14:1-11.
Let heaven fill thoughts—Colossians 3:1,2.
Lust in one's thoughts—Matthew 5:28.
Myths—1 Timothy 1:4; 2 Timothy 4:4; Titus 1:14; 2 Peter
1:16.
Old wives' tales—1 Timothy 4:7.

Imitating Jesus

Be humble like Jesus—Philippians 2:3-8.
Be transformed—2 Corinthians 3:18.
Follow Jesus' lead—John 13:12-15.
Love like Jesus—John 13:34,35.
Obey like Jesus—John 15:9-11.
Paul imitated Christ—1 Corinthians 11:1.
Predestined to become Christ-like—Romans 8:29,30.
Walk as Jesus walked—1 John 2:6.
See Model.

Immaturity

Infants in Christ—1 Corinthians 3:1,2.
Leave immaturity behind—Proverbs 9:6.
No longer infants—Ephesians 4:14.
Stop thinking like children—1 Corinthians 14:20.
Worldly Christians—1 Corinthians 3:3.
You need milk, not solid food—Hebrews 5:12,13.

Immorality

Darkened heart and mind—Matthew 5:27,28.
Immoral lives—Jude 4.
No immoral living—Romans 13:13.
Playing with fire—Proverbs 6:27.
Prostitute—Jeremiah 3:1,2.
Repent of sexual immorality—2 Corinthians 12:21.
Run from immoral woman—Proverbs 5:8.

Satan tempts believers to immorality—1 Corinthians
7:5.

Watch out for immoral women—Proverbs 2:16; 5:3.

Immortality

Better things waiting for us in eternity—Hebrews
10:34.

Elijah carried by whirlwind into heaven—2 Kings 2:11.

Free gift of God is eternal life—Matthew 25:46;
Romans 6:23.

God is mine forever—Psalm 73:26.

Hold tightly to eternal life—1 Timothy 6:12.

Jesus gives us eternal life—John 10:28.

Jesus is the resurrection and the life—John 11:25,26.

See Eternal Life; Heaven.

Immutability of God

See God, Immutability of.

Impartiality of God

Does not tolerate partiality—Deuteronomy 10:17;
2 Chronicles 19:7; Acts 10:34.

Has no favorites—Romans 2:11; Ephesians 6:9; Colossians 3:25; 1 Peter 1:17.

See Favoritism, Examples of.

Impenitence

Blind and stubborn—Psalm 81:11,12.

Deaf to truth—Acts 7:51.

Do not harden your hearts—Hebrews 3:8.

Dog returns to its vomit—Proverbs 26:11.

Growing increasingly bold in wickedness—Psalm 52:7.

No remorse—Jeremiah 44:10.

Pay no attention to God—Proverbs 1:24.

Rebellion is as bad as the sin of witchcraft—1 Samuel
15:23.

Rebels from earliest childhood—Isaiah 48:8.

Refusal to give hearts to God—Psalm 78:8.

Refusal to obey—Psalm 106:25.
Stubbornly follow evil desires—Jeremiah 16:12.
Unbending necks—Isaiah 48:4.
See Apostasy; Carnality; Rebellion.

Incarnation, Necessity of Christ's

Came as sacrifice for sin—Hebrews 10:1-10.
Came to become our High Priest—Hebrews 5:1,2.
Came to destroy works of devil—1 John 3:8.
Came to fulfill Davidic Covenant—Luke 1:31-33.
Came to give an example for living—1 Peter 2:21.
Came to reveal God—John 1:18.
See Jesus Christ, Humanity of in the Incarnation.

Incest Forbidden

With aunt—Leviticus 20:19.
With close relative—Leviticus 18:6.
With daughter-in-law—Leviticus 20:12.
With father's wife—Leviticus 20:11; Deuteronomy 22:30;
    27:20.
With sister—Leviticus 20:17.
See Immorality; Lasciviousness.

Inconsistency

Get log out of your own eye—Matthew 7:3.
Scribes and Pharisees do not practice what they preach—
    Matthew 23:3,4.

Indecency

See Immorality.

Indecision

Hearts of people are fickle—Hosea 10:2.
No one can serve two masters—Matthew 6:24.
Spirit strong, body weak—Matthew 26:41.
Waver back and forth—1 Kings 18:21; James 1:8.

Industry

Hard work means prosperity—Proverbs 12:11.
Hard workers get rich—Proverbs 10:4.
Hard workers have plenty of food—Proverbs 28:19.
Never be lazy in your work—Romans 12:11.
Wealth from hard work grows—Proverbs 13:11.
Whatever you do, do well—Ecclesiastes 9:10.
Work brings profit—Proverbs 14:23.
Work hard and become a leader—Proverbs 12:24.
Work six days—Exodus 23:12; Deuteronomy 5:13.

Infant

Baby Jesus was worshiped—Matthew 2:2.
Herod killed infant boys—Matthew 2:16.
Jesus, born as holy babe—Luke 1:35.
Moses, baby in basket—Exodus 2:3.
Pharaoh's daughter finds baby Moses in basket—
    Exodus 2:5.
Twins—Genesis 48:5.
See Children.

Infanticide

Herod's order—Matthew 2:16.
Pharaoh's order—Exodus 1:16.
See Abortion.

Infertility

See Barren.

Influence

Evil

See Bad Example.

Good

Be example to other Christians—1 Thessalonians 1:7.
Influence spouse—1 Corinthians 7:16.
Influence unbelieving neighbors—1 Peter 2:12.
Influence world as salt—Matthew 5:13.

153

Let your light shine—Mark 4:21; Luke 11:33.

Inheritance, Spiritual

Inheritance from God—Ephesians 1:11.
Inheritance of Christ's treasures—Romans 8:17.
Inheritance of eternal life—Titus 3:7.

Injustice

Cursed is anyone who is unjust—Deuteronomy 27:19.
Do not exploit widows or orphans—Exodus 22:22.
Do not falsely charge anyone—Exodus 23:7.
Do not oppress foreigners—Exodus 22:21.
Do not pass along false reports—Exodus 23:1.
Do not twist justice—Exodus 23:6; Deuteronomy
16:19,20.
Judge neighbors fairly—Leviticus 19:15.
Scales and weights must be accurate—Leviticus 19:36.
See Justice.

Innocence

Clean, innocent behavior—Romans 16:19; Philippians
2:15.
Do not punish innocent man—Exodus 23:7; Proverbs
17:26.
God sees no one as innocent—Job 9:2.
Innocent lifestyle—1 Timothy 3:2-4.
Pilate, "I am innocent of this man's blood"—Matthew
27:24.

Insanity

Feigning insanity—1 Samuel 21:13.
Madness as a judgment—Deuteronomy 28:28.
Paul denied insanity—Acts 26:24,25.
Saul raved like a madman—1 Samuel 18:10.

Insensitive

Hardening of hearts—Psalm 95:8.
Seared conscience—1 Timothy 4:1,2.
Unconcerned about right and wrong—Ephesians 4:19.

Unconcerned for God or man—Luke 18:1-5.

Insomnia

Bothersome dreams—Daniel 2:1.

Disturbed sleep—Psalm 56:8.

King could not sleep—Esther 6:1; Daniel 6:18.

Restlessness—Job 7:3,4.

Worry about problems—Ecclesiastes 5:12.

See Sleep.

Instability

Do not be attracted by strange ideas—Hebrews 13:9.

Doubtful mind is unsettled—James 1:6.

Excuses, excuses—Luke 9:59.

Failure to love Christ as at first—Revelation 2:4.

Fickle hearts—Hosea 10:2.

Galatians turned from gospel of grace—Galatians 1:6.

Neither hot nor cold—Revelation 3:15,16.

No one can serve two masters—Matthew 6:24.

You are no longer like children—Ephesians 4:14.

Instruction of Children

Bring children up with discipline—Ephesians 6:4.

Teach children about God—Exodus 10:2;
    Deuteronomy 4:9; Psalm 78:4.

Teach children to choose right path—Proverbs 22:6.

Insult

Go away, you baldhead—2 Kings 2:23.

Hail! King of the Jews—John 19:3.

Prophesy to us, you Messiah—Matthew 26:68.

Rebuild the temple in three days, can you?—Mark
    15:29.

Scoffers in the last days—2 Peter 3:3,4.

See Criticism; Scoffing.

Integrity

Elder must be blameless—Titus 1:7.

155

Fix thoughts on what is true, honorable, right—
Philippians 4:8.
Godly walk with integrity—Proverbs 20:7.
Live by Golden Rule—Luke 6:31.
People with integrity have firm footing—Proverbs 10:9.

Intercession of Man with God

Elders pray over the sick—James 5:14.
Pray for all people, including government—1 Timothy
2:1,2.
Pray for Christians everywhere—Ephesians 6:18.
We are God's priests—1 Peter 2:5,9.
See Prayer; Prayerfulness.

Interstellar Space ("Heavens")

Do not try to read future in stars—Jeremiah 10:2.
Do not worship sun, stars, or moon—Deuteronomy 4:19;
17:2,3.
God can restrain movement of stars—Job 38:31.
God counts and names all stars—Psalm 147:4,5.
God made moon to mark seasons—Psalm 104:19.
God stretched out heavens—Job 26:7; Psalm 104:2.
Heavens cannot be measured—Jeremiah 31:37.
Heavens tell of the glory of God—Psalm 19:1.
Stars cannot be counted—Jeremiah 33:22.
Sun will be darkened—Matthew 24:29; Acts 2:19,20.

Intoxication

Be filled with Spirit, not drunk on wine—Ephesians 5:18.
Brings affliction—Proverbs 23:29,30.
Do not carouse with drunkards—Proverbs 23:20.
Leads to brawls—Proverbs 20:1.
Leads to shame—Joel 1:5; Psalm 69:12.
Robs people of clear thinking—Hosea 4:11.
Wine is not the way to riches—Proverbs 21:17.

Jealousy

Arouses husband's fury—Proverbs 6:34.

Corinthians jealous—1 Corinthians 3:3; 2 Corinthians 12:20.

Destructive nature—Proverbs 27:4.

God is a jealous (protective) God—Exodus 20:5; 34:14; Psalm 78:58.

Mark of the flesh—Galatians 5:19,20.

Sadducees jealous—Acts 5:17.

See Covetousness; Envy.

Jesus Christ

Annunciations

To Joseph—Matthew 1:18-25.

To Mary—Luke 1:26-37.

Ascension of

Ascension to Father—John 7:33; 16:28; 20:17; Ephesians 4:8.

Entered glory—Luke 24:26; John 7:39.

Jesus going to prepare a place—John 14:2.

Jesus left, then sent Comforter—John 16:7.

Jesus prayed for restoration to state of glory—John 17:5.

Jesus told disciples He was going away—John 14:12,28; 16:5.

Taken up into heaven—Mark 16:19; Luke 24:51; John 6:62; 1 Timothy 3:16.

Taken up into the sky—Acts 1:9.

Birthplace of
See Nazareth.

Compassion of

Compassion for peoples' hunger—Matthew 15:32; Mark 8:2.

Compassion for people without shepherd—Mark 6:34.

Great pity for the crowds—Matthew 9:36.

Had compassion and healed the sick—Matthew 14:14; 20:34.

Understands all our weaknesses—Hebrews 4:15.

Creator

Beginner of God's creation—Revelation 3:14.

Created everything—John 1:3; Colossians 1:16.

Laid foundation of the earth—Hebrews 1:10.

Universe made through Jesus—1 Corinthians 8:6; Hebrews 1:2.

World made through Jesus—John 1:10.

Death of

Atoning sacrifice—1 John 2:2.

Beaten and bloodied—Isaiah 52:14.

Betrayed and crucified—Matthew 26:2.

Betrayed, flogged, mocked, killed, and raised—Matthew 17:22,23; Mark 10:33,34.

Bore our sins in His body—1 Peter 2:24.

Buried and raised—1 Corinthians 15:3,4; 1 Thessalonians 4:14.

Gave His life as ransom—Mark 10:45; 1 Timothy 2:5,6.

Good Shepherd laid down life for sheep—John 10:11,14,15,17,18.

In the heart of the earth for three days—Matthew 12:40.

Killed, then raised—Matthew 16:21; Mark 8:31; 9:31.

Lamb who was killed—Isaiah 53:7; Revelation 5:12; 13:8.

Part of God's plan—Acts 2:23.

Pierced hands and feet—Psalm 22:16; Zechariah 12:10.

Purchased salvation by blood—Revelation 5:9.

Reconciliation through His death—Romans 5:10; 2 Corinthians 5:18,19.

Redeemed humanity by blood—Galatians 3:13; 1 Peter 1:18,19.

Sacrifice of atonement—Romans 3:25; Ephesians 5:2.

Took up our infirmities—Isaiah 53:4,5.

We preach Christ crucified—1 Corinthians 1:23.

Deity of
- Alpha and Omega—Revelation 1:8; 22:13,16.
- Created everything—John 1:3; Colossians 1:16; Hebrews 1:10.
- Elohim, Mighty God—Isaiah 9:6.
- Equated with the "I AM" of Exodus 3:14—John 8:58.
- Eternal—Isaiah 9:6; Micah 5:2.
- Father addressed Jesus as God—Hebrews 1:8.
- Final Judge of humankind—Matthew 25:31,32.
- First and the Last—Revelation 1:17.
- Forgives sins (which only God can do)—Mark 2:5-12.
- Fullness of deity lives in bodily form—Colossians 2:9.
- God and Savior—2 Peter 1:1 (compare with Isaiah 43:11).
- God the One and Only—John 1:18.
- Great God and Savior—Titus 2:13.
- Has life in Himself—John 1:4.
- Has nature of God—Philippians 2:6.
- He and the Father are one—John 10:30.
- Image of the invisible God—Colossians 1:15.
- Immanuel, God with us—Matthew 1:23.
- Is God—John 1:1.
- Is prayed to as God—Acts 7:59.
- King of kings and Lord of lords—Revelation 17:14; 19:16.
- Omnipresent—Matthew 28:20; Ephesians 1:22,23.
- Omniscient, knows all that goes on in churches—Revelation 2–3.
- Preexisted creation—John 17:4,5.
- Prophecy of Messiah as God—Isaiah 40:3; Matthew 3:3.
- Raised people from dead—John 5:21; 11:25-44.
- Reflects God's own glory—Hebrews 1:3.
- Sinless—John 8:29.
- Sustains universe as God—Colossians 1:17.
- Thomas called Jesus God—John 20:28.
- Unchanging (immutable)—Hebrews 13:8.

J

159

Worshiped as God—Matthew 28:16,17; Hebrews 1:6.

Eternity of
Everlasting Father—Isaiah 9:6.
Existed before Abraham—John 8:58.
Existed before everything else began—Colossians 1:17.
Existed from the beginning—1 John 1:1.
Existed long before John the Baptist—John 1:15.
First and the Last—Revelation 1:17.
From eternity past—Micah 5:2.
Glory before the creation—John 17:5.
Is, was, and is still to come—Revelation 1:8.

J

Exaltation of
Ascended higher than all the heavens—Ephesians 4:10.
Crowned with glory and honor—Hebrews 2:9.
Exalted to God's right hand—Luke 22:69; Acts 2:33,34; 5:31; Colossians 3:1.
Name above every other name—Philippians 2:9.
Sat down in the place of honor—Romans 8:34; Ephesians 1:20; Hebrews 1:3; 8:1.

Holiness of
Born as holy babe—Luke 1:35.
Holy and blameless—Hebrews 7:26.
Holy One sent from God—Mark 1:24; Luke 4:34.
Holy, righteous one—Acts 3:14.
Holy servant—Acts 4:27,30.
Never sinned—2 Corinthians 5:21; Hebrews 4:15; 1 Peter 2:22.
Sinless, spotless Lamb of God—1 Peter 1:19.

Humanity of in the Incarnation
Became flesh—John 1:14; Hebrews 2:14,17,18.
Became human—John 1:14.
Born in Bethlehem—Luke 2:11.
Born of a virgin—Isaiah 7:14.
Born of a woman—Genesis 3:15; Galatians 4:4.
Called a man—1 Timothy 2:5.

Called "man of sorrows"—Isaiah 53:3.
Called "son of Abraham"—Matthew 1:1.
Called "son of David"—Mark 10:47.
Came to earth in real body—2 John 7.
Child is born to us—Isaiah 9:6.
Flesh and bones body—Luke 24:39.
Grew in wisdom as man—Luke 2:52.
Grew tired—John 4:6.
Had a human nature—Romans 1:2,3.
Hungered—Matthew 4:2.
Slept—Matthew 8:23,24.
Son of Man—Matthew 16:27; Mark 10:45; Luke 19:10.
Tempted—Hebrews 4:15.
Thirsted—John 19:28.
Took on human appearance—Philippians 2:7.
Wept—John 11:35.

J

Humility of

Ate with sinners—Matthew 9:10.
He is humble—Matthew 21:5.
Led as a sheep to the slaughter—Acts 8:32.
Made Himself nothing—Philippians 2:7.
Washed disciples' feet—John 13:5.

Incarnation of

See Jesus Christ, Humanity of in the Incarnation.

Judge

Great Judge is coming—James 5:9.
Judge of all—Acts 10:42.
We must all stand before Christ—2 Corinthians 5:10.
Will bring our deepest secrets to light—Romans 2:16;
   1 Corinthians 4:5.
Will judge the world—Acts 17:31.

King

Authority over everything—Matthew 11:27.
Bless the King—Luke 19:38.
Complete authority—Matthew 28:18.

Government will rest on His shoulders—Isaiah 9:6.
Heir to David's throne—Isaiah 11:10; Acts 2:30.
King is coming—John 12:15.
King of kings—1 Timothy 6:15; Revelation 17:14; 19:16.
King of the Jews—Matthew 2:2; John 19:19.
Kingdom not of this world—John 18:36.
Kingship—John 18:37.
Powerful dominion—Psalm 110:2.

Lamb of God
See Lamb of God.

Lord

J

Christ the Lord—Luke 2:11.
Confess that Jesus is Lord—Romans 10:9.
Do all in name of the Lord—Colossians 3:17,23,24.
Every knee will bow before Lord Jesus—Philippians 2:9-11.
Grow in knowledge of the Lord—2 Peter 3:18.
Holy Spirit enables us to say, "Jesus is Lord"—1 Corinthians 12:3.
Hypocrites give lip service to Lord—Luke 6:46.
In your heart, set apart Jesus as Lord—1 Peter 3:15.
Lord of lords—Revelation 17:14.
One Lord—1 Corinthians 8:6.
Paul asks identity of Lord—Acts 9:5.
We live to the Lord—Romans 14:8,9.
We preach Jesus as Lord—2 Corinthians 4:5.

Love of
Christ's love controls us—2 Corinthians 5:14.
Compassion—Matthew 9:36; 14:14; 15:32; Luke 7:13.
Died for us—Matthew 8:17; John 10:11; 1 John 3:16.
Full of love—2 Corinthians 8:9.
Loves us deeply—John 13:34; 14:21; 15:9; Revelation 1:5.

Meekness of
Gentle and kind—2 Corinthians 10:1.

Humble—Matthew 21:5.
Humble and gentle—Matthew 11:29.
Humble position of servant—Philippians 2:7,8.
Lamb silent before the slaughter—Acts 8:32.

Miracles of

Blind see, lame walk, lepers cured, deaf hear—
    Matthew 15:30; Luke 7:21,22.
Cast out demons—Mark 1:34.
Healed blind and deaf man—Matthew 12:22.
Healed diseases—Matthew 4:23,24; 14:14; Luke 4:40.
Healed Peter's mother-in-law—Matthew 8:14,15.
Miraculous fish catching—John 21:6.
Miraculous signs—John 2:23; 3:2.
Turned water into wine—John 4:46.

Mission of

Appointed to preach Good News—Luke 4:18.
Came as a light—John 12:46.
Came to die for sinners—Romans 5:6.
Came to fulfill law—Matthew 5:17.
Came to give life as ransom—Matthew 20:28; Mark
    10:45.
Came to rescue us from evil world—Galatians 1:4.
Came to save His people from sins—Matthew 1:21.

Names and Titles of

Alpha and Omega—Revelation 1:8; 22:13.
Bread of Life—John 6:48.
Carpenter—Mark 6:3.
Cornerstone—Ephesians 2:20; 1 Peter 2:4.
Eternal High Priest—Hebrews 6:20.
Faithful and True—Revelation 19:11.
Faithful and true witness—Revelation 3:14.
First and the Last—Revelation 1:17.
God and Savior—2 Peter 1:1.
God's Chosen One, the Messiah—Luke 23:35.
God's Messenger and High Priest—Hebrews 3:1.

J

163

Good Shepherd—John 10:11.

Great God and Savior—Titus 2:13.

Great High Priest—Hebrews 4:14.

Great Shepherd—Hebrews 13:20.

Head of body, the church—Ephesians 5:23; Colossians 1:18.

Holy One sent from God—Mark 1:24.

Immanuel—Isaiah 7:14; Matthew 1:23.

King of kings and Lord of lords—Revelation 19:16.

King of the Jews—Matthew 2:2; 27:37.

Lamb and Shepherd—Revelation 7:17.

Lamb of God—John 1:29.

Last Adam—1 Corinthians 15:45.

Light of the world—John 8:12.

Lion of tribe of Judah—Revelation 5:5.

Lord—Mark 1:2,3 (see Isaiah 40:3); Acts 2:21 (see Joel 2:32); Philippians 2:11.

Lord and Savior—2 Peter 1:11.

Lord over all lords and King over all kings—Revelation 17:14.

Mediator—1 Timothy 2:5.

Messiah—Matthew 1:1; 16:20; Luke 9:20; 23:2; Mark 14:61; John 1:41.

Mighty God—Isaiah 9:6.

Mighty Savior—Luke 1:69.

Nazarene—Matthew 2:23.

Passover Lamb—1 Corinthians 5:7.

Prince and Savior—Acts 5:31.

Prophet—Deuteronomy 18:15,18; Matthew 21:11.

Resurrection and the life—John 11:25.

Righteous One—Acts 7:52; 22:14.

Ruler of Israel—Micah 5:2.

Savior—Luke 2:11,30; Titus 1:4; 1 John 4:14.

Shepherd—Mark 14:27.

Son of God—Matthew 26:63-65; Luke 1:35; John 1:49; Acts 9:20.

Son of Man—Mark 2:28.

Son of the Most High—Luke 1:32.
Teacher—John 3:2.
True light—John 1:9.
True vine—John 15:1.
Way, truth, and life—John 14:6.
Wonderful Counselor, Mighty God, Everlasting Father, Prince of Peace—Isaiah 9:6.
Word—John 1:1; Revelation 19:13.

Obedience of

Came to do Father's will—Matthew 26:39,42; Mark 14:36; Luke 22:42; John 4:34.
Does exactly what Father commands—John 14:30,31; 15:10; 17:4.
Learned obedience—Hebrews 5:8.
Obedient to Father even as a child—Luke 2:49-51.
Obedient to death—Philippians 2:8.
Sought to please Father—John 8:29.
Totally obedient—Romans 5:18,19.

Omnipotence of

Cast out evil spirits, healed disease—Matthew 10:1.
Complete authority in heaven and on earth—Matthew 28:18.
Great power—2 Peter 1:16.
Mighty God—Isaiah 9:6.
Opens doors no one can shut—Revelation 3:7.
Raised people from the dead—John 11:1-44.
Resurrected Himself—John 2:19.
Sustains universe by His mighty power—Colossians 1:17; Hebrews 1:3.
Wind and waves obey Him—Matthew 8:27.

Omnipresence of

Fills everything with His presence—Ephesians 1:23.
Jesus is with us always—Matthew 28:20.
Where two or three are, He is among them—Matthew 18:20.

Omniscience of

Knew Nathanael's situation from afar—John 1:48.
Knew what scribes were discussing—Mark 2:8.
Knew who would betray Him—John 13:11.
Knows everything—John 16:30; 21:17.
Knows Father as Father knows Him—Matthew 11:27.
Knows motives—Matthew 22:18.
Knows thoughts—Matthew 12:25; Luke 6:8.
Searches out intentions of every person—Revelation 2:23.
Spirit of knowledge upon Him—Isaiah 11:2.

Preaching and Teaching

Olivet Discourse—Matthew 24–25.
People were amazed at His teaching—Matthew 7:28,29.
Preached and healed—Matthew 9:35.
Preached good news to the poor—Luke 4:18.
Preached of the kingdom—Matthew 4:23,24.
Sermon on the Mount—Matthew 5–7.
Upper Room Discourse—John 14–16.

Preexistence

Before Abraham, "I am"—John 8:58.
Existed before creation—Colossians 1:15.
Existed before the beginning—John 1:1.
From days of eternity—Micah 5:2.
Glory before world began—John 17:5.

Present Activities of

Answers our prayers—John 14:13,14.
Builds the church—Matthew 16:18.
Head of the church—Ephesians 1:20-23.
Helps us bear fruit—John 15:1-10.
Intercedes for us—John 17:15; Hebrews 7:25; 1 John 2:1.
Preparing an eternal abode for us—John 14:1-3.
Sympathetic High Priest—Hebrews 4:15.

Priesthood

Eternal High Priest—Hebrews 6:20.

166

God's Messenger and High Priest—Hebrews 3:1.

Great High Priest—Hebrews 4:14,15.

High Priest who gave perfect sacrifice—Hebrews 10:12.

High Priest with superior ministry—Hebrews 8:6.

Merciful and faithful High Priest—Hebrews 2:17.

Priest forever in line of Melchizedek—Hebrews 5:6; 7:11,17,21.

Prophecies of

Betrayed for 30 pieces of silver—Zechariah 11:12,13.

Born from line of David—2 Samuel 7:12,13.

Born in Bethlehem—Micah 5:2.

Born of a virgin—Isaiah 7:14.

Born of seed of a woman—Genesis 3:15.

Born of seed of Abraham—Genesis 12:1-3.

Crucified—Zechariah 12:10.

Disciples scattered after crucifixion—Zechariah 13:7.

Enemies stare at—Psalm 22:6,7,17.

Mocked and shamed—Psalm 69:7; 109:25.

Resurrected—Psalm 16:10.

Slain for our iniquities—Isaiah 53:3-7.

Relation to Father

All that the Father has is Jesus'—John 16:15.

Came from the Father—John 16:28.

Came to do Father's will—John 6:38; 14:31.

Does what Father does—John 5:19.

Existed with Father in beginning—John 1:1,2.

Father and Jesus are one—John 10:30.

Father draws people to Jesus—John 6:44.

Father gave Jesus authority—John 3:35; 1 Corinthians 15:27.

Father is "greater" positionally—John 14:28.

Father is with Jesus—John 16:32.

Father made universe through Jesus—Hebrews 1:2.

Jesus honors the Father—John 8:49.

Jesus knows the Father—John 10:15.

Jesus obeys the Father—John 15:10.

Jesus pleased the Father—2 Peter 1:17.

Jesus prayed to Father—Matthew 26:39; John 11:41; 17:1.

Jesus reflects glory of Father—Hebrews 1:3.

Jesus sits at Father's right hand—Acts 2:33.

Jesus speaks message of Father—John 7:16; 8:28; 12:50; 14:24.

Jesus was sent into world by Father—John 3:34; 4:34; 7:29,33; 8:29; 12:49.

Jesus will turn kingdom over to Father—1 Corinthians 15:24.

Lord (Father) said to my Lord (Jesus)—Psalm 110:1.

Resurrection

Alive forever and ever—Revelation 1:18.

Angel announced, He is risen—Matthew 28:6,7; Mark 16:6; Luke 24:1-12.

Appeared for 40 days—Acts 1:3.

Christ's resurrection, part of the gospel—1 Corinthians 15:1-4.

Exalted above the heavens—Hebrews 7:26.

Exalted to the highest place—Philippians 2:9-11.

Father raised Jesus from the dead—Acts 13:30.

First to rise from the dead—Revelation 1:5.

Firstfruits of resurrection—Colossians 1:18.

Flesh and bones body—Luke 24:39.

If Christ not raised, our faith is in vain—1 Corinthians 15:17,20.

Jesus in tomb three days and nights—Matthew 12:40.

Jesus promised, raised third day—Matthew 16:21; 20:19; Mark 8:31; 10:34.

Jesus raised Himself—John 2:19-22.

Like Jesus, we will be raised—1 Corinthians 6:14.

Physically and visibly ascended—Acts 1:9.

Prophecy, body won't rot in grave—Psalm 16:10.

Risen Christ is worshiped—Matthew 28:9.

Sign of the prophet Jonah—Matthew 16:4.

Will never die again—Romans 6:9.
See Resurrection, Appearances of Christ.

Savior

Birth of the Savior—Luke 2:11.
Came into world to save sinners—1 Timothy 1:15.
Came to seek and save the lost—Luke 19:10.
Eternal life is in Jesus Christ—Romans 6:23.
Faith in the Savior—Acts 16:31.
God's promised Savior—Acts 13:23.
Great God and Savior—Titus 2:13.
Grow in the knowledge of the Savior—2 Peter 3:18.
Jesus will save His people—Matthew 1:21.
Lord and Savior—2 Peter 2:20.
Prince and Savior—Acts 5:31.
Salvation in no one else—Acts 4:12.
Savior—Ephesians 5:23; Philippians 3:20;
   1 Timothy 1:1,10.
Savior has appeared—2 Timothy 1:10.
Savior of all men—1 Timothy 4:10.
Savior of the world—John 4:42; 1 John 4:14.
We await the Savior—Philippians 3:20.

Second Coming

See Second Coming of Christ.

Sinlessness

Always pleases the Father—John 8:29,46.
Committed no sin—2 Corinthians 5:21; 1 Peter
   2:22,23.
Holy, blameless—Hebrews 7:26-28.
Holy One—Luke 1:35.
In Him is no sin—1 John 3:4,5.
Lamb without blemish—1 Peter 1:18,19.
Righteous One—Acts 3:14.
Unblemished—Hebrews 9:14.
Without sin—Hebrews 4:15.

J

Son of God

Authority of Son—1 Corinthians 15:28.

Centurion recognizes Jesus as Son—Matthew 27:54; Mark 15:39.

Charge of blasphemy for claiming to be Son—John 19:7.

Devil challenges Son—Matthew 4:3,6; Luke 4:9.

Evil spirits recognize Jesus as Son—Mark 3:11.

Father says, You are my Son—Psalm 2:7; Hebrews 1:5.

Father's beloved Son—Matthew 3:17; 17:5; Mark 1:11; 9:7.

Glory of the Son—John 1:14.

Messiah, Son of God—John 11:27; 20:31.

Sacrifice of the Son—1 John 4:10.

Son brings glory to Father—John 14:13.

Son can do nothing by Himself—John 5:19.

Son destroys work of devil—1 John 3:8.

Son has life in Himself—John 5:26.

Son of the blessed God—Mark 14:61.

Son of the Most High God—Mark 5:7; Luke 8:28.

Temptation of

Faced same temptations we do—Hebrews 4:15.

Never sinned—2 Corinthians 5:21; Hebrews 4:15; 1 Peter 2:22.

Overcame world—John 16:33.

Sinless, spotless Lamb of God—1 Peter 1:19.

Tempted by the devil—Matthew 4:1-11; Mark 1:12,13.

There is no sin in Him—1 John 3:5.

Three Major Discourses of

Olivet Discourse—Matthew 24–25.

Sermon on the Mount—Matthew 5–7.

Upper Room Discourse—John 14–16.

True Shepherd

Good Shepherd—John 10:1-28.

Great Shepherd—Hebrews 13:20.

Head Shepherd—1 Peter 5:4.

Worship of

Angels worshiped Him—Hebrews 1:6.

At the name of Jesus every knee will bow—Philippians 2:10.

Disciples worshiped—Matthew 14:33.

Magi worshiped—Matthew 2:2,11.

Jewels

Armbands, bracelets, rings, earrings—Numbers 31:50.

Earrings, rings—Exodus 35:22.

Jewelry, bracelets, and beautiful necklaces—Ezekiel 16:11,12.

Silver and gold jewelry—Genesis 24:53; Exodus 3:22.

Joy

Cheerful look brings joy—Proverbs 15:30.

Comes from abiding in Christ—John 15:10,11.

Filled with joy and with the Holy Spirit—Acts 13:52.

Fruit of the spirit—Galatians 5:22.

Fullness of joy in God's presence—Psalm 16:11.

God anoints with oil of joy—Psalm 45:7.

God turns mourning into joy—Jeremiah 31:13.

God's commands bring joy to heart—Psalm 19:8.

Good children bring joy to father—Proverbs 23:24.

Humble will be filled with fresh joy—Isaiah 29:19.

Joy at answered prayer—John 16:24.

Joy for those whose rebellion is forgiven—Psalm 32:1,2.

Joy from the Holy Spirit—Romans 14:17; 1 Thessalonians 1:6.

Joy in trusting God—Psalm 40:4.

Knowledge will fill you with joy—Proverbs 2:10.

Long hair is a woman's joy—1 Corinthians 11:15.

Look forward to joys of heaven—Colossians 1:5.

Mourning turns into joyful dancing—Psalm 30:11.

Plant in tears, harvest joy—Psalm 126:5.

Serve God with joy—Psalm 100:2.

Shout for joy—Psalm 71:22,23.
Take joy in doing God's will—Psalm 40:8.
Trials, count it all joy—James 1:2.
Worthy wife is her husband's joy—Proverbs 12:4.
See Contentment; Happiness.

Judge

See God, Judge.
See Jesus Christ, Judge.

Judgment

After death comes judgment—Hebrews 9:27.
Believers judged by Christ—1 Corinthians 3:10-15;
2 Corinthians 5:10.
Day of judgment coming—2 Peter 3:7.
God will bring every deed to judgment—Ecclesiastes
12:14.
God will judge righteously—Romans 2:1-3,5.
God will judge the good and bad—Ecclesiastes 3:17.
God will judge whole earth—Psalm 96:13.
Great White Throne judgment—Revelation 20:12.
Jesus is judge of all men—John 5:22; Acts 17:31.
Judge yourself, and you will not be judged—
1 Corinthians 11:31.
Judgment awaits all of us—Matthew 12:36;
Romans 14:10,12.
Judgment in the family of God—1 Peter 4:17.
Nations will be judged at Second Coming—Joel 3:2;
Matthew 25:31-46.

According to Works

God gives what is due—1 Corinthians 4:5.
Judgment according to deeds—1 Peter 1:17; Revelation
20:12.
Judgment according to what people have done—Psalm
62:12; Proverbs 24:12.
People will be paid back for wrong—Colossians 3:25.
People will get what they deserve—Proverbs 11:31.

Reward according to work—1 Corinthians 3:8.

Justice

Blessed are those who seek justice—Psalm 106:3.
Christ's sacrifice demonstrates God's justice—Romans 3:25,26.
Do not pervert justice—Leviticus 19:15.
Do not show partiality—Deuteronomy 16:19.
God loves justice—Psalm 99:4; Isaiah 61:8.
God will bring about justice—Luke 18:7,8.
God will judge world with justice—Acts 17:31.
Good comes to those who seek justice—Psalm 112:5.
Jesus will reign in justice—Isaiah 9:7.
Justice at the Second Coming—Revelation 19:11.
Justice can be perverted—Habakkuk 1:4.
Justice gives a country stability—Proverbs 29:4.
Lord is a God of justice—Isaiah 30:18.
Lord works justice for the oppressed—Psalm 103:6.
Pharisees are unjust—Matthew 23:23.
The righteous care for justice—Proverbs 29:7.

Of God
See God, Just.

Justification

Abram declared righteous—Genesis 15:6.
Blessed is he who is forgiven—Psalm 32:1,2.
Justified by faith—Acts 13:39; Romans 3:28; 5:1; Galatians 2:16.
Justified by God's grace—Romans 3:23,24.
Justified in the name of Jesus—1 Corinthians 6:11.
Law does not justify—Romans 3:20.
Tax collector went home justified—Luke 18:14.
See Salvation.

K

Key

Key to bottomless pit—Revelation 9:1; 20:1.
Keys of death and Hades—Revelation 1:18.
Keys of Kingdom of Heaven—Matthew 16:19.

Kidnapping

Kidnappers must be killed—Exodus 21:16; Deuteronomy
24:7.

Kindness

Always be kind—1 Thessalonians 5:15.
Be clothed with mercy and love—Colossians 3:12-14.
Be considerate—Romans 15:1-5.
Be kind and compassionate—Ephesians 4:32.
Be kind to everyone—2 Timothy 2:24.
Blessed are those who help the poor—Proverbs 14:21.
Do good to enemies—Luke 6:35.
Do good to everyone—Galatians 6:10.
Fruit of the spirit includes kindness—Galatians 5:22.
Give to those who ask—Matthew 5:42; Luke 6:30.
Kind words cheer people up—Proverbs 12:25.
Kindhearted woman—Proverbs 11:16.
Kindness of wife—Proverbs 31:26.
Kindness to the poor—Proverbs 19:17.
Love is patient and kind—1 Corinthians 13:4.
Love one another with tender hearts—1 Peter 3:8.
Maintain brotherly kindness—2 Peter 1:5-7.
Show mercy and kindness—Zechariah 7:9.

Of God

See God, Kindness of.

Kingdom of Heaven

Become like children to enter—Matthew 18:3.
Belongs to children—Matthew 19:14; Mark 10:14.
Hard for rich person to enter—Matthew 19:23,24; Mark
10:23.

Keys of Kingdom of Heaven—Matthew 16:19.

Kingdom more important than relatives—Luke 18:29,30.

Parable of the growing seed—Mark 4:26-29.

Parable of the hidden treasure and pearl—Matthew 13:44-46.

Parable of the mustard seed—Mark 4:30-34.

Parable of the mustard seed and the yeast—Matthew 13:31-43.

Parable of the net—Matthew 13:47-52.

Parable of the talents—Matthew 25:14-30.

Parable of the ten virgins—Matthew 25:1-13.

Parable of the wedding banquet—Matthew 22:1-14.

Parable of the weeds—Matthew 13:24-30.

Parable of the workers in the vineyard—Matthew 20:1-16.

Parable of unmerciful servant—Matthew 18:21-35.

Secrets of the kingdom of God—Luke 8:10.

Kingship of Jesus Christ

See Jesus Christ, King.

Kiss

Greet each other with holy kiss—Romans 16:16; 2 Corinthians 13:12.

Judas betrayed Jesus with kiss—Luke 22:48.

Wound of friend better than kiss of enemy—Proverbs 27:6.

Knowledge

Fear of Lord is beginning of knowledge—Proverbs 1:7.

Gift of special knowledge—1 Corinthians 12:8.

Intelligent people are open to new ideas—Proverbs 18:15.

Knowing Christ is priceless—Philippians 3:8.

Knowing God, most important—Hosea 6:6.

Knowledge will fill you with joy—Proverbs 2:10.

Lord gives understanding—1 Kings 3:9.

175

Lord teaches good judgment—Psalm 119:66.
Wise man is mighty—Proverbs 24:5.
Wise person is hungry for truth—Proverbs 15:14.
See Wisdom.

Of God

    See God, Knowledge of.

K

L

Labor

Do not be lazy—Romans 12:11; 2 Thessalonians 3:7.
Hard work means prosperity—Proverbs 10:4; 12:11.
People who work hard sleep well—Ecclesiastes 5:12.
Rest seventh day—Exodus 23:12; 34:21.
Whatever you do, do well—Ecclesiastes 9:10.
Work brings profit—Proverbs 14:23.
Work hard and become a leader—Proverbs 12:24.
Work six days—Exodus 20:9.
Work with your hands—1 Thessalonians 4:11.

Lake of Fire

Beast and false prophet thrown in—Revelation 19:20.
Death and Hades thrown in—Revelation 20:14.
Devil thrown in—Revelation 20:10.
Sinners thrown in—Revelation 21:8.
Those not in Book of Life thrown in—Revelation 20:15.

Lamb of God

Apostles of the Lamb—Revelation 21:14.
Believers belong to the Lamb—Revelation 13:8.
Blood of the Lamb—Revelation 12:11.
Lamb stands in front of the throne—Revelation 7:17.
Lamb takes away sin of the world—John 1:29.
Lamb victorious—Revelation 17:14.
Lamb's Book—Revelation 21:27.
Light in the eternal city—Revelation 21:23.
Throne of God and of the Lamb—Revelation 22:3.
Wife of the Lamb—Revelation 21:9.
Wrath of the Lamb—Revelation 6:16.

Lameness

Messiah heals the lame—Matthew 11:5; 15:31; 21:14;
Luke 7:22.
Messianic promise, lame will leap like deer—Isaiah
35:6.

Lamp, Figurative

Eye is a lamp for the body—Matthew 6:22.

God's Word is a lamp for our feet—Psalm 119:105.

Lamp of your life can be snuffed out—Proverbs 20:20.

Life of the godly is full of light—Proverbs 13:9.

Light of eternal city—Revelation 21:23.

Prophets' words, a light in darkness—2 Peter 1:19.

Language

Avoid foul or abusive language—Romans 3:13,14; Ephesians 4:29.

Good words come from good heart—Matthew 12:35.

Let your conversation be gracious—Colossians 4:6.

Rid mouth of filthy language—Colossians 3:8.

Lasciviousness

Avoid lustful passions—1 Thessalonians 4:4,5.

Body not made for sexual immorality—1 Corinthians 6:13.

David and Bathsheba—2 Samuel 11.

Do not chase evil desires—1 Peter 4:2,3.

Have nothing to do with sexual sin—Colossians 3:5.

Immoral lives—Jude 4.

Indulgence in pagan revelry—Exodus 32:6.

King Solomon loved many foreign women—1 Kings 11:1.

No immoral living—Romans 13:13.

No indulging in sexual sin—1 Corinthians 6:9.

Repent of sexual immorality—2 Corinthians 12:21.

Run from immoral woman—Proverbs 5:8.

Sexual immorality comes from heart—Mark 7:21.

Sexual immorality emerges from sinful nature—Galatians 5:19.

Wisdom saves one from immoral woman—Proverbs 2:16.

Late Sleeper

See Rising, Late.

178

Laughter

God laughs at the wicked—Psalm 37:13.

Job, a laughingstock to friends—Job 12:4.

Laughter changed to mourning—James 4:9.

Sarah laughed at God's promise—Genesis 18:13.

There is a time to laugh—Ecclesiastes 3:4.

Woe to you who laugh now—Luke 6:25.

Law

Function of

Reveals holiness of God—Romans 7:12.

Reveals what sin is—Romans 7:7.

Tutor that leads us to Christ—Galatians 3:24.

God's

Delight in God's law—Psalm 1:1-3.

God's law in human hearts—Romans 2:14,15.

Jesus came to fulfill law—Matthew 5:17-20.

Law is holy—Romans 7:12.

Law of Lord revives the soul—Psalm 19:7.

Law shows sin—Romans 7:7.

Meditate on God's law—Psalm 119:97-104.

No one is justified by the law—Galatians 3:10-14.

Those who sin are opposed to God's law—1 John 3:4.

We are set free from law of sin and death—Romans 8:1-3.

Temporary

Christ accomplished whole purpose of law—Romans 10:4.

Jesus ended the law—Ephesians 2:15.

Law of Moses was only a shadow—Hebrews 10:1.

Lawsuits

Come to terms quickly with enemy—Matthew 5:25.

Do not be in hurry to go to court—Proverbs 25:8.

L

179

Why file a lawsuit against Christians?—1 Corinthians 6:1.

Lawyer

Expert in religious law—Matthew 22:35; Luke 10:25; 11:45.

Tertullus pressed charges against Paul—Acts 24:1,2.

Zenas the lawyer—Titus 3:13.

Laziness

Be lazy and become a slave—Proverbs 12:24.

Do not be lazy—Hebrews 6:12.

Jesus on laziness—Matthew 25:26,27.

Laziness leads to poverty—Proverbs 10:4.

Lazy people are a pain to their employer—Proverbs 10:26.

Lazy people are full of excuses—Proverbs 22:13; 26:13.

Lazy people have trouble all through life—Proverbs 15:19.

Lazy people want much but get little—Proverbs 13:4.

Never be lazy in your work—Romans 12:11.

Sluggard reaps no harvest—Proverbs 20:4.

Take a lesson from the ants—Proverbs 6:6.

Whoever does not work should not eat—2 Thessalonians 3:10.

Leadership

Apostles—Luke 17:5; 22:14; Acts 1:13,26; 1 Corinthians 4:9; 9:1; 2 Corinthians 11:5; Ephesians 2:20; 4:11; Revelation 21:14.

Christ head over all authorities—Colossians 2:9,10.

Confidence in leader—1 Corinthians 3:21.

Humble leaders—Exodus 3:11; Judges 6:15; Isaiah 6:5; Jeremiah 1:6.

Imitate church leaders—Hebrews 13:7.

Importance of prayer by leaders—Luke 6:12-16.

Jewish leaders headed for judgment—Matthew 23:33.

Joseph, good leader—Genesis 47:13-26.

Lead gently—Galatians 6:1,2.

Leaders lead by good example—1 Peter 5:3.
Man appointed to lead over creation—Genesis 1:26.
Obey spiritual leaders—Hebrews 13:17.
Overbearing authority to be avoided—2 Corinthians 13:10.
Priests—Genesis 14:18; Exodus 18:1; Joshua 3:6; 2 Chronicles 11:13.
Prophets—Numbers 12:6; 1 Samuel 10:11; 1 Kings 18:4; 2 Chronicles 20:20.
Rebellious leaders—Isaiah 1:23.
Respect church leadership—1 Thessalonians 5:12,13.
Servant leaders—Matthew 20:28; Mark 10:43,44; John 13:3-9; Titus 2:7.
Some leaders are like wolves—Ezekiel 22:27.
Transfer of leadership—Deuteronomy 34:9; 2 Samuel 2:1-7.
Work hard and become a leader—Proverbs 12:24.
See Government; Rulers, Wicked.

Lease
House rental—Acts 28:30.
Vineyard rental—Matthew 21:33; Mark 12:1; Luke 20:9.

Leaven
Beware the yeast of the Pharisees—Mark 8:15; Luke 12:1.
Kingdom of Heaven is like yeast—Matthew 13:33.
No yeast in grain offerings—Leviticus 2:11.
No yeast on Passover—Exodus 12:19,20.
Yeast of Pharisees and Sadducees—Matthew 16:6.
Yeast spreads quickly—Galatians 5:9.

Legalism
Avoid quarrels about the law—Titus 3:9.
Breaking the Sabbath—Mark 2:24; Luke 6:2; 13:14; John 5:10.

181

Dead to the law—Romans 7:4.

Don't let any judge you regarding Sabbath days—Colossians 2:16.

Gentiles and circumcision—Acts 15:5.

Letter kills, Spirit gives life—2 Corinthians 3:6.

No food is unclean in itself—Romans 14:14.

Paul previously zealous for law—Acts 22:3; Galatians 1:14.

Weighty burden—Luke 11:45,46.

Lending

All goes well for the generous—Psalm 112:5.

Be willing to loan to anyone—Luke 6:34,35.

Borrower is servant to lender—Proverbs 22:7.

Do not charge interest—Exodus 22:25; Deuteronomy 23:19.

Every seventh year, cancel debts—Deuteronomy 15:1.

Give to those who ask—Matthew 5:42.

Help relative in poverty—Leviticus 25:35.

Helping the poor is lending to the Lord—Proverbs 19:17.

The godly give generous loans—Psalm 37:26.

Leprosy

Follow instructions of Levitical priests—Deuteronomy 24:8.

Jesus heals leper—Matthew 8:3; Luke 5:13; 17:14.

King Uzziah had leprosy until day he died—2 Chronicles 26:21.

Leper ceremonially unclean—Leviticus 22:4.

Lord struck king with leprosy—2 Kings 15:5.

Liars/Lies

Devil, father of lies—John 8:44.

Do not lie—Proverbs 24:28; Colossians 3:9.

Do not pass along false reports—Exodus 23:1.

Do not spend time with liars—Psalm 26:4.

Do not testify falsely—Exodus 20:16; Deuteronomy 5:20.

L

False apostles lie—Revelation 2:2.
False witness is a traitor—Proverbs 14:25.
Followers of Jesus lied about—Matthew 5:11.
From the heart comes lying—Matthew 15:19.
God cannot lie—Numbers 23:19; Titus 1:2.
If we claim no sin, we lie—1 John 1:10.
Liars die young—Psalm 55:23.
Liars headed for hell—Revelation 21:8.
Lord hates liars—Proverbs 12:22.
Lord, rescue me from liars—Psalm 120:2.
Satan tempts believers to lie—Acts 5:3.

Liberalism

See Apostasy.

Liberty

Be free from concerns of life—1 Corinthians 7:32.
Christ led captives free—Ephesians 4:8.
Christ purchased our freedom—1 Timothy 2:6.
Christ's blood freed us from sin—Revelation 1:5.
In Christ no slave or free—Galatians 3:28.
Son sets you free—John 8:32-36.
We are set free from law of sin and death—Romans 8:1-3.

Life
Brevity of

All must die eventually—2 Samuel 14:14.
Be mindful of brevity of life—Psalm 39:4.
Days are swift—Job 7:6.
Days on earth are like a shadow—1 Chronicles 29:15.
Days on earth are transient—Job 8:9.
Fade away like a flower—James 1:10.
Gone in a moment—Psalm 78:39.
Human existence frail as breath—Psalm 39:11.
Humanity frail—Job 14:1.
Job near death—Job 17:1.

L

183

Life is like morning fog—James 4:14.

Life passes swiftly—Job 9:25.

Little time left—Job 10:20.

No one can escape power of grave—Psalm 89:48.

Only a step away from death—1 Samuel 20:3.

Remember how short life is—Psalm 89:47.

Seventy years are given to us—Psalm 90:10.

We are like a breath of air—Psalm 144:4.

We blossom for a moment, then wither—Job 14:2.

Wither like grass—Psalm 102:11; Isaiah 40:6,7,24; 51:12; 1 Peter 1:24.

Everlasting

All who believe in Jesus have eternal life—John 6:47,50.

Christ gives eternal life—John 10:28.

Confidence of eternal life—Titus 1:2.

Death is swallowed up in victory—1 Corinthians 15:53,54.

Death will be swallowed up forever—Isaiah 25:8.

Eternal body made for us by God—2 Corinthians 5:1.

Eternal life, free gift of God—Romans 6:23.

Eternal life in Jesus—1 John 5:11.

Hold tightly to eternal life—1 Timothy 6:12.

Righteous will go into eternal life—Matthew 25:46.

Rise up to everlasting life—Daniel 12:2.

Spiritual

Belief in Jesus necessary—John 5:24.

Bread of Life necessary—John 6:33,35,41,47,48.

Consider yourselves dead to sin—Romans 6:11.

Jesus is the resurrection and the life—John 11:25, 26.

Jesus is the way, the truth, and the life—John 14:6.

Jesus' purpose is to give life—John 10:10.

Must be born again—John 3:3.

You have become slaves of God—Romans 6:22.

You have been given new life—Romans 6:13.

184

Lifespan
See Life, Brevity of.

Lifestyle
See Conduct, Proper.

Light
Believers are full of light—Ephesians 5:8.
Brilliant light from heaven came upon Saul—Acts 9:3.
Children of the light—1 Thessalonians 5:5.
Creation, let there be light—Genesis 1:3;
    2 Corinthians 4:6.
Eye is a lamp for body—Luke 11:34.
God is light—1 John 1:5.
God lives in unapproachable light—1 Timothy 6:16.
God's Word is a lamp—Psalm 119:105.
Jesus' face shone like the sun—Matthew 17:2.
Jesus' followers, light of the world—Matthew 5:14-16.
Jesus is the light of the world—John 8:12; 9:5.
Let your lives shine brightly—Philippians 2:15.
Light in the eternal city—Isaiah 60:19; Revelation
    21:23.
Light to the Gentiles—Isaiah 49:6.
The Lord is my light—Psalm 27:1.

Lightning
God lays out path for lightning—Job 38:25.
God sends lightning—Psalm 135:7; Jeremiah 10:13;
    51:16.
God's lightning flashes—Psalm 97:4.
Second Coming like lightning—Matthew 24:27.
Throne of God, flashes of lightning—Revelation 4:5.

Liquor
See Alcohol.

L

185

Litigation

Come to terms quickly with your enemy—Matthew 5:25.
Do not file lawsuit against Christians—1 Corinthians 6:1.
Try to settle the matter—Luke 12:58.

Loan

See Lending.

Logic

Come now, let us reason—Isaiah 1:18; 43:26.
Jesus confounds critics with logic—Mark 11:29-33.

Loneliness

Christ is with us always—Matthew 28:20.
Even if mother and father forsake you, God will not—
Psalm 27:10.
Fear not, God is with you—Isaiah 41:10.
God will never forsake us—Hebrews 13:5.
Lord is with you like a shepherd—Psalm 23.
Poor man's friends desert him—Proverbs 19:4.

Longevity

Aaron died at 123—Numbers 33:39.
Fear of Lord lengthens life—Proverbs 10:27.
God gives long life—Psalm 91:16.
Honor father and mother, live long—Exodus 20:12.
Jacob died at 147—Genesis 47:28.
Joseph died at 110—Genesis 50:26.
Joshua died at 110—Joshua 24:29.
Longevity in millennial kingdom—Isaiah 65:20.
Moses died at 120—Deuteronomy 34:7.
Obedience to God yields long life—Proverbs 3:2.
Seventy years are given to us—Psalm 90:10.
Wisdom will multiply your days—Proverbs 9:11.

Lord's Prayer

Lord's Prayer—Matthew 6:9-13; Luke 11:2-4.
See Prayer; Prayerfulness.

Lord's Supper

Jesus celebrates—Matthew 26:26-28; Mark 14:22-24; Luke 22:19,20.

Paul on the Lord's Supper—1 Corinthians 11:23-29.

Lordship of Jesus Christ

See Jesus Christ, Lord.

Lost Sheep

Astray like a lost sheep—Psalm 119:176; 1 Peter 2:25.

Good shepherd seeks out—John 10:1-27.

Shepherd looks for single lost sheep—Matthew 18:12; Luke 15:4.

Love

For God

Be careful to love Lord—Joshua 23:11.

Choose to love Lord—Deuteronomy 30:6,16,20.

Desire only God—Psalm 73:25.

God brings good to those who love Him—Romans 8:28.

God first loved us—1 John 4:19–5:3.

God gives us spirit of love—2 Timothy 1:7.

God pours His love in our hearts—Romans 5:5.

Lord protects those who love Him—Psalm 145:20.

Love God, most important law—Mark 12:29-33.

Love God with whole heart and soul—Deuteronomy 6:5; 10:12; 11:13; 13:3.

Love means doing what God commands—2 John 6.

Pharisees neglect love of God—Luke 11:42.

Of Fellow Man

Be an example in love—1 Timothy 4:12.

Be filled with love—Ephesians 5:2; 1 Timothy 1:5.

Be Good Samaritan—Luke 10:25-37.

Disregard people's faults—Proverbs 17:9.

Do everything with love—1 Corinthians 16:14.

L

187

Do loving deeds—1 Thessalonians 1:3.

Do not just pretend to love others—Romans 12:9,10.

Fruit of Holy Spirit, love—Galatians 5:22.

God commands us to love each other—John 15:12,13.

Godliness leads to love—2 Peter 1:7.

Golden Rule—Matthew 7:12; Luke 6:31.

He who loves fulfills law—Romans 13:8-10; Galatians 5:13,14.

Let love be your highest goal—1 Corinthians 14:1.

Let love overflow—Philippians 1:9.

Live together in unity—Psalm 133:1-3.

Love covers all offenses—Proverbs 10:12.

Love each other—John 13:34,35; 15:12; Hebrews 13:1; 1 John 3:23; 2 John 1:5.

Love for God shows itself in love for others—1 John 4:7-12,20.

Love is supreme—1 Corinthians 13:1-13.

Love one another with tender hearts—1 Peter 3:8.

Love shows our commitment to Christ—1 John 2:9-11; 3:10,11,16-18.

Love strangers—Deuteronomy 10:19.

Love your Christian brothers and sisters—1 Peter 2:17.

Love your neighbor as yourself—Leviticus 19:18; James 2:8.

Many waters cannot quench love—Song of Solomon 8:7.

Show deep love for each other—1 Peter 4:8.

Show sincere love—1 Peter 1:22.

Of God
See *God, Love of.*

Of Jesus Christ
See *Jesus Christ, Love of.*

Loyalty
Be loyal to Christ—John 14:21-24.

Be loyal to friends—Ruth 1:14; Proverbs 17:17; 27:6.

Be loyal to God—Matthew 6:24; Luke 9:62;
   1 Corinthians 10:21.
Cannot serve two masters—Matthew 6:24.
Loyalty tested—John 21:15-17.

Lukewarmness

Abandoned your first love—Revelation 2:4.
From bad to worse—Jeremiah 9:3.
Hearts of the people are fickle—Hosea 10:2.
Neither hot nor cold—Revelation 3:15,16.

Lust

Abstain from fleshly lusts—1 Peter 2:11.
Avoid lust for physical pleasure—1 John 2:16.
Do not covet neighbor's wife—Exodus 20:17.
Do not even look at woman with lust—Matthew 5:28.
Don't gratify sinful nature—Romans 13:14.
Eve's sin began with lusting—Genesis 3:6.
Live by the Spirit to overcome lusts—Galatians 5:16.
Obey God, do not lust—Proverbs 6:24,25.
Run from youthful lusts—2 Timothy 2:22.
Sin nature full of lust—Ephesians 4:22.

L

M

Magician

Magic arts—Revelation 9:21.
Magic charms—Ezekiel 13:18.
Magic spells—Isaiah 47:12.
Magicians of Egypt mimicked Moses—Exodus 7:11,12,22; 8:7,18.
See Occultism.

Malice

Devil and malice—John 8:44.
Do not bear grudge—Leviticus 19:18.
Get rid of malicious behavior—Ephesians 4:31; Colossians 3:8; 1 Peter 2:1.
Lord hates malice—Zechariah 8:17.
See Bitterness; Resentment.

M

Mammon

Be trustworthy with worldly wealth—Luke 16:11.
No one can serve two masters—Matthew 6:24; Luke 16:13.
Use worldly resources to benefit others—Luke 16:9.
See Money.

Man

Creation of

All nations descended from one man—Acts 17:26.
Created a little lower than angels—Psalm 8:3-6; Hebrews 2:7,8.
Created in God's image—Genesis 1:26,27; 9:6; 1 Corinthians 11:7.
Created in likeness of God—Genesis 5:1; James 3:9.
Created to live on earth—Isaiah 45:12.
Eve formed from Adam's rib—Genesis 2:21-23.
God formed spirit within man—Zechariah 12:1.
God made male and female—Genesis 5:2; Mark 10:6.
God made us wonderfully complex—Psalm 139:14.

Man formed by God's own hands—Job 10:8-12; Isaiah 64:8.

Spirit and body created by God—Genesis 2:7.

Dichotomy View of

Man is body and soul—Matthew 10:28.

Man is body and spirit—Genesis 2:7; 2 Corinthians 7:1.

Spirit and soul equivalent—Luke 1:46,47.

Dominion of

Animals tamed by man—James 3:7.

Created to rule and subdue—Genesis 1:26,28.

Man rules over animals—Genesis 9:2,3; Jeremiah 27:6; 28:14; Daniel 2:38.

Ruler over all God's works—Psalm 8:6.

Insignificance of

Knows so little—Job 38:4,12,13.

Like a grasshopper—Isaiah 40:22.

Like a worm—Job 25:6.

What are mere mortals?—Psalm 8:3,4; 144:3,4.

Mortal

See Mortality.

Sinful

See Sin.

Trichotomy View of

Man is body, soul, and spirit—1 Thessalonians 5:23.

Word of God divides between soul and spirit—Hebrews 4:12.

Manna

Bread from heaven—Psalm 78:24; John 6:31.

Complaints about manna—Numbers 11:6.

Food from heaven rained down—Exodus 16:4.

M

Manners

Bad manners—Judges 8:35; 1 Samuel 25:21; 2 Kings 2:23,24.

Good manners—Leviticus 19:32; Job 29:7,8; 1 Corinthians 13:5; Colossians 4:5,6.

See Behavior; Conduct, Proper; Courtesy.

Marriage

Do not marry pagans—Deuteronomy 7:3,4.

Do not marry unbelievers—2 Corinthians 6:14.

Good wife, favor from the Lord—Proverbs 18:22.

If husband dies, wife can remarry—Romans 7:2,3.

Jesus on divorce—Matthew 5:31,32.

Keep marriage bed pure—Hebrews 13:4.

Man and woman become one—Genesis 2:24,25.

No marriage in afterlife—Matthew 22:30; Mark 12:25.

Paul on marriage and divorce—1 Corinthians 7:2-4, 7,8,10-14.

Rejoice in wife of youth—Proverbs 5:18.

Wife of noble character—Proverbs 12:4; 31:10,30,31.

Wives submit, husbands love—Ephesians 5:22-28,33.

See Divorce; Husband; Wife.

Figurative

Wedding feast of Lamb—Revelation 19:7.

Your Creator will be your husband—Isaiah 54:5.

Martyrdom

Family members may betray you—Matthew 10:21; Mark 13:12; Luke 21:16,17.

Give life up for Jesus, find true life—Matthew 10:39; 16:25; Luke 9:24.

Martyrs under God's throne—Revelation 6:9.

Prophets killed—Revelation 16:6.

Two witnesses martyred—Revelation 11:7.

See Persecution.

Mary

Asked Jesus to turn water to wine—John 2:1-11.
Mother of Jesus—Matthew 1:16.
Sword will pierce soul (at Jesus' crucifixion)—Luke 2:35.
Virgin will conceive a child—Isaiah 7:14; Matthew 1:23.

Materialism

Cannot have two masters—Matthew 6:24.
Danger of greed—1 Peter 5:2,3.
Dishonest money dwindles—Proverbs 13:11.
Do not be greedy for money—1 Peter 5:2.
Do not love money—1 Timothy 3:2,3; Hebrews 13:5.
False confidence in wealth—Psalm 49:6; Proverbs 11:28; Jeremiah 48:7.
Gold a snare—Judges 8:24-27.
Money lovers never satisfied—Ecclesiastes 5:10.
Store treasure in heaven, cannot be stolen—Matthew 6:19,20.
See Affluence; Greed.

M

Maturity

Avoid youthful passions—2 Timothy 2:22.
Be steadfast—1 Peter 5:10.
Be strong, resist evil—1 John 2:14.
Content in all situations—Philippians 4:12.
Discipline from God fosters maturity—Hebrews 12:6-9.
Grow in faith and love—2 Thessalonians 1:3.
Grow in grace and knowledge—2 Peter 3:18.
Grow to completion—Philippians 1:6.
Manual of maturity—Book of Proverbs.
Mature through Scripture—2 Timothy 3:16,17.
Partake of deeper truths—Hebrews 5:14.
Put away childish things—1 Corinthians 13:11.
Stand firm—Philippians 1:27-30.

Stay calm—2 Timothy 4:5.
Strive for Christ's ideal—Ephesians 4:13.
Think like adults—1 Corinthians 14:20.
*See Disciples and Discipleship; Growing Spiritually;
Immaturity.*

Mediator

See Advocate, Spiritual.

Medicine

Cheerful heart is good medicine—Proverbs 17:22.
Healing leaves in heaven—Revelation 22:2.
Medicinal wine—1 Timothy 5:23.
Ointments, bandages—Isaiah 1:6; 38:21.
Strong drink for the dying—Proverbs 31:6.
See Disease; Health.

Meditation

Meditate on God's Law—Joshua 1:8.
Meditate on God's principles—Psalm 119:23,48.
Meditate through the night—Psalm 63:6.
Ponder God's great works—Psalm 143:5.
Reflect on God's ways—Psalm 119:15.
See Devotions.

Meekness

Avoid conceit—Galatians 5:26.
Be humble and gentle—Ephesians 4:2.
Clothe yourselves with humility—Colossians 3:12.
God blesses the gentle and lowly—Matthew 5:5.
God leads the humble—Psalm 25:9.
Humble will be filled with fresh joy—Isaiah 29:19.
Lord supports the humble—Psalm 147:6.
Love is not proud—1 Corinthians 13:4.
Unfading beauty of a gentle and quiet spirit—1 Peter 3:4.

Merchant

Selling lambs, rams, and goats—Ezekiel 27:21.

M

Selling pearls—Matthew 13:45.

Selling Solomon's horses—1 Kings 10:28.

Selling variety of wares—Nehemiah 13:20.

Selling wheat, figs, honey, oil, and balm—Ezekiel 27:17.

See Commerce.

Mercy

Clothe yourselves with mercy—Colossians 3:12.

God blesses the merciful—Matthew 5:7.

God's mercy and compassion—Deuteronomy 4:31; Psalm 116:5.

God's mercy goes out to those who fear Him—Luke 1:50.

New mercies every morning—Lamentations 3:22,24.

Those who confess sins find mercy—Proverbs 28:13.

Messiah

Crucifixion prophesied—Zechariah 12:10.

Descendant of Abraham—Genesis 12:1-3.

Enables deaf to hear—Matthew 11:5.

God's Chosen One, the Messiah—Luke 23:35.

Heals the lame—Matthew 11:5; 15:31; 21:14; Luke 7:22.

Helps the blind see—Matthew 11:5.

Inaugurates New Covenant—Jeremiah 31:31-34.

Jesus is Messiah—Matthew 1:1; 16:20; Luke 9:20; 23:2; Mark 14:61; John 1:41.

Miracles prove Jesus is Messiah—John 20:31.

Prophecy of Messiah as God—Isaiah 40:3; Matthew 3:3.

Redeems from sin—1 Peter 1:18-20.

Rules on David's throne—Isaiah 9:7.

To be born in Bethlehem—Micah 5:2.

To be born of a virgin—Isaiah 7:14; Matthew 1:23.

Work of Messiah described—Isaiah 53.

M

Meteorology and Celestial Phenomena

At crucifixion, darkness fell across land—Matthew 27:45; Luke 23:44.

Flaming star will fall out of sky—Revelation 8:10.

God can restrain movement of stars—Job 38:31.

God commands sun and stars—Job 9:7.

God made moon to mark seasons—Psalm 104:19.

God stretched out heavens—Psalm 104:2.

Signs in the sun, moon, and stars—Luke 21:25.

Sun will be darkened—Joel 2:31; Matthew 24:29; Revelation 6:12.

Wonders in the heavens—Acts 2:19,20.

See Astronomy.

Military

Devout centurion—Acts 10:1,2,22.

God, a military leader—Judges 3:1,2.

Peter chained between soldiers, angel rescued—Acts 12:6,7.

Soldiers of Christ—2 Timothy 2:1-4.

Soldiers pierced Jesus' side—John 19:34.

War in heaven—Revelation 12:7.

Millennial Kingdom

1000-year period, Christ rules—Revelation 20:1-3.

Time of full knowledge of Lord—Isaiah 11:9.

Time of peace—Isaiah 19:24,25.

Time of productivity—Isaiah 35.

Time of righteousness—Isaiah 11:4.

See Jesus Christ, King; Second Coming of Christ.

Ministry

Build up church—2 Corinthians 12:19.

Entrusted with gospel—1 Thessalonians 2:4.

Exhort Christians—Titus 1:9; 2:15.

Feed believers—Acts 20:28; 1 Peter 5:2.

Issue warnings—Acts 20:30,31.

M

196

Jesus, High Priest with superior ministry—Hebrews
  8:6.
Mandate for ministry—2 Timothy 4:1-5.
Ministry in Lord's name—3 John 7.
Power for ministry—1 Thessalonians 1:4,5.
Preach the gospel—1 Corinthians 1:17.
Qualifications for elders—1 Timothy 3:1-7; Titus
  1:7-9.
Strengthen faith—Acts 14:22.
Teach doctrine—2 Timothy 2:2.
Upward call—Philippians 3:14.
Watch over souls—Hebrews 13:17.

Miracles

Convincing Effect of

Crowds listened intently—Acts 8:6.
Disciples believed in Christ—John 2:11,22,23.
Egyptians fearful—Exodus 14:25.
God convinces by miracles—Romans 15:19.
Nebuchadnezzar responds—Daniel 3:28,29.
Pharaoh responds—Exodus 10:16,17; 12:31.
Prove that Jesus is Messiah—John 20:31.

Of Jesus Christ

See Jesus Christ, Miracles of.

Of the New Testament, Notable

5000 fed—Matthew 14:15-21.
Centurion's servant cured of paralysis—Matthew
  8:5-13.
Fig tree withered—Matthew 21:18-22.
Lazarus raised from the dead—John 11:38-44.
Net full of fishes—Luke 5:1-11.
Paralytic cured—Matthew 9:1-8.
Peter's mother-in-law healed—Matthew 8:14-17.
Resurrection of Jesus Christ—Luke 24:6.
Ten lepers cleansed—Luke 17:11-19.
Walking on water—Matthew 14:25-33.

M

197

Water turned into wine—John 2:1-11.
Widow's son raised from the dead—Luke 7:11-17.
Windstorm stilled—Matthew 8:23-27.
Woman with flow of blood healed—Matthew 9:20-22.

Of the Old Testament, Notable

Daniel in lion's den—Daniel 6:22.
Dead man revived by touching Elisha's bones—2 Kings 13:21.
Fifty men destroyed by God's fire—2 Kings 1:10.
God divides sea—Exodus 14:13-22.
Jonah swallowed by great fish—Jonah 1:17.
Lord appeared in burning bush—Exodus 3:2.
Lot's wife became pillar of salt—Genesis 19:26.
Miraculous perception of angels—2 Kings 6:17.
Moses' staff became snake—Exodus 4:3-5.
Shadrach, Meshach, and Abednego in furnace—Daniel 3:19-30.
Sun stands still—Joshua 10:12,13.

M

Mission of Jesus Christ

See Jesus Christ, Mission of.

Missionary Work

Be ready with an answer—1 Peter 3:15.
Christ's ambassadors—2 Corinthians 5:18-21.
Confess Christ—Matthew 10:32.
Contend for faith—Jude 3.
Evangelize—Matthew 28:19,20.
Jonah—Jonah 3:2.
Message of missionaries—1 Timothy 2:5-7.
Message to entire world—Acts 10:9-20.
Paul's first missionary journey—Acts 13–14.
Paul's second missionary journey—Acts 15:36-41; 16–17; 18:1-22.
Paul's third missionary journey—Acts 18:23-28; 19–20; 21:1-15.
Spread of gospel—Colossians 1:6.

Teach doctrine—Colossians 3:16; Hebrews 3:13.

See Ambassadors, God's; Evangelism; Gospel.

Mixed Marriages (Believers with Unbelievers)

Bad results from marrying unbelievers—Genesis 6:1-4.

Don't be yoked with unbeliever—2 Corinthians 6:14-16.

God's anger provoked—Joshua 23:12,13.

Two cannot walk together unless agreed—Amos 3:3.

Mocking

Am I my brother's keeper?—Genesis 4:9.

Go away, you baldhead—2 Kings 2:23.

Hail! King of the Jews—John 19:3.

Let the false gods save you—Judges 10:14.

Prophesy to us, you Messiah—Matthew 26:68.

Rebuild temple in three days, can you?—Mark 15:29.

You would convert me?—Acts 26:28.

M

Model

Be example by doing good deeds—Titus 2:7; 1 Timothy 4:12.

Do not be influenced by bad example—3 John 11.

Do not be stumbling block—1 Corinthians 8:9,13.

Imitate apostles and Lord—1 Thessalonians 1:6.

Imitate church leaders—Hebrews 13:7.

Imitate the ants—Proverbs 6:6,9.

Leaders lead by good example—1 Peter 5:3.

Prophets, examples of patience—James 5:10.

Modesty

Examples of—1 Samuel 9:21; Esther 1:11,12; Job 32:4-7.

Women should be modest—1 Timothy 2:9.

Money

Abram very rich—Genesis 13:2.

Cannot buy gift of God—Acts 8:20.

Cannot have two masters—Matthew 6:24.

Dishonest money dwindles—Proverbs 13:11.

Do not be greedy for money—1 Peter 5:2.

Do not love money—1 Timothy 3:2,3; Hebrews 13:5.

Give to Caesar what belongs to him—Matthew 22:21.

Judas sold out for 30 pieces of silver—Matthew 27:3.

Money lovers never satisfied—Ecclesiastes 5:10.

Monotheism

God is one—James 2:19.

Lord is one—Deuteronomy 6:4.

One God and Father of all—Ephesians 4:5,6.

Only one God—Deuteronomy 4:35; Isaiah 46:9.

There is no God but one—1 Corinthians 8:4.

Moon

God made moon to mark seasons—Psalm 104:19.

God made moon to preside at night—Genesis 1:16.

Moon will become red as blood—Joel 2:31; Acts 2:20; Revelation 6:12.

Moon will grow dark—Joel 3:15; Matthew 24:29; Mark 13:24; Revelation 8:12.

Worship of moon forbidden—Deuteronomy 17:3.

Morality

Bad company corrupts good character—1 Corinthians 15:33.

Be holy for God is holy—1 Peter 1:15.

Fruit of Holy Spirit—Galatians 5:22,23.

Human morality proves a moral source—Romans 2:14-16.

Kingdom of God requires righteousness—Romans 14:17.

Morality and Christian leadership—1 Timothy 3:1-13; 2 Timothy 2:24,25.

Morality exemplified in Sermon on the Mount—Matthew 5–7.

M

Morality exemplified in Ten Commandments—Exodus 20:1-17.

Scripture fosters morality—2 Timothy 3:16,17.

Mortality

All people die—Job 30:23; Ecclesiastes 7:2; 1 Corinthians 15:21,22.

Death resulted from sin—Romans 5:12.

Each person dies once—Hebrews 9:27.

Man is like withering grass—Psalm 90:5,6; 103:15,16; James 1:10; 1 Peter 1:24.

No one has power over death—Ecclesiastes 8:8.

Return to ground—Genesis 3:19.

We quickly disappear—Job 14:1,2.

What are mere mortals?—Psalm 8:3,4; 144:3,4.

See Death.

Moses

Baby in basket—Exodus 2:3.

Commissioned to deliver Israelites—Exodus 3:10.

Fled from Pharaoh—Exodus 2:15.

God appeared to in burning bush—Exodus 3:2.

God made him seem like a god to Pharaoh—Exodus 7:1.

"Let my people go"—Exodus 5:1.

Pharaoh's daughter got baby in basket—Exodus 2:5.

Stone tablets, Ten Commandments—Exodus 34:29.

Tended flock of father-in-law—Exodus 3:1.

Was taught all the wisdom of the Egyptians—Acts 7:22.

Mother

Do not curse or strike mother—Exodus 21:15,17.

Do not despise mother's experience—Proverbs 23:22.

Do not neglect mother's teaching—Proverbs 1:8; 6:20.

Foolish child brings grief to mother—Proverbs 10:1.

Foolish children despise mother—Proverbs 15:20.

M

Honor your mother—Exodus 20:12; Matthew 19:19; Luke 18:20; Ephesians 6:2.

Love Jesus more than mother—Matthew 10:37.

Mother is disgraced by undisciplined child—Proverbs 29:15.

Respect mother—Leviticus 19:3.

Mountain

Devil took Jesus to peak of high mountain—Matthew 4:8.

Faith can move mountain—Matthew 17:20; 21:21; Mark 11:23.

Mount Sinai shook in presence of Lord—Judges 5:5.

Sermon on the Mount—Matthew 5–7.

Mourning, Examples of

Abraham mourned Sarah—Genesis 23:2.

Loud wailing throughout Egypt—Exodus 12:30.

Mourning throughout Bethlehem—Matthew 2:18.

Reuben and Jacob mourned Joseph—Genesis 37:29,34,35.

See Bereavement and Loss; Grief; Tears.

Murder

Capital punishment instituted for murder—Genesis 9:6.

Commandment against murder—Exodus 20:13; Deuteronomy 5:17.

Devil is a murderer—John 8:44.

From the heart comes murder—Matthew 15:19; Mark 7:21.

God abhors murderers and deceivers—Psalm 5:6.

God will avenge—Deuteronomy 32:43; Psalm 9:12.

Lord detests murderers—Psalm 5:6.

Murder comes from sin nature—Galatians 5:21.

Murder forbidden—Genesis 9:5.

Murderers do not have eternal life—1 John 3:15.

Murmuring

Against Christ—Luke 5:30; John 6:41-43,52.

Against disciples—Mark 7:2; Luke 5:30.

Against God—Proverbs 19:3.

Angers God—Numbers 14:2,11; Deuteronomy 9:8,22.

Complaining wife—Proverbs 21:19.

Do not grumble—1 Corinthians 10:10.

Examples of—Exodus 14:11; 15:24; 16:2; 17:3; Numbers 11:1; 14:27; Psalm 77:3.

God hears all complaints—Numbers 14:27.

Stay away from complaining and arguing—Philippians 2:14.

Wicked people engage in—Jude 10.

Music and Musical Instruments

Harp and flute—Genesis 4:21.

Harps and lyres for musicians—1 Kings 10:12.

Harps, lyres, tambourines, sistrums, and cymbals—2 Samuel 6:5.

Hymns and spiritual songs—Colossians 3:16.

Lyres, tambourines, flutes, and harps—1 Samuel 10:5.

Praise God with harp—Psalm 43:4; 71:22; 98:5; 144:9; 147:7; 149:3; 150:3,4.

Prayer accompanied by harp—Habakkuk 3:19.

Promotes joy—Ecclesiastes 2:8-10.

Psalm accompanied by harp—Psalm 4:1; 6:1; 55:1; 61:1; 67:1; 76:1.

Song of Moses—Exodus 15:1-18.

Tambourine and harp—Job 21:12.

Tambourines and flutes—Isaiah 5:12.

Trumpets and cymbals and other instruments—1 Chronicles 16:42.

Used at coronation of kings—2 Chronicles 23:11-13.

Used at religious feasts—2 Chronicles 30:21.

Used in funeral ceremonies—Matthew 9:23.

Used in Temple—1 Chronicles 16:4-6; 2 Chronicles 29:25.

Used to celebrate victory—1 Samuel 18:6,7.

M

Names of God

El Elyon is the Most High—Isaiah 14:13,14.

El Olam is the Everlasting God—Isaiah 40:28.

El Roi is the Strong One who sees us—Genesis 16:13.

El Shaddai is God Almighty—Genesis 17:1-21.

Elohim created the universe—Genesis 1:1.

Elohim is Yahweh—Deuteronomy 6:4.

Elohim's name should not be taken in vain—Exodus 20:7.

Yahweh delivered Israel from Egypt—Exodus 20:2.

Yahweh sent Moses to Egypt—Exodus 3:14.

Yahweh-Jireh provides for us—Genesis 22:13,14.

Yahweh-Sabbaoth is the Lord of hosts—1 Samuel 1:3.

Yahweh-Shalom is our peace—Judges 6:24.

Yahweh-Shammah is present with us—Ezekiel 48:35.

Names of Jesus Christ

See Jesus Christ, Names and Titles of.

Nations

Every nation came from one man—Acts 17:26.

God has plan for whole earth—Isaiah 14:26.

God has plans for Israel—Romans 9–11.

Nations will beat swords into plowshares—Isaiah 2:4; Micah 4:3.

What joy for the nation whose God is the Lord—Psalm 33:12.

Nativity

See Christmas.

Nature, World of

All nature praises God—1 Chronicles 16:31-33; Psalm 69:34; 96:11,13.

Beautiful flowers—Song of Solomon 2:12.

Christ upholds creation—Colossians 1:17.

Earth entrusted to man—Psalm 115:16.
Living creatures—Genesis 1:20.
New heavens, new earth—Isaiah 65:17; 66:22; 2 Peter 3:13; Revelation 21:1.
Not even Solomon was dressed like lilies—Matthew 6:29.
Revelation through nature—Psalm 19:1-14; Romans 1:18-20.
Wilderness will rejoice and blossom—Isaiah 35:1.

Nazareth
Can anything good come from Nazareth?—John 1:46.
God sent angel Gabriel to Nazareth—Luke 1:26,27.
Jesus, a Nazarene—Matthew 2:23; Mark 1:24.
Jesus, prophet from Nazareth—Matthew 21:11; Luke 24:19.
Jesus' boyhood home—Luke 4:16.

Necromancy
Consulting mediums and psychics—Isaiah 8:19.
Do not call forth spirits of the dead—Deuteronomy 18:10-12.
Medium at Endor—1 Samuel 28:7.
See Occultism.

Neighbor
Do not plot against neighbors—Proverbs 3:29.
Do not testify falsely against neighbor—Exodus 20:16.
Love your neighbor as yourself—Matthew 19:19; 22:39; Romans 13:9; James 2:8.

Nepotism, Examples of
David appointed nephew commander—2 Samuel 19:13.
Joseph gave best land to family—Genesis 47:11.
Saul's cousin Abner was appointed commander—1 Samuel 14:50.

New Heavens and New Earth
New heavens, new earth—Isaiah 65:17; 66:22; 2 Peter 3:13; Revelation 21:1.

205

Night

Darkness was called night—Genesis 1:5.

Jesus prayed to God all night—Luke 6:12.

Jesus walked on water during night hours—Matthew 14:25.

Meditating on God during night—Psalm 63:6.

Moon gives light at night—Genesis 1:16.

No night in heaven—Revelation 22:5.

Ponder God's promises during night—Psalm 119:148.

Noah

Became a farmer—Genesis 9:20.

Built an altar on land—Genesis 8:20.

Entered the Ark—Genesis 7:1.

Lived 350 years after flood—Genesis 9:28.

Lived to 950 years old—Genesis 9:29.

Made the Ark—Genesis 6:14.

See Ark, Noah's.

N

Oaths, Examples of

Abram's oath—Genesis 14:22.
David's oath—1 Samuel 20:3.
Elijah's oath—2 Kings 2:2.
Esau's oath—Genesis 25:33.
Peter's oath—Mark 14:71.
Ruth's oath—Ruth 1:17.
Saul's oath—1 Samuel 19:6.

Obedience

Abraham's obedience—Genesis 17:23.
Be careful to obey everything—Joshua 23:6.
Be devoted to obedience—Psalm 119:45.
Blessed are those that obey—Psalm 119:2,12; Luke 11:28.
Christ's sheep follow Him—John 10:27.
Disobey, be least in the kingdom—Matthew 5:19.
Do will of God with whole heart—Ephesians 6:6.
Ezra's obedience—Ezra 7:10.
Friendship and obedience—John 15:14.
God loves the obedient—Deuteronomy 5:10; Psalm 25:10.
Happiness and obedience—Psalm 112:1; 119:55,56.
Hurry to obey—Psalm 119:60.
Jesus' obedience—John 4:34.
Jonah's obedience—Jonah 3:3.
Joseph's obedience—Matthew 1:24.
Joshua's obedience—Joshua 10:40.
Levites' obedience—Deuteronomy 33:9.
Life and obedience—Proverbs 19:16.
Love and obedience—John 14:21; 1 John 5:3.
Mary's obedience—Luke 1:38.
Moses' and Aaron's obedience—Exodus 7:6.
Obedience and assurance—1 John 2:3.
Obedience and eating hearty—Isaiah 1:19.

Obedience and family of God—Matthew 12:50; Mark 3:35; Luke 8:21.

Obedience and fellowship—1 John 3:24.

Obedience and long life—1 Kings 3:14.

Obedience better than sacrifice—1 Samuel 15:22.

Obedience of angels—Psalm 103:21.

Obey and all will be well—Jeremiah 7:23.

Obey and live forever—John 8:51; 1 John 2:17.

Obey as God's children—1 Peter 1:14.

Obey God over humans—Acts 4:19; 5:29.

Obey God's commands with all purity—1 Timothy 6:14.

Obey wholeheartedly—Joshua 24:14; Romans 6:17.

Peace and obedience—Proverbs 1:33.

Perpetual obedience—Psalm 119:44.

Prayer and obedience—1 John 3:22.

Wisdom and obedience—Psalm 119:100.

Of Jesus Christ
See Jesus Christ, Obedience of.

Obesity

Eglon was fat—Judges 3:17,22.

Eli was fat—1 Samuel 2:29; 4:18.

Gluttony—Proverbs 23:2.

Gorging—Proverbs 23:20,21.

Overeating—Proverbs 25:16.

Stomach is god—Philippians 3:19.

Take care of body—1 Corinthians 6:19,20.

Obligation

See Responsibility.

Obscenity

Avoid foul or abusive language—Romans 3:13,14; Ephesians 4:29.

Avoid perverse talk—Proverbs 4:24.

Corrupt speech, wicked men—Proverbs 2:12.

Do not speak evil—James 4:11; 1 Peter 3:10.

208

Evil words destructive—Proverbs 11:9.

Mouths full of cursing, lies, and threats—Psalm 10:7.

Obscene stories and coarse jokes—Ephesians 5:4.

Wicked speak only what is corrupt—Proverbs 10:32; 15:28.

Occultism

Astrologers cannot interpret dreams—Daniel 4:7.

Astrologers cannot save you—Isaiah 47:13.

Consulting mediums brings judgment—Leviticus 20:6.

Diviners will be disgraced—Micah 3:7.

Do not call forth spirits of the dead—Deuteronomy 18:11.

Do not listen to fortunetellers—Jeremiah 27:9.

Do not listen to mediums, psychics—Leviticus 19:31; Isaiah 8:19.

Do not practice fortunetelling—Leviticus 19:26.

Do not try to read future in stars—Jeremiah 10:2.

Egyptian magicians, secret arts—Exodus 7:11,22; 8:7,18.

Egypt's mediums and psychics—Isaiah 19:3.

Execute mediums, psychics, sorcerers—Exodus 22:18; Leviticus 20:27.

Fortuneteller—Acts 16:16,18.

Incantation books burned—Acts 19:19.

Josiah exterminated mediums and psychics—2 Kings 23:24.

Magicians, enchanters, sorcerers stood before king—Daniel 2:2.

Medium at Endor—1 Samuel 28:7.

No fortunetelling or sorcery—Deuteronomy 18:10,11.

No more fortunetellers—Micah 5:12.

Reading stars—Isaiah 47:13.

Saul consulted medium—1 Chronicles 10:13.

Sorcery and divination—2 Kings 21:6.

Using cups—Genesis 44:2,5.

Wizards—1 Samuel 28:3.

O

Offering
See Tithes.

Jesus as
High Priest offered Himself—Hebrews 10:12.
Lamb of God—John 1:29; Revelation 5:6.
Offering for our sin—2 Corinthians 5:21.
Passover Lamb—1 Corinthians 5:7.
Sacrifice—Ephesians 5:2.

Offerings

Figurative
Give your bodies to God—Romans 12:1.
Sacrifice of praise—Hebrews 13:15.

Piety Must Accompany
Broken spirit desired—Psalm 51:17.
Do what is right—Proverbs 21:3.
No hypocrisy—Amos 5:21.
Obedience required—1 Samuel 15:22.

Old Age
Extended age prior to flood—Genesis 6:3.
God sustains us even in old age—Isaiah 46:4.
Gray hair is a crown of glory—Proverbs 16:31.
Instructions for older men—Titus 2:2,3.
Satisfying long life—Psalm 91:16.
Seventy years are given to us—Psalm 90:10.
Wisdom belongs to the aged—Job 12:12.

Omnipotence
See God, Omnipotence of.
See Jesus Christ, Omnipotence of.

Omnipresence
See God, Omnipresence of.
See Jesus Christ, Omnipresence of.

Omniscience

See God, Omniscience of.
See Jesus Christ, Omniscience of.

Opposition

By family members—Matthew 10:21.
By powers of darkness—Ephesians 6:12.
By the devil—1 Thessalonians 2:18; 1 Peter 5:8,9.
Gently teach those who oppose truth—2 Timothy 2:25.
God opposes the proud—James 4:6; 1 Peter 5:5.
Godly suffer persecution—2 Timothy 3:12.
Love your enemies—Luke 6:27.
Mob against Paul and Silas—Acts 17:5,7.
Moses chose affliction over pleasures of sin—Hebrews 11:25.
Opposition to Christ—Matthew 26:3,4.
Opposition to God—2 Thessalonians 2:3,4.
Opposition to Holy Spirit—Acts 7:51.
Opposition to ministry—1 Corinthians 16:9.
Opposition to those who speak truth—Isaiah 30:10; Jeremiah 11:21.
Paul beaten, jailed, and mobbed—2 Corinthians 6:5.
Paul persecuted Christians in ignorance—Galatians 1:13.
Pray for those who persecute you—Romans 12:14.
Sheep among wolves—Matthew 10:16.
Soft speech crushes opposition—Proverbs 25:15.
Those who sin are opposed to God's law—1 John 3:4.
When God is for us...—Romans 8:31.
Wicked despise the godly—Proverbs 29:27.

Oppression

Do not oppress foreigners—Exodus 22:21; 23:9.
Do not oppress widows, orphans, poor people—Zechariah 7:10.

211

Egyptians oppressed Israelites—Exodus 3:9.
God rescues the oppressed—Psalm 9:9; 12:5.
Lord helps those treated unfairly—Psalm 103:6.
Lord, rescue me from oppression—Psalm 119:134.
Oppression and extortion wrong—Habakkuk 2:6.
Unjust laws—Isaiah 10:1,2.

Optimism

Be confident—2 Corinthians 5:6.
Be joyful always—1 Thessalonians 5:16.
Be strong and take heart—Psalm 31:24.
Cheerful heart is good medicine—Proverbs 17:22.
God has plans for us—Jeremiah 29:10,11.
Hope in God—Psalm 42:5.
Let us rejoice and be glad—Psalm 118:24.
Lift up eyes to the hills—Psalm 121:1.
No fear of bad news—Psalm 112:7,8.
There is a future—Psalm 37:37.

Outer Space

See Astronomy; Meteorology and Celestial Phenomena.

O

P

Pagans

Detestable acts—Deuteronomy 12:31.

Human sacrifice in fire—2 Kings 16:3; 17:17.

Idolatry—Deuteronomy 27:15.

Indulgence in pagan revelry—1 Corinthians 10:7.

Many so-called gods—1 Corinthians 8:5.

Sacrifice of sons and daughters—Psalm 106:37.

Sacrifices to demons—Deuteronomy 32:17; Psalm 106:37; 1 Corinthians 10:20.

Sacrificing to false god—Exodus 22:20.

Shrine prostitutes—1 Kings 14:24; 15:12.

Sorcery and divination—2 Kings 21:6.

See Abomination; Heathen; Idol.

Paradise

Paul caught up to paradise—2 Corinthians 12:4.

Thief with Christ in paradise—Luke 23:43.

Tree of life in paradise—Revelation 2:7.

See Heaven.

Paralysis

Paralyzed man healed—Matthew 9:2-6; Mark 2:3-9; Luke 5:18.

Paralyzed people healed—Acts 8:7.

Parents

Bring children to Christ—Matthew 19:13,14.

Do not curse parents—Exodus 21:17; Proverbs 20:20; 30:11.

Do not despise and defy parents—Deuteronomy 27:16; Micah 7:6.

Do not mistreat parents—Proverbs 19:26.

Do not provoke children—Ephesians 6:4; Colossians 3:21.

Do not rise against parents—Mark 13:12.

Do not rob parents—Proverbs 28:24.

Do not strike parents—Exodus 21:15.

Even if parents forsake you, God will not—Psalm 27:10.

Evil influence over children—1 Kings 22:52; Jeremiah 9:14; Amos 2:4.

Father-son rivalry—2 Samuel 15:1-37.

Fool despises parents' discipline—Proverbs 15:5.

Good influence over children—1 Kings 9:4; 2 Chronicles 17:3; 2 Timothy 1:5.

Listen to what parents teach—Proverbs 1:8; 6:20; 23:22.

Obey parents—Ephesians 6:1; Colossians 3:20.

Pagan parents eat children—Ezekiel 5:10.

Parents correct children—Proverbs 13:24; 19:18; 22:15.

Parents exercise control over children—1 Timothy 3:4.

Parents influence children for paganism—Jeremiah 17:2.

Parents nurture children—Ephesians 6:4.

Parents provide for children—2 Corinthians 12:14.

Parents the pride of their children—Proverbs 17:6.

Partiality of parents—Genesis 25:28; 37:3; 48:22; 1 Chronicles 26:10.

Pray for children—1 Thessalonians 5:17.

Show compassion to children—Psalm 103:13.

Show respect for parents—Leviticus 19:3.

Treat children fairly—Deuteronomy 21:15-17.

See Children; Daughter; Son.

P

Partiality

See Favoritism, Examples of.

Passover

Celebrate Passover—Ezekiel 45:21.

Christ, our Passover Lamb—1 Corinthians 5:7.

Jesus' betrayal, near time of Passover—Matthew 26:2; Mark 14:1.

Pastor

Appointed by God—2 Corinthians 3:6; 4:1; 5:18; Ephesians 3:7; Colossians 1:23.

Feed and shepherd God's flock—Acts 20:28; 1 Peter 5:2.

God gives pastors to the church—Ephesians 4:11.

Not heavy drinker—1 Timothy 3:3; Titus 1:7.
Not lover of money—1 Timothy 3:3.
Not quick-tempered—Titus 1:7.
Pray over the sick—James 5:14.
Pray, preach, and teach—Acts 6:4.
Preach Christ crucified—1 Corinthians 1:23.
Preach Jesus as Lord—2 Corinthians 4:5.
Preach the Word—Mark 16:15; 1 Timothy 4:2,13.
Serve God—Revelation 22:3.
Set example for flock—1 Peter 5:3.
Should be paid well—1 Timothy 5:17.
See Clergy.

Patience

Be patient in trouble—Romans 12:12.
Be patient until Lord's coming—James 5:7-10.
Be patient with everyone—Ephesians 4:2;
    1 Thessalonians 5:14.
Clothe yourselves in patience—Colossians 3:12.
Cool-tempered person stops fights—Proverbs 15:18.
Do not be quick-tempered—Ecclesiastes 7:8,9.
Fruit of Spirit includes patience—Galatians 5:22.
Love is patient—1 Corinthians 13:4.
Patient endurance—2 Corinthians 1:6; 2 Peter 1:6;
    Revelation 1:9.
Patient man has understanding—Proverbs 14:29.
Patiently endure troubles—2 Corinthians 6:4.
Patiently endure unfair treatment—1 Peter 2:19.
Preach with patience—2 Timothy 4:2.
Wait patiently and confidently—Romans 8:25.
Wait patiently for Lord—Psalm 37:7.
Wisdom gives patience—Proverbs 19:11.

Of God
    See God, Patience of.

Paul

Apostle—1 Corinthians 9:1.
Began preaching—Acts 9:20.

P

Dragged out to be stoned—Acts 14:19.
Eager to destroy Lord's followers—Acts 9:1.
Educated under Gamaliel—Acts 22:3.
Jew of Tarsus—Acts 21:39.
Lord appears to Paul—Acts 9:3-9.
Member of Pharisees—Philippians 3:5.
People tried to worship Paul—Acts 14:11-15.
Persecuted church—Acts 8:3.
Witnessed Stephen's execution—Acts 7:58–8:1.

Peace of Mind

Be at peace, Christ has overcome world—John 16:33.
Fruit of Holy Spirit—Galatians 5:22.
Holy Spirit controls mind, peace—Romans 8:6.
Let not your heart be troubled—John 14:27.
Let peace of God rule your heart—Colossians 3:15.
Mind stayed on God is in perfect peace—Isaiah 26:3.
Peace and joy in the Holy Spirit—Romans 14:17.
Peace of God guards your heart—Philippians 4:7.
Peace with God—Romans 5:1.

P

Penitence

Angels rejoice when sinners repent—Luke 15:7-10.
Broken and repentant heart—Psalm 51:17.
God answers prayers of the penitent—2 Chronicles 7:14.
God comforts the penitent—Matthew 5:4.
God forgives the penitent—Micah 7:18.
God gives Holy Spirit to the penitent—Acts 2:38.
God gives life to the penitent—Ezekiel 18:21.
God pardons sins of penitent—Isaiah 55:7.
Lord is close to the brokenhearted—Psalm 34:18.

Pentecost

Holy Spirit fell on Day of Pentecost—Acts 2.
See Charismatic Issues; Holy Spirit.

Perfection

Abram called to be blameless—Genesis 17:1.

Be perfect—Matthew 5:48.

Believers do not claim perfection—Philippians 3:12.

Church will ultimately attain to perfection—Ephesians 4:13.

Father in heaven is perfect—Matthew 5:48.

God's law is perfect—Psalm 19:7.

God's power made perfect in weakness—2 Corinthians 12:9.

God's way is perfect—2 Samuel 22:31.

God's work is perfect—Deuteronomy 32:4.

Impossibility of attaining perfection in this life—Psalm 119:96.

Jesus, High Priest, perfect sacrifice—Hebrews 10:12.

Mind stayed on God is in perfect peace—Isaiah 26:3.

Now we see imperfectly—1 Corinthians 13:9-12.

Perfect faithfulness of God—Isaiah 25:1.

Perfect in Christ—1 Corinthians 2:6; Philippians 3:15; Colossians 1:28.

Pray for perfection—Hebrews 13:20,21; 1 Peter 5:10.

Whatever is good and perfect comes from God—James 1:17.

Perfectionism

See Sinlessness.

Perfections of Jesus Christ

See Jesus Christ, Sinlessness.

Perjury

Corrupt witness—Proverbs 19:28.

Do not lie—Leviticus 19:11.

Do not pass along false reports—Exodus 23:1.

Do not testify falsely—Exodus 20:16; Deuteronomy 5:20.

False accusations—Acts 6:11.

217

False witness is a traitor—Proverbs 14:25.

False witness tells lies—Proverbs 12:17.

Perjurers—1 Timothy 1:10.

Peter commits—Mark 14:71.

Persecution

All the godly suffer persecution—2 Timothy 3:12.

Blessed are those persecuted for righteousness—Matthew 5:10,11.

Brother will betray brother—Matthew 10:21.

Do not be surprised if world hates you—1 John 3:13.

God blesses those mocked for following Jesus—Luke 6:22,23.

Great wave of persecution broke out—Acts 8:1-3.

Moses chose affliction over pleasures of sin—Hebrews 11:24,25.

Paul beaten, jailed, and mobbed—2 Corinthians 6:4,5.

Persecution after Stephen's death—Acts 11:19.

Pray for those who persecute you—Matthew 5:44.

Rejoice in being counted worthy to suffer—Acts 5:41.

Sheep among wolves—Matthew 10:16.

Suffer for doing good—1 Peter 3:17.

Suffer with Christ now, be glorified with Christ later—Romans 8:17.

Time of great persecution—Luke 21:12.

Wicked despise the godly—Proverbs 29:27.

You will be persecuted—Revelation 2:10.

See Martyrdom.

Perseverance

Be faithful to the end—Hebrews 3:14.

Do not tire of doing good—Galatians 6:9; 2 Thessalonians 3:13.

Endure suffering—2 Timothy 2:3.

God's children shall never perish—John 10:28,29.

God's Word assures us—1 John 5:13.

Hold on to pattern of right teaching—2 Timothy 1:13.

P

218

Hold on to what is good—1 Thessalonians 5:21.
Hold tightly to hope—Hebrews 10:23.
Jesus prays for us—John 17:11,12.
Lord rescues us—2 Timothy 4:18.
Nothing can separate us from Christ—Romans 8:38,39.
Remain faithful—2 Timothy 3:14.
Run with endurance—Hebrews 12:1.
Stand firm—2 Corinthians 1:21; Ephesians 6:13; Colossians 1:23.
Stand true—1 Corinthians 16:13.
Stay alert—Ephesians 6:18.
Watch out for attacks from devil—1 Peter 5:8.
Watch out, do not be carried away with error—2 Peter 3:17.

Personhood of Holy Spirit
See Holy Spirit, Personhood of.

Pessimism
All is meaningless—Ecclesiastes 1:2.
Dread fulfilled—Job 3:25.
Elijah gripes—1 Kings 19:4-10.
Focusing on affliction—Psalm 116:10,11.
Focusing on troubles—Psalm 25:17.
Spies with bad attitude—Numbers 13:25-31.

Pestilence
Consuming pestilence—Deuteronomy 32:24.
Deadly pestilence—Psalm 91:3,6.
Plagues that destroy—Leviticus 26:25.
Wasting diseases—Leviticus 26:16.
See Disease.

Pets
See Animals.

Pharisees

Apostle Paul—Acts 23:6.
Brood of snakes—Matthew 3:7.
Hypocrites—Matthew 6:2; Luke 12:1.
Tried to trap Jesus—Matthew 19:3; 22:15.
Wanted miraculous sign—Matthew 12:38,39.
Worship is a farce—Matthew 15:9.
See Formalism; Hypocrisy; Legalism.

Philanthropy

See Alms (Good Deeds); Generosity.

Philosophy

Brilliant ideas—1 Corinthians 2:1.
Cosmological argument—Romans 1:20.
Empty philosophy—Colossians 2:8.
Epicurean and Stoic philosophers—Acts 17:18.
High-sounding ideas—1 Corinthians 1:17.
Human wisdom—1 Corinthians 1:19,21,22; 2:13.
Wisdom that belongs to this world—1 Corinthians 2:6.

Physician

P

Doctor Luke—Colossians 4:14.
Physician, heal yourself—Luke 4:23.
Sick people need a doctor—Matthew 9:12; Mark 2:17.
See Healing, God Does Not Always Grant; Health.

Physiology

God clothed us with skin and flesh—Job 10:11.
God put us together—Psalm 139:13,15.
Humans are wonderfully complex—Psalm 139:14.

Pleasure, Worldly

Constant partying leads to destruction—Isaiah
5:11-13.
Fools think only about having good time—Ecclesiastes
7:4.

Love of pleasure leads to poverty—Proverbs 21:17.

Love pleasure rather than God—2 Timothy 3:4.

Moses chose God's way over fleeting pleasures—Hebrews 11:25.

Pleasures of life can stifle spiritual interests—Luke 8:14.

Sin nature craves for lustful pleasures—Galatians 5:19-21.

Slaves to evil pleasures—Titus 3:3.

Wicked love to indulge in evil pleasures—2 Peter 2:13.

Worldly pleasures do not satisfy—Ecclesiastes 2:8-11.

See Carnality; Hedonism.

Politics

Corruption—Psalm 12:8; Daniel 6:4-15.

Electioneering—2 Samuel 15:2-6.

End-time government—Revelation 17:12.

God controls governments—Romans 13:1.

Obey government—Romans 13:1,5.

Political marriage—1 Kings 3:1; 2 Chronicles 18:1; Daniel 11:6.

Political murder—2 Kings 21:23,24; Jeremiah 41:2; Acts 12:1-4.

Politicians should be diligent—Romans 12:8.

Pray for kings and others in authority—1 Timothy 2:2.

Rebellious leaders—Isaiah 1:23.

Some leaders are like wolves—Ezekiel 22:27.

Submit to government—Titus 3:1.

Wicked ruler is dangerous—Proverbs 28:15.

Wicked rulers ruined Israel—Isaiah 3:14.

Polygamy

Church leaders, faithful to one wife—1 Timothy 3:2,12.

Solomon loved many foreign women—1 Kings 11:1-4.

See Husband; Marriage; Wife.

P

Polytheism

False gods—Isaiah 2:8; Jeremiah 2:11; 1 Corinthians 12:2; Galatians 4:8.

Many so-called gods—1 Corinthians 8:5.

See God, Unity; Monotheism.

Poor

Duty to

Be kind to the poor—Psalm 41:1.

Feed Christ's brothers—Matthew 25:35,36.

Feed the hungry—Isaiah 58:7,10.

Give generously to others in need—Ephesians 4:28.

Give helping hand to the poor—Proverbs 31:20.

Give money to the poor—Matthew 19:21; Luke 18:22.

Give to those who ask—Matthew 5:42.

Help the oppressed—Isaiah 1:17.

Share money generously—Romans 12:8.

Speak up for the poor—Proverbs 31:9.

Oppression of

A common practice—Ecclesiastes 5:8.

Borrower is servant to lender—Proverbs 22:7.

Deprivation of the poor—Isaiah 10:2.

Oppression of the poor leads to poverty—Proverbs 22:16.

Poor are despised—Proverbs 14:20.

Poor are kicked aside—Job 24:4.

Robbery of the poor—Amos 8:4.

Trampling the poor—Amos 5:11.

Popularity

Absalom popular—2 Samuel 15:2-6,13.

Better to be sincere—Colossians 3:22.

David popular—2 Samuel 3:36.

Felix desired popularity—Acts 24:27.

Festus desired popularity—Acts 25:9.

Herod desired popularity—Acts 12:1-3.

Love for praise of men—John 12:43.

222

Pharisees feared crowd—Matthew 21:45,46.
Priests feared Jesus' popularity—Mark 11:18.
See Public Opinion.

Poverty

Better to be poor and godly—Proverbs 16:8.
Give me neither poverty nor riches—Proverbs 30:8.
Love sleep, end in poverty—Proverbs 20:13.
Playing around brings poverty—Proverbs 28:19.
See Poor, Duty to; Poor, Oppression of.

Power

All-surpassing power is from God—2 Corinthians 4:7.
Be strong in Lord's power—Ephesians 6:10.
God gives power to weak—Isaiah 40:29; 2 Peter 1:3.
God gives us spirit of power—2 Timothy 1:7,8.
God's power made perfect in weakness—2 Corinthians
    12:9.
Gospel, power of God for salvation—Romans 1:16.
Jesus teaches with power—Luke 4:36.
Jesus' miraculous power—Luke 6:19.
No one has power over death—Ecclesiastes 8:8.
Power from Holy Spirit—Acts 1:8; Ephesians 3:16.
Power of the Most High—Luke 1:35.
Powerful testimony of apostles—Acts 4:33.
Wicked man's power vanishes at death—Proverbs
    11:7.

Of Christ

Authority over everything—John 3:35.
Complete authority in heaven and earth—Matthew
    28:18.
Created everything—John 1:3; Colossians 1:16.
Disarmed evil rulers and authorities—Colossians 2:15.
Healed paralyzed man—Matthew 9:6.
Healed those oppressed by devil—Acts 10:38.
Holds all creation together—Colossians 1:17.
Overcame the world—John 16:33.

P

Resurrection—John 2:19; 10:18.
Sustains universe—Hebrews 1:3.
Wind and waves obey Him—Matthew 8:27.
See Jesus Christ, Omnipotence of.

Of God

All-powerful—Job 36:22.
Be strong with the Lord's mighty power—Ephesians 6:10.
Created everything—Revelation 4:11.
Heavens are the work of His hands—Psalm 102:25.
Made the earth by His power—Jeremiah 10:12.
Miracles—1 Chronicles 16:9.
No false god can do what God does—Deuteronomy 3:24.
Nothing is too hard for Him—Genesis 18:14; Jeremiah 32:27.
Performs miracles without number—Job 5:9.
Spread out the heavens above—Isaiah 48:13.
With God everything is possible—Matthew 19:26.
See God, Omnipotence of.

Of the Holy Spirit

Begot Jesus—Luke 1:35.
Demons cast out by Spirit of God—Matthew 12:28.
Jesus filled by Spirit's power—Luke 4:14.
Made the heavens beautiful—Job 26:13.
Power from the Holy Spirit—Acts 1:8; Acts 2.
Raised Jesus from the dead—Romans 8:11.
Spirit fills believers with power—Luke 24:49; Acts 1:8; Ephesians 3:16.
Spirit of power—2 Timothy 1:7.
See Holy Spirit, Deity of.

Praise

Give thanks always—Ephesians 5:20.
Give thanks to the Lord—1 Chronicles 16:8.
God's praise always on my lips—Psalm 34:1.
Great multitude praising God—Revelation 19:6,7.
Let all things praise the Lord—Psalm 103:1-5,20-22.

Offer sacrifice of praise—Hebrews 13:15.
Praise be to God—Ephesians 1:3.
Praise God forever—Psalm 145:1-7; Revelation 7:12.
Praise God with song—Psalm 69:30.
Praise the Lord—Psalm 148:1-5; 150:1.
Sing a new song to the Lord—Psalm 96:1; 98:1.
Sing songs of praise—James 5:13.
Worship Lord with gladness—Psalm 100.

Prayer

Ask and it will be given—Matthew 7:7,8.
Ask in Jesus' name—John 14:13,14.
Believe and you will receive—Matthew 21:22.
Call on the Lord—Psalm 145:18.
Earnest prayer—James 5:17,18.
Lift up hands in prayer—1 Timothy 2:8.
Pray and seek God's face—2 Chronicles 7:14.

Confession In

Confess and receive mercy—Proverbs 28:13.
Confess sins—Psalm 32:5; 38:18; 51:4.
Refuse to confess, misery results—Psalm 32:3.
See Guilt; Sin, Confession of.

P

Prayerfulness

Always be prayerful—Romans 12:12.
Daniel prayed three times a day—Daniel 6:10.
Keep on praying—1 Thessalonians 5:17.
Pray as long as you have breath—Psalm 116:2.

Preaching

Apostles sent out to preach—Mark 3:14.
Be persistent in preaching—2 Timothy 4:2.
Builds believers up—Ephesians 4:11,12.
Called to preach—2 Timothy 1:11.
Compulsion to preach—1 Corinthians 9:16.
Faithfully preach truth—2 Corinthians 6:7-9.
Imprisoned for preaching—Ephesians 3:1.

Jesus appointed to preach Good News—Luke 4:18,19.
Jesus preached of the kingdom—Matthew 4:23.
John the Baptist preached repentance—Matthew 3:1,2.
Preach about righteousness—Acts 24:25; 1 Timothy 4:11-16; 2 Peter 2:5.
Preach Christ crucified—1 Corinthians 1:23.
Preach God's message with sincerity—2 Corinthians 2:17.
Preach Jesus as Lord—2 Corinthians 4:5.
Preach on riches in Christ—Ephesians 3:8.
Preach the Word—Mark 16:15,16; Ephesians 6:20; 1 Timothy 4:2,13.
Preach without fear—Ephesians 6:19,20.

Preaching of Jesus Christ

See Jesus Christ, Preaching and Teaching.

Predestination

Father draws people—John 6:44.
Father gave followers to Jesus—John 6:39.
God chose us in Christ—Ephesians 1:4.
God has a prearranged plan—Acts 2:23.
God set Jeremiah apart from birth—Jeremiah 1:5.
God's plan is from all eternity—Ephesians 3:11.
Many are called, few are chosen—Matthew 22:14.
Paul chosen before birth—Galatians 1:15.
Planned long before the world began—2 Timothy 1:9.
See Election; God, Foreknowledge of; God, Sovereign.

Preexistence of Jesus Christ

See Jesus Christ, Preexistence.

Preservation, God's Ministry of

See God's Ministry of Preservation.

Pride

Better to be lowly in spirit—Proverbs 16:19.
Do not be conceited—Romans 12:16.
Ego illustrated—Genesis 11:4.

God humbles the proud—Isaiah 13:11; Daniel 4:37.
God mocks proud mockers—Proverbs 3:34.
God opposes the proud—James 4:6; 1 Peter 5:5.
In last days, lots of proud people—2 Timothy 3:2.
Lord detests pride—Proverbs 8:13; 16:5.
Love is not proud—1 Corinthians 13:4.
Pride goes before destruction—Proverbs 16:18; 18:12.
Pride is sinful—Proverbs 21:4.
Self-confident boasting—2 Corinthians 11:17.
Self-deification—Ezekiel 28:2.
Voice of a god—Acts 12:22.
See Arrogance; Humility.

Priest

Beautiful garments—Exodus 28:2.
Cleansing of—Leviticus 16:24.
Jesus our eternal High Priest—Hebrews 6:20.
Melchizedek—Genesis 14:18.
Must be purified—Exodus 19:22.
Never be defiled—Ezekiel 44:25,26.

Priesthood of Jesus Christ

See Jesus Christ, Priesthood.

P

Priority

Better to be a servant than ambitious—Luke 22:26.
Better to be free from concerns of life—1 Corinthians 7:32,33.
Better to be godly and have little—Psalm 37:16; Proverbs 16:8.
Better to lose one part of body than go to hell—Matthew 5:29,30; 18:9.
Do not store treasures on earth—Matthew 6:19.
Frankness better than flattery—Proverbs 28:23.
God and His will, top priority—Matthew 6:33.
Good reputation better than riches—Proverbs 22:1.

227

Kingdom more important than relatives—Luke 18:29,30.

Living is for Christ, dying is even better—Philippians 1:21.

Love Jesus more than mother or father—Matthew 10:37; Luke 14:26.

More blessed to give—Acts 20:35.

Obedience better than sacrifice—1 Samuel 15:22.

Open rebuke better than hidden love—Proverbs 27:5.

Return to first love—Revelation 2:4.

Store up treasure in heaven—Luke 12:33.

Value of kingdom, parable of hidden treasure and pearl—Matthew 13:44-46.

Virtuous wife worth more than rubies—Proverbs 31:10.

Wise speech worth more than gold and rubies—Proverbs 20:15.

Wound of friend, better than kiss of enemy—Proverbs 27:6.

Problems

See Adversity.

Promiscuity

See Sexual Aberrations.

Promises

See Oaths, Examples of; Vow.

Proofs of God's Existence

Creation proves a Creator—Psalm 19:1-4; Hebrews 3:4.

Design of universe proves Designer—Romans 1:18-20.

Human morality proves a Moral Source—Romans 2:14-16.

Human personhood proves Divine Person—Acts 17:29.

Prophecies of Jesus Christ

See Jesus Christ, Prophecies of.

Propitiation

Jesus took our punishment—Romans 3:25.
Peace with God through Christ—Romans 5:1.
Reconciled through Christ—2 Corinthians 5:10,11,18,19.
Took away our sins—1 John 2:2.
See Salvation.

Prosperity

Could lead one to forget God—Deuteronomy 6:10-12.
Could lead to a denial of God—Proverbs 30:9.
Could lead to rebellion—Deuteronomy 32:15.
Crooked heart will not prosper—Proverbs 17:20.
Danger of—Psalm 73:12; Mark 10:24; Luke 18:25.
False confidence in prosperity—Psalm 30:6; 49:6,7; Proverbs 18:11; Jeremiah 48:7.
God blesses, prospers you in everything—Deuteronomy 28:8.
God prospers the humble—Job 5:11.
Hard work means prosperity—Proverbs 12:11.
Prosperity of Joseph—Genesis 39:2.
Spiritual prosperity—Psalm 23:1; 3 John 2.
Trusting Lord leads to prosperity—Proverbs 28:25.
Wicked prosper—Job 21:7.
See Affluence; Wealth.

Prostitute

See Harlot.

Protection

See Refuge; Safety.

Providence

Of God in Circumstances
All things work for good—Romans 8:28.
Father cares for us—Matthew 10:29-31.

P

229

Joseph betrayed by brothers, led to good—Genesis 45:8; 50:20.

Length of life—Job 14:5; Psalm 139:16.

Of God in History

Controls nations—Job 12:23,24; Psalm 22:28; Jeremiah 27:5,6; Daniel 4:17.

Determines when and where people are born—Acts 17:25-27.

Divine plan—Acts 4:27,28.

Sets up kings, deposes them—Daniel 2:21.

Of God in Nature

Birds are fed—Matthew 6:26, Psalm 147:9.

Grass grows for cattle—Psalm 104:14.

Sends rain—Job 5:10; Psalm 65:9,10; 147:8; Jeremiah 10:13; Acts 14:17.

Provisions

God is sufficient—2 Corinthians 9:8.

God always provides—Isaiah 58:11.

God provides for those who walk uprightly—Psalm 84:11.

God will supply all needs—Philippians 4:19.

Seek first God's kingdom, all else will be added—Matthew 6:33.

Those who seek Lord lack nothing—Psalm 34:10.

Prudence

Prudent carefully consider their steps—Proverbs 14:8,15,16.

Prudent man keeps quiet—Amos 5:13.

Prudent person foresees danger—Proverbs 22:3; 27:12.

Prudent wife is from the Lord—Proverbs 19:14.

See Discernment; Wisdom.

Public Opinion

Priests feared Jesus' popularity—Mark 11:18.

Seek God's approval, not that of the public—John 12:42,43.

Who do people say Son of Man is?—Matthew 16:13.
See Popularity.

Punishment

According to Deeds

God gives people their due rewards—Jeremiah 17:10.

God gives what is deserved—Ezekiel 16:59.

God repays people according to deeds—Job 34:11; Psalm 62:12; Matthew 16:27.

See Judgment, According to Works.

Death Penalty

See Capital Punishment.

Delayed

God delays His wrath—Isaiah 48:9.

God delays punishment—1 Kings 21:29.

God waited patiently—1 Peter 3:20.

Punishment delayed, incentive to do wrong— Ecclesiastes 8:11.

Eternal

Eternal fire—Matthew 25:41.

Eternal judgment—Hebrews 6:2.

Eternal punishment—Matthew 25:46.

Smoke of their torment rises forever—Revelation 14:11.

Torment forever and ever—Revelation 20:10.

See Hell.

P

Purity of Heart

Focus mind on pure things—Philippians 4:8.

God blesses those with pure hearts—Matthew 5:8.

God can purify us from sins—Psalm 51:7; 1 John 1:9.

Keep yourself pure—1 Timothy 5:22.

Purify your hearts—2 Corinthians 7:1; James 4:8.

See Holiness, Personal; Virtue.

Q

Quarantine

Isolation seven days—Numbers 31:19.
Keep a distance—Luke 17:12.
Live outside camp—Leviticus 14:3,8; Numbers 5:2.
Prevent spread of infection—Leviticus 13:45,46.
Separate house—2 Kings 15:5.
See Disease.

Quarrel

Act quickly to settle—Matthew 5:25.
Anger causes quarrels—Proverbs 30:33.
Constant quarrels—Proverbs 18:6.
Contentiousness—Psalm 120:7; 140:2; Proverbs 15:18;
17:19; 18:6; 26:21.
Family quarrels—Genesis 21:10; Proverbs 18:19; 19:13;
21:9; 27:15.
Fools insist on quarreling—Proverbs 20:3.
Quarreling, jealousy, outbursts of anger—2 Corinthians
12:20.

Quickening

God restores us—Psalm 71:20.
God revives us—Psalm 80:18.
God will raise us from dead—Romans 8:11.
See Regeneration; Revival.

Quiet Time

See Devotions.

R

Race
Ethnic
All nations descended from one man—Acts 17:26.
Eve, mother of all people—Genesis 3:20.
We are all children of the same Father—Malachi 2:10.
See Nations.

Spiritual
Do not lose the race—Philippians 2:16.
Keep your eyes on Jesus (the finish line)—Hebrews 12:2.
Run in such a way that you will win—1 Corinthians 9:24.
Run with endurance—Hebrews 12:1.
See Games, Spiritual.

Rain
Disobey, and God withholds rain—Deuteronomy 11:17;
1 Kings 8:35,36.
Elijah prevented rain for three and a half years—James 5:17.
God directs rain to fall—Job 37:6.
No false god can send rain—Jeremiah 14:22.
Obedience brings God's seasonal rains—Isaiah 30:23; Jeremiah 5:24.
The Genesis flood, judgment—Genesis 7:4,10,17.

Rape
Enemies rape women—Isaiah 13:16; Lamentations 5:11; Zechariah 14:2.
Rape brings death penalty—Deuteronomy 22:25.

Rapture of Church
All will be changed—1 Corinthians 15:50-52.
Christ will bring raptured church to place He prepared—John 14:1-3.

R

233

Church delivered from time of trouble—Revelation 3:10.

Church not appointed to wrath—1 Thessalonians 1:10; 5:9.

Church will be raptured—1 Thessalonians 4:13-17.

See Second Coming of Christ; Tribulation Period.

Rashness

Do not be in hurry to go to court—Proverbs 25:8.

Do not be quick-tempered—Ecclesiastes 7:9.

Do not make rash promises to God—Ecclesiastes 5:2.

Do not speak without thinking—Proverbs 29:20.

Hasty shortcuts lead to poverty—Proverbs 21:5.

Hasty temper yields mistakes—Proverbs 14:29.

Person moving too quickly may go wrong way—Proverbs 19:2.

Reasoning

Be ready with answer—1 Peter 3:15.

Come now, let us reason—Isaiah 1:18; 43:26.

Job wanted to argue his case—Job 13:3.

Paul reasoned with Jews and Gentiles—Acts 17:2; 18:4,19.

Reasonable people—1 Corinthians 10:15.

See Discernment; Logic.

R

Rebellion

End-times rebellion—2 Thessalonians 2:3.

Joy for those whose rebellion is forgiven—Psalm 32:1,2.

Lord, show me my rebellion—Job 13:23.

Lucifer rebelled against God—Isaiah 14:12-15; Ezekiel 28:13-18.

One-third of angels followed Lucifer in rebellion—Revelation 12:4.

Overcoming captivity to rebellious ideas—2 Corinthians 10:5.

Rebel against right teaching—Titus 1:10.

Rebellion against God—1 Samuel 15:23; Psalm 68:6; Isaiah 30:1; 65:2.

Rebellion against God's prophet—Jeremiah 42:2-22.

Rebellion is as bad as sin of witchcraft—1 Samuel 15:23.

Rebellious leaders—Isaiah 1:23.

Rebels from earliest childhood—Isaiah 48:8.

Seven-year period of rebellion—Revelation 4–18.

Rebuke

Disciples rebuked for unbelief—Mark 16:14.

Dying thief rebukes companion—Luke 23:39-41.

Michael would not rebuke devil—Jude 9.

Nathan rebukes David—2 Samuel 12:7,9.

Open rebuke better than hidden love—Proverbs 27:5.

Patiently correct, rebuke, and encourage—2 Timothy 4:2.

Rebuke when necessary—Titus 1:13.

Rebuking a fool—Proverbs 26:5.

Samuel rebukes Saul—1 Samuel 13:13.

Warn each other—Hebrews 3:13.

Whoever hates correction will die—Proverbs 15:10.

See Reproof.

Reconciliation Between God and Man

Made right in God's sight—Romans 5:1.

Reconciled through Christ—2 Corinthians 5:18; Colossians 1:20.

Restored to friendship with God—Romans 5:10.

See Salvation.

Reconnaissance

Scout out the land—Judges 18:2.

Spy out the land—Joshua 2:1.

Recreation

Get away and rest—Mark 6:31,32.

R

235

Physical rest commanded—Exodus 23:12; Leviticus 23:3; Mark 6:31.

See Rest.

Redemption

Angels interested in plan of redemption—1 Peter 1:12.

Brings about forgiveness of sin—Ephesians 1:7.

Brings about justification—Romans 3:24.

Brings us into God's family—Galatians 4:4,5.

Christ redeemed man by blood—Galatians 3:13; Hebrews 9:12; 1 Peter 1:18,19.

Creation eagerly awaits redemption—Romans 8:19-21.

Heavenly destiny of the redeemed—Revelation 7:9-17.

Holy Spirit seals believers unto day of redemption—Ephesians 4:30.

Planned before creation—1 Peter 1:18-20.

Redeemed from bondage of law—Galatians 4:5.

Redeemed from death—Hosea 13:14.

Redeemed from evil world—Galatians 1:13-15.

Redeemed from grave—Psalm 49:15.

Redeemed from sin—Titus 2:14.

Redemption through Christ—Romans 3:24; Colossians 1:14; 2 Peter 2:1.

Rooted in God's love and compassion—John 3:16; Romans 6:8; 1 John 4:10.

White robe for the redeemed—Revelation 6:11; 7:9,13.

Worst sinners can be saved—1 Timothy 1:15,16.

See Salvation.

Refuge

Cities of refuge—Exodus 21:13; Numbers 35:25-28.

Divine wings, a refuge—Psalm 17:8,9.

God is our hiding place—Psalm 32:7.

God is our refuge—Deuteronomy 33:27; Psalm 27:5; 31:20; 46:1; 144:2.

God is our rock and fortress—Psalm 71:3; Proverbs 14:26.

R

Godly have a refuge when they die—Proverbs 14:32.
Happy are those who take refuge in God—Psalm 34:8.

Regeneration

God creates clean heart—Psalm 51:10.
God creates new hearts—Ezekiel 36:26,27.
God creates tender hearts—Ezekiel 11:19.
God removes all impurities—Isaiah 1:25.
God writes law on hearts—Jeremiah 31:33.
Jesus gives living water—John 4:10.
Jesus is a life-giving vine—John 15:1,3.
Jesus is bread from heaven—John 6:50,51,57.
New birth—John 3:1-5; 1 Peter 1:23.
See Born Again.

Regret

See Remorse.

Relationships

Be kind to fainting friend—Job 6:14.
Caution in friendship—Proverbs 12:26.
Children, honor father and mother—Matthew 15:4;
19:19; Luke 18:20.
Children must obey parents—Ephesians 6:1,4;
Colossians 3:20.
Do not forsake friend—Proverbs 27:10.
Friend loves at all times—Proverbs 17:17.
Husband and wife, marriage—Genesis 2:23,24.
Husband, live happily with woman you love—
Ecclesiastes 9:9.
Husbands, love your wives—Colossians 3:19.
Husbands, one wife only— 1 Timothy 3:2-5.
Lay down life for friends—John 15:13-15.
Love your neighbor—Matthew 22:39; John 13:35.
Relationships with believers—Matthew 25:40; Luke
8:21; John 21:23.
Wife is her husband's joy—Proverbs 12:4.

R

Religion

False

Clean outside, dirty inside—Matthew 23:25-28.
Hypocrites tithe, but no religion—Matthew 23:23.
Just going through the motions—Hosea 6:6.
Leaving Christ out of the picture—John 5:39,40.
Legalism—Matthew 12:1-8.
"Lord, Lord"—Matthew 7:21-23.
Mere lip service—Mark 7:6,7.
Paul prior to conversion—Acts 26:5.
Scribes and Pharisees—Matthew 23.
See Cults; Doctrine, False; Heathen; Heresy; Pagans.

True

Fear God, keep His commandments—Ecclesiastes 12:13.
Fear God, walk in His ways—Deuteronomy 10:12,13.
Look after orphans and widows—James 1:27.
Love everyone—Romans 13:10.
Love God with whole heart—Mark 12:33.
Walk humbly—Micah 6:8.

Remarriage

Divorced people—Deuteronomy 24:1-4.
Paul's instructions—Romans 7:1-3.
Widows—1 Corinthians 7:8,9; 1 Timothy 5:11.
See Divorce; Husband; Marriage; Wife.

Remorse

Broken heart—Lamentations 1:20.
God heals the brokenhearted—Psalm 147:3.
Humble and contrite—Isaiah 66:2; 1 Peter 5:5.
Impenitent have no remorse—Jeremiah 44:10.
Judas filled with remorse—Matthew 27:3.
Prayer of remorse—Psalm 51.
See Contrite; Guilt; Sorrow.

R

Repentance

Angels rejoice in heaven over repenting sinner—Luke 15:7,10.

Be humble and repent—2 Chronicles 7:14.

Confess and find mercy—Proverbs 28:13.

God commands repentance—Acts 17:30.

God desires all to repent—2 Peter 3:9.

Godly sorrow brings repentance—2 Corinthians 7:10.

God's kindness leads to repentance—Romans 2:4.

John the Baptist preached repentance—Matthew 3:1,2.

Produce fruit of repentance—Matthew 3:8.

Prove repentance by deeds—Acts 26:20.

Repent and believe good news—Mark 1:15.

Repent and live—Ezekiel 18:32.

Repent and turn to God—Acts 3:19.

Repent, kingdom is near—Matthew 4:17.

Repentance and forgiveness—Luke 24:47.

Return to God with whole heart—Joel 2:12,13.

Unless you repent, you perish—Luke 13:3.

See Penitence.

Reproof

Do not bother rebuking mockers—Proverbs 9:8.

Do not ignore criticism—Proverbs 13:18.

Fool despises parent's discipline—Proverbs 15:5.

Listen to constructive criticism—Proverbs 15:31.

Love discipline—Proverbs 12:1.

Open rebuke better than hidden love—Proverbs 27:5.

Patiently correct, rebuke, and encourage—2 Timothy 4:2.

Privately point out person's fault—Matthew 18:15.

Reject criticism, harm only yourself—Proverbs 15:32.

Speak truth in love—Ephesians 4:15.

Valid criticism is treasured—Proverbs 25:12.

Warn each other—Hebrews 3:13.

R

239

Whoever hates correction will die—Proverbs 15:10.

Wound from friend better than kiss from enemy—
Proverbs 27:6.

See Counsel; Criticism; Rebuke.

Reputation, Good

Choose a good reputation—Proverbs 22:1.

Good reputation is valuable—Ecclesiastes 7:1.

See Conduct, Proper; Honor; Respect.

Resentment

Against God—Isaiah 45:9.

Godless harbor resentment—Job 36:13.

Love covers all offenses—Proverbs 10:12.

Mocker resents correction—Proverbs 15:12.

Pharisees against Jesus—Luke 15:1,2.

Prodigal son's brother—Luke 15:11-32.

Resentment kills a fool—Job 5:2.

See Attitude; Bitterness; Jealousy.

Respect

Live so others respect you—1 Thessalonians 4:12.

Respect aged people—Leviticus 19:32; Job 32:6; Proverbs
23:22; 1 Timothy 5:1,2.

Respect church leadership—Philippians 2:29;
1 Thessalonians 5:12,13.

Respect host—Luke 14:10.

Respect parents—Leviticus 19:3; Ephesians 6:1,2.

Respect rulers by not exalting yourself—Proverbs 25:6.

Respect Scripture—Nehemiah 8:5.

Treat deaf with respect—Leviticus 19:14.

Wives must be respected—1 Timothy 3:11.

Wives respect husbands—Ephesians 5:33.

Responsibility

Individual responsibility—Ezekiel 18:20.

Making excuses—Genesis 3:12,13.

Manual of responsible living—Book of Proverbs.

Responsible for words spoken—Matthew 12:36,37.
Responsible to God—Ezekiel 18:20; Romans 3:19; 14:12.
Trustworthy people are given more responsibility—Luke 16:10.
Wife is responsible to husband—1 Corinthians 11:3.
See Commitment.

Rest

Jesus and disciples rested—Mark 6:31.
Jesus rested in midst of storm—Matthew 8:24.
Rest on seventh day—Exodus 23:12; 34:21.
See Sleep.

Spiritual

Enter God's place of rest—Hebrews 4:1.
Find rest in God—Psalm 62:1.
God gives rest in green meadows—Psalm 23:2.
God gives rest to the weary—Jeremiah 31:25.
You will find rest for your souls—Matthew 11:28,29.

Restitution

Compensate for loss of life—Exodus 21:30.
Compensate for stolen animals—Leviticus 24:18.
Compensate for stolen goods—Exodus 22:1.
Make full restitution—Numbers 5:7.
Zacchaeus's restitution—Luke 19:8.

Restoration, Final

Disciples' question—Acts 1:6.
Final restoration of all things—Acts 3:21.
New heaven and new earth—Revelation 21:1.
See New Heavens and New Earth.

Resurrection

Believers will be resurrected—Job 19:25-27; Psalm 49:15; Isaiah 26:19; John 6:39,40,44,54; 1 Corinthians 6:14; 1 Thessalonians 4:13-17; Revelation 20:4-6.
Dead will hear Christ's voice—John 5:25,28,29.
Eternal body made for us by God—2 Corinthians 5:1.

R

241

Glorious bodies—Philippians 3:21.

If Christ not raised, our faith in vain—1 Corinthians 15:12-21.

Jesus is the resurrection and the life—John 11:24,25.

Perishable body will become imperishable—1 Corinthians 15:42.

Resurrection of Jesus—Acts 4:33.

Resurrection of righteous and wicked—Acts 24:15.

Resurrection will swallow up death—Isaiah 25:8.

United with Christ in resurrection—Romans 6:5.

We will all be changed—1 Corinthians 15:50-52.

Appearances of Resurrected Christ

To 10 disciples—Luke 24:36-43.

To 11 disciples—John 20:26-29.

To disciples on road to Emmaus—Luke 24:13-35.

To Mary Magdalene—John 20:11-17.

To more than 500—1 Corinthians 15:6.

To Peter—1 Corinthians 15:5.

To seven disciples by Galilee—John 21:1-23.

To some women—Matthew 28:9,10.

To the 11 at the ascension—Matthew 28:16-20.

Retaliation

See Revenge.

Revelation

General revelation found in creation—Psalm 19:1-4; Romans 1:18-21.

God is revealed in His provisions for man—Acts 14:17.

God is the source of revelation—Hebrews 1:1,2.

God reveals more to those who seek Him—Acts 10:1-31; Hebrews 11:6.

Special revelation in Jesus, the ultimate revelation—Hebrews 1:2.

See Bible.

Revenge

Do not repay evil for evil—1 Thessalonians 5:15;
1 Peter 3:9.
God will avenge—Deuteronomy 32:43; Psalm 9:12.
Never avenge yourselves—Leviticus 19:18; Romans
12:17,19.
Vengeance is God's—Psalm 94:1.

Reverence to God

Abram fell face down—Genesis 17:3.
Be sure to fear the Lord—1 Samuel 12:24.
Live in the fear of the Lord—Acts 9:31.
Show reverence for God's sanctuary—Leviticus 19:30.
Take off your sandals—Exodus 3:5.
Worship God with reverence—Hebrews 12:28.
See Fear, Of the Lord.

Revival

Day of Pentecost—Acts 2:1-42,46,47.
Due to work of Messiah—Isaiah 35:4-6.
God renews hearts—Ezekiel 11:19.
Pray for—Habakkuk 3:2.
Prophecy of future revival—Joel 2:28,29.
Restoration—Hosea 6:2.
Return to the Lord—Lamentations 3:40.
Revival of evil—2 Chronicles 33:1-7.
Under Elijah—1 Kings 18:17-40.
Under Joshua—Joshua 5:2-9.
Under Josiah—2 Kings 22–23.

Reward

Children are a reward from God—Psalm 127:3.
Confidence will be rewarded—Hebrews 10:35.
Do good in secret, God will reward—Matthew 6:1-6.
Eternal rewards—1 Corinthians 3:5-10.

R

God rewards according to deeds—1 Corinthians 3:13,14;
Revelation 22:12.

God rewards those who seek Him—Hebrews 11:6.

Good will be rewarded—Ephesians 6:8.

Great is your reward in heaven—Matthew 5:12.

Inheritance as a reward—Colossians 3:24.

Rewarded with long life—Exodus 20:12; Deuteronomy
4:40.

Righteous are rewarded—Psalm 58:11.

Riches

Better to be poor and godly—Proverbs 16:8.

Better to have little with fear—Proverbs 15:16.

Blessing of Lord makes person rich—Proverbs 10:22.

Do not store up treasures on earth—Matthew 6:19.

Do not weary yourself trying to get rich—Proverbs 23:4,5.

Greedy person tries to get rich quick—Proverbs 28:22.

Lord makes one poor and another rich—1 Samuel 2:7.

Lure of wealth—Mark 4:19.

Riches do not last—Proverbs 27:24.

Riches will not help on day of judgment—Proverbs 11:4.

Trust in money and down you go—Proverbs 11:28.

Righteousness

R

Abraham believed, credited as righteousness—Genesis
15:6.

Eyes of Lord are on the righteous—Psalm 34:15; 1 Peter
3:12-18.

Fruit of the righteous is a tree of life—Proverbs 11:30.

Lord hears prayers of righteous—Proverbs 15:28,29.

No one declared righteous by obeying law—Romans
3:10-20.

Prayer of righteous man is effective—James 5:16.

Righteous will live by faith—Romans 1:17.

Of God

See God, Righteousness of.

Rising

Early

Do not get up early to do evil—Micah 2:1.
Do not get up early to drink—Isaiah 5:11.
Jesus' example, early devotions—Mark 1:35.
New strength every morning—Isaiah 33:2.
Prayer in the morning—Psalm 5:3; 119:147.
Wife gets up before dawn—Proverbs 31:15.

Late

A little extra sleep leads to poverty—Proverbs 24:33,34.
Lazybones, how long will you sleep?—Proverbs 6:9.
Love sleep, end in poverty—Proverbs 20:13.
Son who sleeps during harvest is shameful—Proverbs 10:5.

Robbery

Do not cheat or rob anyone—Leviticus 19:13.
Do not steal—Exodus 20:15; Leviticus 19:11; Deuteronomy 5:19.
If you are a thief, stop stealing—Ephesians 4:28.
Lord hates robbery—Isaiah 61:8.
Robbing the poor is wrong—Amos 8:4.
Satan steals seed from heart—Matthew 13:19; Mark 4:15.

Rock, Figurative

Christ is a rock—1 Corinthians 10:4.
God is a solid rock—2 Samuel 22:32,47.
Lord is a rock—Psalm 18:2.
Rock of Israel—2 Samuel 23:3.

Roman Empire

Roman citizenship and the law—Acts 16:37; 22:25.
Roman court—Acts 25:10,16.
Roman emperor, Augustus—Luke 2:1.

R

Roman emperor, Tiberius—Luke 3:1.

Ruby

Virtuous wife worth more than rubies—Proverbs 31:10.
Wise speech worth more than rubies—Proverbs 20:15.
See Jewels.

Rulers, Wicked

Destruction certain for unjust judges—Isaiah 10:1.
King Ahaz of Israel—2 Chronicles 28:19.
Leaders of Israel—Hosea 5:10.
Officials and judges alike demand bribes—Micah 7:3.
Only a stupid prince oppresses his people—Proverbs 28:16.
Prophecy against leaders of Israel—Ezekiel 34:2.
Rebellious leaders—Isaiah 1:23.
Some leaders are like wolves—Ezekiel 22:27.
Wicked ruler is dangerous—Proverbs 28:15.
Wicked rulers ruined Israel—Isaiah 3:14.
See Government.

R

S

Sabbath

Day of rest—Exodus 16:23.

Do not let anyone judge you regarding Sabbath days— Colossians 2:16.

God rested seventh day—Genesis 2:2,3.

Lord of the Sabbath—Matthew 12:8.

Sabbath-rest—Hebrews 4:9.

Sacrifice

Body is a living sacrifice—Romans 12:1.

Christ our example—1 John 3:16.

Christ, the ultimate sacrifice—Hebrews 10:1-10.

God's covenants confirmed by—Genesis 15:9-17; Exodus 24:5-8.

Obedience is better than sacrifice—1 Samuel 15:22.

Offered to false gods—Leviticus 17:7; Deuteronomy 32:17.

Old Testament sacrifices pointed to Christ's— Ephesians 5:2; Hebrews 10:1.

Sacrifice cannot take away sin—Hebrews 9:9; 10:1-11.

Sacrifice of praise—Hebrews 13:15.

Sacrifice of sons and daughters—Psalm 106:37.

Sacrifice of thanksgiving—Psalm 116:17.

Sadducees

Beware of their yeast—Matthew 16:6.

Brood of snakes—Matthew 3:7.

Denied belief in resurrection—Matthew 22:23; Mark 12:18; Luke 20:27; Acts 23:8.

Safety

Daniel protected in lion's den—Daniel 6:13-24.

Go your way in safety—Proverbs 3:23.

God is our shield—Deuteronomy 33:29.

God will not let your foot slip—Psalm 121:3.

S

God's people live securely—Isaiah 32:18.
Listen to God and live in safety—Proverbs 1:33.
No harm befalls the righteous—Proverbs 12:21.
No harm will befall you—Psalm 91:10.
See Refuge.

Salary

See Employee; Employer; Wages.

Salt

Add salt to grain offerings—Leviticus 2:13.
Lot's wife became pillar of salt—Genesis 19:26.
Salt of the earth—Matthew 5:13.
Valley of Salt—2 Kings 14:7.

Salvation

Adoption into God's family—Galatians 4:5.
Believe and be saved—John 3:14-17; 5:24; 6:29,47;
   11:25,26; 20:31; Acts 16:31.
By grace through faith—Ephesians 2:8,9.
Imputation of righteousness—Romans 4:5.
Jesus died in our place—Matthew 20:28; 2 Corinthians
   5:21.
Justification—Romans 3:28; 5:1,2,9.
Lord is my salvation—Exodus 15:2.
Must become like little children—Matthew 18:3.
New birth—John 3:3.
Propitiation—1 John 2:2.
Reconciliation to God—2 Corinthians 5:18.
Redemption—2 Peter 2:1.
Salvation only in Christ—John 14:16; Acts 4:12;
   1 Timothy 2:5,6.
Sanctification—1 Corinthians 6:11.
Sins become white as snow—Isaiah 1:18.
Son of Man came to seek and save the lost—Luke 19:10.
Works not involved—Romans 11:6.

S

See Justification; Reconciliation Between God and Man; Redemption.

Plan of

Jesus accomplished His role—John 17:4.

Plan slowly revealed—Colossians 1:26.

Planned in eternity past—Ephesians 1:1-11.

There is a timetable for the plan—Galatians 4:4.

Security of

See Assurance of Salvation.

Samson

Eyes gouged out—Judges 16:21.

Great strength—Judges 14:6,19.

Lord blessed him as he grew up—Judges 13:24.

Spirit of Lord took control of him—Judges 14:19.

Sanctification

Avoid sexual immorality—1 Thessalonians 4:3.

Positional sanctification—1 Corinthians 6:11.

Sanctified by faith—Acts 26:17,18.

Sanctified by truth—John 17:17,19.

Sanctified in Christ—1 Corinthians 1:2.

Sanctified through and through—1 Thessalonians 5:23.

Sanctifying work of the Holy Spirit—2 Thessalonians 2:13; 1 Peter 1:1,2.

Transformed—2 Corinthians 3:18.

S

Sanctuary

Construction of—Exodus 26.

Do not desecrate—John 2:16.

House of prayer—Isaiah 56:7; Matthew 21:13.

Praise God in His sanctuary—Psalm 150:1.

Sacred residence for Lord—Exodus 25:8.

Show reverence for—Leviticus 19:30.

See Tabernacle; Temple.

249

Sanitation

Disinfection

After childbirth—Leviticus 12:2-5; Ezekiel 16:4.
After touching dead animals—Leviticus 11:24-40.
Burn unclean things—Leviticus 7:19.
Cleansing ceremony—Leviticus 14:8,9.
Related to disease—Leviticus 15.

Food

Do not eat blood—Leviticus 19:26; Deuteronomy 12:16; 15:23.
Do not eat unclean animals—Leviticus 11:26,27,29; Deuteronomy 14:3.
Meat must be eaten on same day offered—Leviticus 7:15.
Never eat fat—Leviticus 7:23.

Quarantine

Call out, "Unclean! Unclean!" Leviticus 13:45.
Infection, quarantine—Leviticus 13:31.
Keep a distance—Luke 17:12.
Live in isolation—Leviticus 13:46.
Live outside camp—Leviticus 14:3; Numbers 5:2.

Satan

Accuses and slanders believers—Job 1:6-11; Revelation 12:10.
Barred from heaven during Tribulation—Revelation 12:9,10.
Deceives whole world—Revelation 12:9.
Entered into Judas—Luke 22:3; John 13:27.
Fatherhood of the devil—John 8:44.
Fosters spiritual pride—1 Timothy 3:6.
God of this evil world—2 Corinthians 4:4.
Has followers—1 Timothy 5:15.
Hinders answers to prayers—Daniel 10:12-20.
Instigates jealousy—James 3:13-16.
Is a cherub—Ezekiel 28:14.

S

Jesus came to destroy—Hebrews 2:14; 1 John 3:8.
Jesus tempted by devil—Matthew 4:1-11; Mark 1:13; Luke 4:2.
Liar and murderer—John 8:44.
Lied to Eve—Genesis 3:4.
Lucifer (Satan) rebelled against God—Isaiah 14:12-15; Ezekiel 28:13-18.
Masquerades as angel of light—2 Corinthians 11:14.
One-third of angels followed Lucifer in rebellion— Revelation 12:4.
Plants doubt in minds of believers—Genesis 3:1-5.
Prideful—1 Timothy 3:6.
Prince of demons—Matthew 12:24.
Prowls like roaring lion—1 Peter 5:8.
Resist the devil—James 4:7.
Rose up against Israel—1 Chronicles 21:1.
Satanic possession—Mark 3:22.
Spoke to Lord about Job—Job 1:6-9,12.
Synagogue of Satan—Revelation 2:9.
Tempts believers to immorality—1 Corinthians 7:5.
Tempts believers to lie—Acts 5:3.
Wear spiritual armor for protection—Ephesians 6:11-18.
Will be bound in chains for thousand years— Revelation 20:2.
Worked through Peter—Matthew 16:23.
See Demons.

S

Terms Used to Describe
Accuser of brethren—Revelation 12:10.
Beelzebub—Matthew 12:24.
Belial—2 Corinthians 6:15.
Devil—1 Peter 5:8.
Dragon—Revelation 12:3.
Evil one—1 John 5:19.
God of this age—2 Corinthians 4:4.
Lucifer—Isaiah 14:12.

Prince of the power of the air—Ephesians 2:2.
Prince of this world—John 12:31.
Satan—2 Corinthians 11:14.
Serpent—Revelation 12:9.
Tempter—1 Thessalonians 3:5.

Savior

See God, Savior.
See Jesus Christ, Savior.

Scoffing

Avoid scoffers—Psalm 1:1.
Enemies continually taunt—Psalm 42:3.
Lord mocks mockers—Proverbs 3:34.
Mock the Holy One of Israel—Isaiah 5:19.
Mocker refuses to listen—Proverbs 13:1.
Mockers are proud and haughty—Proverbs 21:24.
Mockers will be punished—Proverbs 19:29.
Pharisees scoffed at Jesus—Matthew 12:24.
Prophets were scoffed at—2 Chronicles 36:16.
Scoffers in the last days—2 Peter 3:3,4.
Scoffing at the Almighty—Job 21:15.
Throw out the mocker—Proverbs 22:10.

S Scribe

Jehoshaphat the royal historian—1 Kings 4:3.
Joah the royal historian—2 Kings 18:37.
Jonathan, a scribe—1 Chronicles 27:32.
King's secretaries—Esther 3:12; 8:9.
Seraiah the court secretary—2 Samuel 8:17.
Shebna the court secretary—2 Kings 19:2.
Shemaiah, a secretary—1 Chronicles 24:6.
Sheva the court secretary—2 Samuel 20:25.
Zadok the scribe—Nehemiah 13:13.

Scripture

Inerrancy of

All God's words are true—Psalm 119:160.

Every jot and tittle accurate—Matthew 5:17,18.

Every word of God is flawless—Proverbs 30:5,6.

God's commands are true—Psalm 119:151.

God's word is truth—John 17:17.

God's words are flawless—Psalm 12:6; 18:30.

Law of Lord is perfect—Psalm 19:7.

Letters of words accurate—Matthew 22:41-46.

Ordinances of Lord are sure—Psalm 19:9.

Scripture cannot be broken—John 10:35.

Singular word is accurate—Galatians 3:16.

Verb tense accurate—Matthew 22:23-33.

Words from God—Matthew 4:4.

Inspiration of

All Scripture is inspired—2 Timothy 3:16.

Christ spoke through Paul—2 Corinthians 13:2,3.

God inscribed two stone tablets—Exodus 31:18.

God put His words in Jeremiah's mouth—Jeremiah 1:9; 5:14.

God taught Moses what to speak—Exodus 4:12-16.

Holy Spirit guided apostles into truth—John 14:26; 16:13.

Holy Spirit moved biblical writers—2 Peter 1:21.

Holy Spirit spoke through David—2 Samuel 23:2,3; Acts 1:16; 4:25.

Jeremiah wrote God's words in a book—Jeremiah 30:1,2.

Luke's Gospel recognized as inspired Scripture— 1 Timothy 5:18.

Paul wrote at Lord's command—1 Corinthians 14:37.

Paul's words were God's words—1 Thessalonians 2:13.

Paul's writings recognized as inspired Scripture— 2 Peter 3:16.

S

Scripture cannot be broken—John 10:35.

Words of Scripture "taught" by Holy Spirit—1 Corinthians 2:13.

Seasons

Moon marks seasons—Psalm 104:19.

Seasons remain as long as earth remains—Genesis 8:22.

Signs to mark off the seasons—Genesis 1:14.

Summer—Matthew 24:32.

Second Coming of Christ

Be blameless until He comes—1 Thessalonians 5:23; 1 Timothy 6:13-15.

Be patient as you await Lord's return—James 5:7.

Christ will come like a thief—1 Thessalonians 5:1-3; Revelation 16:15.

Christ will come visibly—Acts 1:9-11.

Coming from heaven—1 Thessalonians 1:10.

Coming soon—Philippians 4:5; Revelation 22:12,20.

Crown of righteousness for those longing His coming— 2 Timothy 4:8.

Every eye will see Him—Zechariah 12:10; Revelation 1:7.

Judgment of the nations follows—Matthew 25:31-46.

No one knows hour—Matthew 24:42,44,46-50.

Rapture—1 Thessalonians 4:13-17.

Return of our Lord Jesus—1 Corinthians 1:7,8; Hebrews 9:28.

Scoffers in the last days—2 Peter 3:4.

Signs in the sun, moon, and stars—Luke 21:25,27.

We eagerly wait—Philippians 3:20; Titus 2:13.

We will be like Him—1 John 3:2.

Will bring us to place He prepared—John 14:3.

Will come back on clouds of heaven—Matthew 26:64.

Will come in glory—Matthew 16:27; 25:31; Mark 8:38; Luke 9:26.

See Millennial Kingdom; Rapture of Church; Tribulation Period.

Secrecy

Confront secretly—Matthew 18:15.
Discuss privately—Proverbs 25:9.
Give secretly—Matthew 6:4.
Pray secretly—Matthew 6:6.

Secretary

Elihoreph and Ahijah were court secretaries—1 Kings 4:3.
King's secretaries—Esther 3:12; 8:9.
Seraiah the court secretary—2 Samuel 8:17.
Shebna the court secretary—2 Kings 18:18,37.
See Scribe.

Security, False

Do not need a thing?—Revelation 3:17.
Long, good life assured?—Job 29:18.
People think God does not care what they do—Psalm 50:21.
People think they are safe—Jeremiah 21:13.
People think they live in a rock fortress—Jeremiah 49:16.
People trust in wealth—Jeremiah 49:4.
Sudden death—Amos 9:10.
When crime not punished, people do wrong—Ecclesiastes 8:11.
Wicked people think God is dead—Psalm 10:4.

Seduction

Evil people who lead astray—1 John 2:26.
Joseph flees from—Genesis 39:6-20.
Seduced away from the faith, evil spirits—1 Timothy 4:1.
Seductive power of false Christs—Mark 13:22.
Seductive woman—Proverbs 7:6-27; Ecclesiastes 7:26.
See Immorality.

S

Self-Condemnation

David recognized his sin—2 Samuel 24:17.
Job's own mouth pronounced him guilty—Job 9:20.
"Why didn't I listen?"—Proverbs 5:13.

Self-Control

Control tongue and live long—Proverbs 13:3; James 1:26; 3:2.
Do not let sin control you—Romans 6:12.
Exhibit self-control—1 Timothy 3:2; Titus 2:2.
Fruit of the spirit—Galatians 5:22,23.
Great value in controlling temper—Proverbs 16:32.
Make every effort—2 Peter 1:5-7.
Reward of self-control—Revelation 21:7.
Self-control over life in general—Acts 24:25.
Those who control anger are wise—Proverbs 14:29.

Self-Denial

Avoid shameful desires—Colossians 3:5; 1 Peter 2:11.
Do not be tied up in affairs of life—2 Timothy 2:4.
Do not hold on to rights—1 Corinthians 9:12-25.
Do not indulge evil desires—Romans 13:14.
Do not let eye cause you to sin—Matthew 5:29,30.
Do not let hand cause you to sin—Mark 9:43.
Do not think only of your own good—1 Corinthians 10:24.
Give up your life for Jesus—Matthew 16:24,25; Mark 8:35; Luke 9:24.
Go and sell all you have—Matthew 19:21.
Leave everything to follow Jesus—Luke 5:11.
Love Jesus more than mother or father—Matthew 10:37; Luke 14:26.
Put aside selfish ambition—Mark 8:34; Luke 9:23.
Turn from godless living—Titus 2:12.
See Unselfishness.

S

Self-Exaltation

Antichrist—2 Thessalonians 2:4.
Boasting—2 Corinthians 10:17,18.
Self-importance—Galatians 6:3.
Sitting near head of the table—Luke 14:7.
See Arrogance; Pride.

Self-Examination

Examine yourself—1 Corinthians 11:28,31;
    2 Corinthians 13:5.
Lord, point out anything in me that offends you—
    Psalm 139:24.
Lord, search me—Psalm 139:23.
Lord, show me my rebellion—Job 13:23.
Lord, test my motives—Psalm 26:2.
Ponder the direction of your life—Psalm 119:59.
Search your soul—Psalm 77:6.

Self-Existence of God

See God, Self-Existent.

Selfishness

Do not just please yourself—2 Corinthians 5:15.
Do not think only about your own affairs—Philippians
    2:4.
Do not think only of your own good—1 Corinthians
    10:24.
Share each other's troubles—Galatians 6:2.

Self-Pity

Asaph fell into self-pity—Psalm 73:13,14.
Asaph recovered—Psalm 73:15-28.
Cure for self-pity—Psalm 37.
Elijah yielded to self-pity—1 Kings 19:4,5.
God confronted Elijah—1 Kings 19:9.
Turn from self-pity—Proverbs 15:13.

S

257

Self-Righteous

Condemnation of other people—Matthew 9:11-13.
Empty claim of no sin—Jeremiah 2:35.
Foolishness involved—Job 9:20.
Get rid of log from own eye—Matthew 7:5.
God detests—Isaiah 65:5.
Holier than thou—Luke 18:9.
Hypocrites call on Lord but will not obey—Luke 6:46.
Hypocrites clean on outside, filthy on inside—Luke 11:39; 16:15.
Involves boastfulness—Matthew 23:30.
Jesus speaks against—Matthew 23:27,28.
Pure in their own eyes—Proverbs 30:12.
Reject God's righteousness—Romans 10:3.
Way of fool seems right—Proverbs 12:15.
See Hypocrisy; Pharisees; Sadducees.

Self-Will

Stubborn—Acts 7:51.
Stubborn and obstinate—Isaiah 48:4.
Stubborn and rebellious son—Deuteronomy 21:18; Psalm 78:8.

Sermon

Paul put someone to sleep—Acts 20:9.
Preach Christ crucified—1 Corinthians 1:23.
Preach Jesus as Lord—2 Corinthians 4:5.
Preach the Word—Mark 16:15,16; 1 Timothy 4:2,13.
Sermon on Mount—Matthew 5–7.

Serpent

Lord sent poisonous snakes—Numbers 21:6-9.
Moses' staff became snake—Exodus 4:3.
Paul bitten by snake—Acts 28:3,5,6.
Seed of woman will crush head of serpent—Genesis 3:15.
Serpent cursed—Genesis 3:14.
Shrewdest of all creatures—Genesis 3:1.

S

Servant, Bond

Be a faithful servant—Matthew 25:23.
Better to be a servant than ambitious—Luke 22:26.
Lord will reward—Ephesians 6:8.
No slave or free in Christ—Galatians 3:28.
Parable of unmerciful servant—Matthew 18:21-35.
Paul became a servant of everyone—1 Corinthians 9:19.
Servant leaders—Matthew 20:28; Mark 10:43,44; John 13:3-9; Titus 2:7.
Voluntary servanthood—Deuteronomy 15:12-18.

Seven

Days

God blessed seventh day, rested from work—Genesis 2:3; Exodus 20:11.
Seventh day, day of rest—Deuteronomy 5:14.

Years

Seven years of famine began—Genesis 41:54.
Seven years of plenty ended—Genesis 41:53.

Seventy

In Babylon for 70 years—Jeremiah 29:10.
Jerusalem must lie desolate for 70 years—Daniel 9:2.
Period of 70 sets of seven—Daniel 9:24.
Seventy of Israel's leaders summoned—Exodus 24:1,9; Numbers 11:16,24,25.
Seventy years of captivity—Jeremiah 25:12.

Sex within Marriage

Marriage bed should be honored by all—Hebrews 13:4.
Sex within marriage good—Matthew 19:5; 1 Corinthians 6:16; Ephesians 5:31.
Two become one flesh—Matthew 19:5; Mark 10:7,8.
See Husband; Marriage; Wife.

S

Sexual Aberrations

Avoid people who indulge in sexual sin—1 Corinthians 5:9.

Body not made for sexual immorality—1 Corinthians 6:13.

David and Bathsheba—2 Samuel 11.

Do not chase evil desires—1 Peter 4:2,3.

Do not have sexual intercourse with mother—Leviticus 18:7.

Homosexuality—Leviticus 18:22.

Immoral lives—Jude 4.

Keep clear of sexual sin—Colossians 3:5; 1 Thessalonians 4:3.

No immoral living—Romans 13:13.

No sex with an animal—Leviticus 18:23.

No sex with close relative—Leviticus 18:6.

No sex with neighbor's wife—Leviticus 18:20.

Sexual immorality brings judgment—1 Corinthians 10:8.

Sexual immorality calls for discipline—1 Corinthians 5:1-11.

Sexual immorality emerges from sinful nature—Galatians 5:19.

Shame

Adam and Eve naked, felt no shame—Genesis 2:25.

After sin, Adam and Eve felt shame—Genesis 3:7.

Avoid shameful desires—Colossians 3:5; 1 Peter 2:11.

Disgraceful for man to have long hair—1 Corinthians 11:14.

Diviners will be disgraced—Micah 3:7.

Fool is put to shame—Proverbs 3:35.

Jesus mocked and shamed—Psalm 69:7; 109:25.

Lord, do not let me be put to shame—Psalm 31:1.

Mother's shame, bad child—Proverbs 29:15.

No shame to suffer as a Christian—1 Peter 4:16.

Noah shamed—Genesis 9:20-27.

S

Pride leads to shame—Proverbs 11:2.

Sin leads to shame and disgrace—Genesis 3:7; Proverbs 3:35; 13:5.

Son who sleeps during harvest is shameful—Proverbs 10:5.

Those who worship idols are disgraced—Psalm 97:7.

Wicked children shameful—Proverbs 17:2.

Sheep, Figurative

Disciples are sheep among wolves—Matthew 10:16.

Israel, God's lost sheep—Matthew 10:6.

Sheep of flock (disciples) will be scattered—Matthew 26:31; Mark 14:27.

Sheep without a shepherd—Matthew 9:36.

Straying sheep—Luke 15:4.

Shepherd

God Is

Carries lambs in His arms—Isaiah 40:11.

God leads His people like a flock—Psalm 78:52.

Head Shepherd—1 Peter 5:4.

Jesus the Good Shepherd—John 10:11.

Jesus the great Shepherd—Hebrews 13:20.

Lord is my Shepherd—Psalm 23.

Shepherd of Israel—Psalm 80:1.

Shepherd, Guardian of your souls—1 Peter 2:25.

Jesus Is

See Jesus Christ, True Shepherd.

Ships

Paul sailed by ship—Acts 20:13.

Tiny rudder makes huge ship turn—James 3:4.

Weather problems assault ship—Acts 27:14-44.

Sickness

See Disease.

S

Sign

Miraculous signs—John 2:11; 3:2.

"Show us a miraculous sign," unbelieving Jews—Matthew 12:38; Mark 8:11,12.

Sign of the coming of the Son of Man—Matthew 24:3,30.

Signs of the times—Matthew 16:3,4.

Sin

All humans have sinned—Isaiah 53:5-6; Romans 3:23; 5:12.

Children of wrath—Ephesians 2:3.

Devastating effects of sin—Romans 1:18–3:20.

Fallen man is totally depraved—Romans 7:18.

God chastens us if we remain in sin—Hebrews 12:6.

God's Word in our hearts prevents sin—Psalm 119:11.

Human heart is deceitful—Jeremiah 17:9.

Natural man does not accept things of God— 1 Corinthians 2:14.

Sin breaks our fellowship with God—Isaiah 59:1,2; 1 John 1:6.

Sin causes death—Romans 6:23.

Sin entered world through Adam—Genesis 3:1-19.

Sin is lawlessness—1 John 3:4.

Sin unto death—1 Corinthians 11:30; 1 John 5:16.

Three areas of sin: lust of flesh, lust of eyes, pride of life— 1 John 2:16.

We are sinful from moment of birth—Psalm 51:5.

Whoever commits sin is servant of sin—John 8:34.

Against Holy Spirit

Blasphemy against the Holy Spirit—Matthew 12:31,32; Mark 3:29; Luke 12:10.

Grieve the Holy Spirit—Isaiah 63:10; Ephesians 4:30.

Lie to the Holy Spirit—Acts 5:3.

Resist the Holy Spirit—Acts 7:51.

Test the Spirit of the Lord—Acts 5:9.

See Holy Spirit.

Confession of
Confess sins to each other—James 5:16.
Confess your sins—1 John 1:9.
Confession cleanses guilt away—Psalm 51:2.
Confession leads to healing—Psalm 41:4.
Model prayer of confession—Psalm 51.
Psalmist confesses—Psalm 32:5; 38:18.

Consequences of
Destruction—Proverbs 13:6.
Enslavement to sinful desires—1 Corinthians 3:3.
Entraps us—Psalm 9:16; Proverbs 12:13; 29:6.
Evil results—Galatians 5:19.
Fall beneath load of sin—Proverbs 11:5.
Fall into own snares—Psalm 141:10.
Full of trouble—Proverbs 12:21.
Held captive by sins—Proverbs 5:22.
No peace—Isaiah 57:21.
No share in Kingdom—1 Corinthians 6:9,10.
Separates us from God—Ephesians 4:17-19.
Shame and disgrace—Genesis 3:7; Proverbs 3:35; 13:5.
Sin nature causes sinful acts—Galatians 5:19-21.
Sow evil, harvest evil—Job 4:8.
Ultimately leads to death—Romans 5:12; 6:23; Galatians 6:8.
We do what we do not want to do—Romans 7:14,15.
Without Christ, leads to Lake of Fire—Revelation 21:8.

Forgiveness of
Cleansing from every sin—1 John 1:7.
Forgiveness and cleansing—1 John 1:9.
God blots out sins—Isaiah 43:25,26.
God forgives *all* our sins—Psalm 65:3; 99:8; Luke 5:21.
Guilt removed—Psalm 32:5.
Jesus has authority to forgive—Luke 5:24.

S

Jesus saves His people from sins—Matthew 1:21.
Joy for those whose rebellion is forgiven—Psalm 32:1,2.
Many sins forgiven—Psalm 25:7,11,18.
Sin against Holy Spirit *not* forgiven—Luke 12:10.
Sins forgiven—Isaiah 6:7; Matthew 9:2.

Known to God

God carefully watches how people live—Job 24:23; 34:21,22.
God hears all complaints—Numbers 14:27.
God knows secrets of every heart—Psalm 44:21.
God sees every sin—Jeremiah 16:17; Hosea 7:2.
God sees secret sins—Psalm 90:8.
Jesus knew who would betray Him—John 13:11.
Jesus knows secret sins—John 4:17.
Lord knows people's thoughts—Psalm 94:11.
Sins cannot be hidden from God—Psalm 69:5.
See God, Omniscience of.

Love of

Dog returns to its vomit—Proverbs 26:11.
Doing wrong is a fool's fun—Proverbs 10:23.
Enjoying evil—Proverbs 2:14.
Enjoying the taste of wickedness—Job 20:12.
Loving darkness—John 3:19,20.
Wandering far from God—Jeremiah 14:10.

S

Separates from God

God hides His face—Deuteronomy 31:18.
Sins cut us off from God—Isaiah 59:2.
See Sin, Consequences of.

Sincerity

Be completely honest—Psalm 32:2.
Be honest and sincere—2 Corinthians 1:12.
Do not just pretend to be good—1 Peter 2:1.
Do not just pretend to love others—Romans 12:9.
Preach God's message with sincerity—2 Corinthians 2:17.

Serve master sincerely—Ephesians 6:5.
Sincere love for each other—1 Peter 1:22.

Single (Unmarried)
See Celibacy.

Sinlessness
Be blameless—1 Thessalonians 3:13.
Be holy in every way—1 Thessalonians 5:23.
Do not compromise—Psalm 119:3.
No one is absolutely sinless—1 John 1:10.

Of Jesus Christ
See Jesus Christ, Sinlessness.

Skepticism
Doubtful mind is unsettled—James 1:6.
Doubting Thomas—John 20:25.
Fools deny God's existence—Psalm 14:1; 53:1.
Satan plants doubt in minds—Genesis 3:1-5.
Skepticism about prayer—Job 21:15.
Waver back and forth—1 Kings 18:21; James 1:8.

Slander
Avoid rumors—Psalm 31:13.
Do not speak evil of anyone—1 Timothy 3:11; Titus 3:2.
False accusations—Psalm 35:11.
False witness—Matthew 26:60.
Get rid of slander—Ephesians 4:31.
Keep your tongue from speaking evil—1 Peter 3:10.
Saying things that harm others—Psalm 52:4.
Slander and telling lies—Psalm 109:2.
Slander of a brother—Psalm 50:20.
Tongue can sting like a snake—Psalm 140:3.
Will give an account for every idle word—Matthew 12:36.

S

Slavery

Be slaves of righteousness—Romans 6:19.
Enslaved to sin—John 8:34; Romans 6:16.
Joseph sold as a slave—Genesis 37:27,28.
No slave or free in Christ—Galatians 3:28.
Onesimus—Philemon 10,11.
Slaves of God—Romans 6:22.
Slaves sold—Ezekiel 27:13.
Slaves to evil pleasures—Titus 3:3.

Sleep

Girl slept in death—Matthew 9:24; Mark 5:39; Luke 8:52.
God gives rest to His loved ones—Psalm 127:2.
Jesus slept—Matthew 8:24; Mark 4:38.
Lazarus fell asleep (in death)—John 11:11.
Lazybones, how long will you sleep?—Proverbs 6:9.

Slothfulness

See Laziness.

Sobriety

Be sober—1 Thessalonians 5:6.
Do not be heavy drinker—1 Timothy 3:3.
Exhibit self-control—1 Timothy 3:2; Titus 2:2.
Live soberly—Titus 2:12.

Sodomy

Burn with lust—Romans 1:27.
Do not practice homosexuality—Genesis 19:5-7; Leviticus 18:22.
Homosexuals have no share in Kingdom—1 Corinthians 6:9.
No intercourse with an animal—Exodus 22:19; Leviticus 18:23; 20:15.
Penalty for homosexual acts—Leviticus 20:13.
Turning against natural feelings—Romans 1:26.
See Abomination; Immorality.

Son

Abraham willing to sacrifice son—Genesis 22:1-18.
Dedicate firstborn sons to God—Exodus
13:2,12,13,15; 34:19; Numbers 8:17.
Father-son rivalry—2 Samuel 15:1-37.
Jesus, an obedient son—Luke 2:41-52.
Joseph a good son—Genesis 46:29; 47:12.
Lord killed firstborn sons in Egypt—Exodus 12:29.
Prodigal son—Luke 15:11-32.
Redemption of firstborn sons—Exodus 22:29,30.
Saul and sons cremated—1 Samuel 31:12.
Sins of Eli and sons—1 Samuel 3:14.
Son cooked—2 Kings 6:28,29.
Son listen to father—Proverbs 1:8; 13:1.
Son who sleeps during harvest, shameful—Proverbs
10:5.
Twin sons—Genesis 38:27.
See Father; Mother.

Of God, Jesus Christ
See Jesus Christ, Son of God.

Song

David sang—2 Samuel 22:1.
God has given us a new song—Psalm 40:3; Revelation
5:9.
Great choir sang wonderful new song—Revelation
14:3.
Moses and people sang to Lord—Exodus 15:1.
Psalms, hymns, and spiritual songs—Ephesians 5:19;
Colossians 3:16.
Sing new songs of praise—Psalm 33:3.
Song of Moses—Revelation 15:3.
See Music and Musical Instruments.

Sorcery

See Occultism.

S

Sorrow

Do not sorrow over dead in Christ—1 Thessalonians 4:13.
God will wipe away all tears—Revelation 21:4.
Godly sorrow produces good—2 Corinthians 7:10,11.
Jesus has borne our griefs—Isaiah 53:4.
Sorrowful, yet rejoicing—2 Corinthians 6:10.
Your heart will rejoice—John 16:22.
See Bereavement and Loss; Comfort; Grief; Tears.

Soul-Winning

See Evangelism.

Sovereignty

See God, Sovereign.

Speaking

Evil

Avoid foul or abusive language—Romans 3:13,14;
  Ephesians 4:29.
Avoid perverse talk—Proverbs 4:24.
Deceitful tongue crushes spirit—Proverbs 15:4.
Do not blaspheme God—Exodus 22:28.
Do not speak evil—James 4:11; 1 Peter 3:10.
False witness is a traitor—Proverbs 14:25.
False witness tells lies—Proverbs 12:17.
Gossiping tongue causes anger—Proverbs 25:23.
Harsh words stir up anger—Proverbs 15:1; Ephesians
  4:31.
Just say *yes* or *no*—Matthew 5:37.
Keep your lips from telling lies—Psalm 34:13.
Mouths full of cursing, lies, and threats—Psalm 10:7.
No one can tame tongue—James 3:8.
Obscene stories and coarse jokes—Ephesians 5:4.
Proud tongues—Psalm 12:3.
Quick retort can ruin everything—Proverbs 13:3.
Tongue can cut like sharp razor—Psalm 52:2.

S

Tongue can do enormous damage—James 3:5.
Tongue can kill—Proverbs 18:21.
Tongue can sting like a snake—Psalm 140:3.
Tongue is a flame of fire—James 3:6.
Twisted tongue tumbles into trouble—Proverbs 17:20.
Wicked are trapped by their words—Proverbs 12:13.
Wicked speak only what is corrupt—Proverbs 10:32;
    15:28.

In Tongues
See Charismatic Issues.

Wisdom in
Be slow to speak—James 1:19.
Control tongue and live long—Proverbs 13:3; James
    1:26.
Curb your tongue—Psalm 39:1.
Do not brag—James 3:13.
Do not let lips speak evil—Job 27:4.
Gentle answer turns away wrath—Proverbs 15:1.
Gentle words bring life and health—Proverbs 15:4.
Godly person gives wise advice—Psalm 37:30;
    Proverbs 10:31,32.
Godly think before speaking—Proverbs 15:28.
Good words come from good heart—Matthew 12:35.
Let conversation be gracious—Colossians 4:6.
Let Lord control what you say—Psalm 141:3.
Let tongue sing about God's Word—Psalm 119:172.
Lord delights in pure words—Proverbs 15:26.
Soft speech crushes opposition—Proverbs 25:15.
Speak encouraging words—Ephesians 4:29.
Wise give good advice—Proverbs 15:7.
Wise person uses few words—Proverbs 17:27.
Wise speech is rare—Proverbs 20:15.
Words of the godly lead to life—Proverbs 10:11.
Words of the godly save lives—Proverbs 12:6.

S

Words of the wise keep them out of trouble—Proverbs 14:3.

Spiritism

See Occultism.

Spirituality, Principles of

Bow down in worship—Psalm 95:6.
Fix thoughts on God—Isaiah 26:3.
Holy Spirit guides us—John 14:17.
Let Word of God guide you in all things—Psalm 119:105.
Love Lord with whole heart—Deuteronomy 6:5.
Obey all commands—Joshua 22:5.
Prayer in the morning—Psalm 5:3; 119:147.
Set sights on heaven—Colossians 3:1.
Trust in God completely—Proverbs 3:5,6.
See Commitment; Disciples and Discipleship; Holiness, Personal.

Stability

See Character, Firmness of.

Stamina

See Endurance.

S Stars

Do not worship stars—Deuteronomy 4:19.
God commands stars—Job 9:7.
God made the stars—Genesis 1:16; Job 9:9.
God set the stars in place—Psalm 8:3.
God spoke, and the stars were born—Psalm 33:6.
One-third of the stars will become dark—Revelation 8:12.
Stars of the sky will fall to the earth—Isaiah 34:4; Mark 13:25; Revelation 6:13.
Stars will no longer shine—Joel 2:10; 3:15.

Stealing

Do not steal—Exodus 20:15; Leviticus 19:11; Deuteronomy 5:19.

If you are a thief, stop stealing—Ephesians 4:28.

Satan steals seed from heart—Matthew 13:19; Mark 4:15.

Store treasure in heaven, where it cannot be stolen—Matthew 6:19,20.

See Robbery.

Stewardship

See Tithes.

Stones, Precious

Crown with gems—1 Chronicles 20:2.

Onyx stones and other gemstones—Exodus 35:27; 39:6.

Precious stones—1 Kings 10:10; Ezekiel 28:13.

See Ruby.

Strength, God Is Our

Can do all things through Christ—Philippians 4:13.

God gives power to the faint—Isaiah 40:29,31.

God will strengthen you—Psalm 27:14; Isaiah 41:10.

God's grace is sufficient—2 Corinthians 12:9.

Lord is my strength—Psalm 28:7.

Strife

Aim for harmony—Romans 14:19.

Contentious wife—Proverbs 19:13; 21:19; 25:24; 27:15.

Fools insist on quarreling—Proverbs 20:3.

Quarreling, jealousy, outbursts of anger—2 Corinthians 12:20.

Stay away from complaining and arguing—Philippians 2:14.

Stay free from anger and controversy—1 Timothy 2:8.

S

271

Stop arguing—1 Corinthians 1:10.

Troublemaker plants seeds of strife—Proverbs 16:28.

Students

Holy Spirit is our teacher—1 Corinthians 2:6-16.

Learn about God and His ways—Deuteronomy 4:10; 11:19; Proverbs 22:6.

Learn Scriptures from childhood—2 Timothy 3:15.

School of the prophets—1 Samuel 19:20.

Students live in poverty—2 Kings 4:1.

Study the Bible—Deuteronomy 17:19; Isaiah 34:16; Acts 17:11; Romans 15:4.

Submission

Be careful to obey God—Exodus 19:5; 23:22; Deuteronomy 4:40; 12:28; 15:5; 28:1.

Jesus submitted to sacrifice—John 18:1-11.

Obey leaders and submit to their authority—Hebrews 13:17.

Submit to God—James 4:7.

Submit to government—Titus 3:1.

Submit to those who are older—1 Peter 5:5.

Wives submit to husbands—Ephesians 5:22-24; Colossians 3:18.

Substance Abuse

See Intoxication.

S

Success

Follow terms of covenant, then you will prosper—Deuteronomy 29:9.

Give God glory for success—Psalm 115:1.

God of heaven gives success—Nehemiah 2:20.

Hard work means prosperity—Proverbs 12:11.

Hard workers get rich—Proverbs 10:4.

Hard workers have plenty of food—Proverbs 28:19.

Lord gave Joseph success—Genesis 39:3.

Many counselors bring success—Proverbs 15:22.
Observe laws, then you will prosper—1 Chronicles 22:13.
Seek first the Kingdom—Matthew 6:33.
Seek Lord and succeed—2 Chronicles 26:5.
Wealth from hard work grows—Proverbs 13:11.
Whatever godly person does prospers—Psalm 1:3.
Work brings profit—Proverbs 14:23.

Suffering

Blessed are those who suffer for doing right—1 Peter 3:14-17.
Christ is our example in suffering—1 Peter 2:21.
Christ's consolation is abundant—2 Corinthians 1:5.
God will restore us—1 Peter 5:10.
If we suffer, we will also reign—2 Timothy 2:12.
No trouble can separate us from Christ—Romans 8:35.
Rejoice in midst of fiery trials—1 Peter 4:12,13.
Rejoice in suffering—Romans 5:3.
Suffering for the gospel—2 Timothy 1:8.
Suffering not comparable to future glory—Romans 8:18.
See Endurance; Persecution; Trial.

For Christ

Christ showed Paul how he would suffer—Acts 9:15,16.
Privilege of suffering for Christ—Philippians 1:29.
We must share Christ's suffering—Romans 8:17.
See Martyrdom; Persecution.

Of Christ

Died for our sins—1 Corinthians 15:3.
Gave up His life for church—Ephesians 5:25; 1 John 3:16.
Laid down life for sheep—John 10:11,15.
Suffered and died—Luke 24:46.

Suffered before entering glory—Luke 24:26.
Suffered physical pain—1 Peter 3:18; 4:1.
Went through suffering and temptation—Hebrews 2:18.
Wounded for us—1 Peter 2:24.

Suicide

Ahithophel's suicide—2 Samuel 17:23.
Assisted suicide—Jonah 1:12 (see 1 Samuel 31:4).
Judas's suicide—Matthew 27:5; Acts 1:18.
Pigs committed pigicide—Luke 8:26-34.
Saul's suicide—1 Samuel 31:4.
Suicide refused—1 Samuel 31:4; 1 Chronicles 10:4.
Temptation of Philippian jailer—Acts 16:27.
Zimri's suicide—1 Kings 16:18.

Sun

Darkness fell across land at crucifixion—Matthew 27:45;
  Mark 15:33; Luke 23:44.
Do not worship sun—Deuteronomy 17:3.
God separated day from night—Genesis 1:14.
Sun stood still—Joshua 10:12,13.
Sun will become dark—Matthew 24:29; Mark 13:24; Acts
  2:20; Revelation 6:12.

Sunday

See Sabbath.

Sympathy

Be compassionate—Luke 6:36.
Be full of sympathy toward each other—1 Peter 3:8.
Be Good Samaritan—Luke 10:30-37.
Bear each other's burdens—Galatians 6:2; Hebrews 13:3.
Do not just pretend to love others—Romans 12:9,10.
Love your neighbor as yourself—Leviticus 19:18; James
  2:8.

Tabernacle

Inventory of the materials used—Exodus 38:21.
Made according to God's design—Exodus 26:30.
Residence built for God—Exodus 25:8.
Tabernacle finished—Exodus 39:32.
See Sanctuary.

Table

Jesus turned over moneychangers' tables—John 2:15.
Table for Bread of the Presence—1 Chronicles 28:16.
Table of idolatry—1 Corinthians 10:21.

Tact

Do not be stumbling block—2 Corinthians 6:3-13.
Gentle answer turns away wrath—Proverbs 15:1.
Jesus' tact with Samaritan woman—John 4:4-26.
Paul became servant of everyone—1 Corinthians 9:19.
Soft speech can crush strong opposition—Proverbs 25:15.
Speak truth in love—Ephesians 4:15.
See Courtesy.

Taste

Evil people enjoy taste of wickedness—Job 20:12.
Food no longer tasty, old age—2 Samuel 19:35.
Food unpalatable—2 Kings 4:40.
Isaac had taste for wild game—Genesis 25:28.
Taste and see that the Lord is good—Psalm 34:8.

Tax

Annual temple tax—Nehemiah 10:32.
Borrow to pay taxes—Nehemiah 5:4.
Collectors, collect only amount owed—Luke 3:13.
In proportion to wealth—2 Kings 23:35.
Jesus and the temple tax—Matthew 17:24.
Jesus associated with tax collectors—Matthew 11:19.
Oppressive taxes—Amos 5:11.

Teachers, False

Do not teach others to break God's law—Matthew 5:19.
False prophets deceive—Matthew 7:15; 24:11; Mark 13:22.
False teachers deceive—Matthew 5:19; 2 Corinthians 11:13; Titus 1:11.
See Apostles, False; Cults; Doctrines, False; Heresy.

Teaching

Admonish each other with wisdom—Colossians 3:16.
Fear of Lord teaches person to be wise—Proverbs 15:33.
Fool ignores Christ's teaching—Matthew 7:26.
God gives teachers to the church—Ephesians 4:11.
Hold on to pattern of right teaching—2 Timothy 1:13.
Holy Spirit reminds us of Jesus' teachings—John 14:26.
Holy Spirit teaches believers—John 16:13-15.
Impress God's Word on children—Deuteronomy 6:7.
Listen to what parents teach—Proverbs 1:8; 6:20; 23:22.
Lord, teach me how to live—Psalm 27:11.
People will turn from right teaching—2 Timothy 4:3.
Wicked rebel against right teaching—Titus 1:10.

Tears

God collects our tears in bottle—Psalm 56:8.
God will wipe away all tears—Revelation 7:17.
Lord, listen to cries for help—Psalm 39:12.
No more sorrow or crying or pain—Revelation 21:4.
See Bereavement and Loss; Comfort; Grief.

Teeth

Enemies grind their teeth—Lamentations 2:16.
Evil spirit caused grinding teeth—Mark 9:18.
Weeping and gnashing of teeth—Matthew 8:12; 13:42,50; 22:13; 24:51; 25:30.
Wicked grind teeth in anger—Psalm 112:10.

T

Temperance

Daniel's temperance—Daniel 1:8.
Deacon, not heavy drinker—1 Timothy 3:8.
Elder, not heavy drinker—1 Timothy 3:3; Titus 1:7.
Older women, not heavy drinkers—Titus 2:3.
See Abstinence from Liquor, Examples of; Intoxication.

Temple

Ark brought to temple—1 Kings 8:1-21; 2 Chronicles 5:2-14.
David's son to build temple—2 Samuel 7:13.
Dedication of temple—2 Chronicles 7:1-10.
Gifts for building temple—1 Chronicles 29:1-9.
Glory of Lord in temple—Ezekiel 10:4.
Moneychangers in temple—John 2:14-16.
Prediction of destruction—Matthew 24:2; Mark 13:2.
Preparations for temple—1 Chronicles 22:2-19.
Solomon built temple—1 Kings 6; Acts 7:47.
Solomon's prayer of dedication—2 Chronicles 6:12-42.
Temple furnishings—1 Kings 7:13-51; 2 Chronicles 4.
Temple turned into den of thieves—Matthew 21:13.

Idolatrous

Temple of Artemis—Acts 19:27.
Temple of Baal—2 Kings 10:21,27.
Temple of Dagon—1 Chronicles 10:10; 1 Samuel 5:2.
Temple of the Ashtoreths—1 Samuel 31:10.

Temptation

T

Beware of temptations—Galatians 6:1.
Do not be tempted to forget God—Deuteronomy 8:11.
Do not let evil get best of you—Romans 12:21.
Do not let Satan outsmart you—2 Corinthians 2:11.
Do not let sin control you—Romans 6:12.
Do not lose secure footing—2 Peter 3:17.
Getting too close to fire burns you—Proverbs 6:27,28.
God can keep you from falling—Jude 24.

God will make way of escape—1 Corinthians 10:13.
Jesus faced temptations and did not sin—Hebrews 4:15.
Jesus helps us in our temptation—Hebrews 2:14,18.
Keep alert and pray—Matthew 26:41; Mark 14:38; Luke 22:46.
Lord, do not let us yield to temptation—Matthew 6:9-13; Luke 11:4.
People who desire wealth fall into temptation—1 Timothy 6:9,10.
Pray that you will not be overcome—Luke 22:40.
Resist the devil—James 4:7.
Satan tempts sexually—1 Corinthians 7:5.
Silver and gold a snare—Deuteronomy 7:25.
Sinful nature loves evil—Galatians 5:17.
Temptations emerge from sin nature—James 1:13-15.
Three kinds of temptations—1 John 2:16.
Watch out for temptation of money—1 Timothy 6:9.

Resistance Illustrated
Jesus resisted devil's temptations—Matthew 4:1-11.
Job made a covenant with his eyes—Job 31:1.
Joseph resisted temptation—Genesis 39:7-9.
Psalmist refused evil—Psalm 119:101.

Tension, Cure for
Let not your heart be troubled—John 14:27.
Mind stayed on God is in perfect peace—Isaiah 26:3.
Peace and joy in the Holy Spirit—Romans 14:17.
Peace of God guards your heart—Philippians 4:7.

Testify on God's Behalf
Acknowledge Christ publicly—Matthew 10:32; Luke 12:8.
Announce everything God has done—Jeremiah 51:10.
Be ready with an answer—1 Peter 3:15.
Confess with your mouth—Romans 10:9.
Declare the wonder of God's name—Hebrews 2:12.
Lamp is placed on a stand—Mark 4:21; Luke 8:16.

T

Let tongue sing about God's Word—Psalm 119:172.

Never be ashamed to tell others—2 Timothy 1:8.

Proclaim God's greatness—1 Chronicles 16:8,9.

Speak of God's miracles—Psalm 26:7.

Tell family—Luke 8:39.

Tell friends—Mark 5:19.

Tell world about God's unforgettable deeds—Psalm 9:11; 145:12; Isaiah 12:4.

Witnesses to the ends of the earth—Acts 1:8.

Thankfulness

Always give thanks—Ephesians 5:20; Colossians 3:15.

Come before God with thanksgiving—Psalm 95:2; 100:4.

Give thanks forever—Psalm 30:12.

Give thanks in front of entire congregation—Psalm 35:18.

No matter what, be thankful—1 Thessalonians 5:18.

Offer sacrifice of thanksgiving—Psalm 116:17.

Thankful each morning and evening—1 Chronicles 23:30.

Thanksgiving before Meals

Give thanks to God before eating—Romans 14:6.

Jesus our example—Matthew 14:19; 15:36; 26:26; Mark 6:41; 8:6; 14:22; Luke 9:16.

Theft and Thieves

Do not cheat or rob anyone—Leviticus 19:11,13.

Do not steal—Exodus 20:15; Deuteronomy 5:19.

Do not try to get rich by robbery—Psalm 62:10.

From the heart comes theft—Matthew 15:19; Mark 7:21.

God hates robbery—Isaiah 61:8.

If you are a thief, stop stealing—Ephesians 4:28.

T

279

Theology

See Doctrine.

Thirst

As deer pants, so psalmist thirsts for God—Psalm 42:1; 63:1; 143:6.

If you are thirsty, come to Christ—John 7:37.

Let the thirsty ones come—Revelation 22:17.

Thirsty for justice—Matthew 5:6.

To all who are thirsty Jesus gives water of life—Revelation 21:6.

Throne, Examples of

Father acknowledges Jesus' eternal throne—Hebrews 1:8.

Isaiah sees God on throne—Isaiah 6:1-5.

Jesus reigns on throne of David—Psalm 132:11; Luke 1:32.

Solomon on throne—1 Kings 2:12,24; 1 Chronicles 29:23.

Throne of God in heaven—Revelation 4:2-6,9,10.

Thunder

Hailstorm against Egypt—Exodus 9:23.

Mount Sinai—Exodus 19:16.

Peals of thunder in heavenly scene—Revelation 4:5.

See Lightning.

Time

Christ created "the ages"—Hebrews 1:2.

Day is like thousand years to the Lord—2 Peter 3:8.

God set boundaries for day and night—Job 26:10.

In the beginning God created—Genesis 1:1.

Signs to mark off seasons—Genesis 1:14.

When the right time came, God sent His Son—Galatians 4:4.

See Eternity.

Tithes

A tenth of everything—Genesis 28:22.

Bring tithes into storehouse—Malachi 3:10.

Set aside a tithe of your crops—Leviticus 27:30; Deuteronomy 14:22.

Tithe, but no religion—Matthew 23:23.

Titles of Jesus Christ

See Jesus Christ, Names and Titles of.

Tolerance

Intolerance of disciples—Mark 9:38,39; Luke 9:49,50.

Jesus tolerated tax collectors—Matthew 9:10.

Paul's tolerance of self-serving preachers—Philippians 1:17,18.

Tolerance for opinions of others—Romans 14:1-8.

Tolerance for the sake of spreading gospel—2 Timothy 2:10.

Tongue

A time to be quiet—Ecclesiastes 3:7.

Babbling fools fall on their faces—Proverbs 10:8.

Confess that Jesus is Lord—Romans 10:8-10.

Do not talk too much—Proverbs 10:19.

God puts new song in mouth—Psalm 40:3.

Guarding mouth averts calamity—Proverbs 21:23.

Keep tight rein on tongue—James 1:26.

Keep tongue from evil—1 Peter 3:10.

Keep tongue from sin—Psalm 39:1.

May words be pleasing—Psalm 19:14.

Offer God sacrifice of praise—Hebrews 13:15.

Reckless words pierce soul—Proverbs 12:18.

Rid mouth of filthy language—Colossians 3:8.

Set guard at mouth—Psalm 141:3.

Speak of God's righteousness—Psalm 35:28.

Wise person uses few words—Proverbs 17:27.

T

Words from mouth come from heart—Matthew 15:17,18.

Tradition

Ancient tradition—Matthew 15:2,3; Mark 7:3.
Human tradition—Colossians 2:8.
Tradition of fathers—Galatians 1:14.
Tradition of hard work—2 Thessalonians 3:6.

Traitor, Ultimate

Devil enticed Judas—Luke 22:3; John 13:2.
Judas Iscariot, the betrayer—Matthew 26:14-16,45,46;
Mark 14:10; Luke 22:48.

Treasure

Parable of the hidden treasure and pearl—Matthew
13:44-46.
Store treasure in heaven—Matthew 6:19,20.
Treasure God's words—Job 23:12.
Valid criticism is treasured—Proverbs 25:12.
We will share Christ's treasures—Romans 8:17.
Where your treasure is, your heart is—Matthew 6:21;
Luke 12:34.

Trial

Public trial—Acts 12:4.
Roman citizenship guarantees trial—Acts 16:37; 22:25.
Stand trial before Caesar—Acts 27:24.
See Lawsuits; Lawyer.

T

Tribulation Period

Antichrist will demand worship—2 Thessalonians 2:4.
Events of Tribulation—Revelation 4–18.
Seven years long—Daniel 9:27.
Time of distress—Daniel 12:1.
Time of Jacob's distress—Jeremiah 30:7.
Worldwide tribulation—Revelation 3:10.

See Antichrist; Millennial Kingdom; Rapture of Church;
Second Coming of Christ.

Trichotomy View of Man

See Man, Trichotomy View of.

Trinity

See God, Trinity.

Trouble

All of us encounter trouble—Job 5:7.
Be patient in trouble—Romans 12:12.
Church delivered from time of trouble—Revelation 3:10.
Do not be troubled, trust Christ—John 14:1.
Fool invites trouble—Proverbs 10:14.
God helps in times of trouble—Psalm 46:1.
Ill-tempered wife is troublesome—Proverbs 21:19.
Lazy person has trouble all through life—Proverbs 15:19.
Let not your heart be troubled—John 14:27.
Life is full of trouble—Job 14:1.
Lord delivers us out of trouble—Psalm 34:17-19.
Patiently endure troubles—2 Corinthians 6:4.
Present troubles insignificant in view of future glory—2 Corinthians 4:17.
Share each other's troubles—Galatians 6:2.
Trust God in times of trouble—Psalm 50:15.
We are troubled but not distressed—2 Corinthians 4:8,9.

Trumpet

Assemble and break camp—Numbers 10:2.
At Mount Sinai—Exodus 20:18.
Called Israel's army to mobilize—2 Samuel 2:28; Ezekiel 7:14.

T

Celebration before God—2 Samuel 6:5; 1 Chronicles 13:8.
Coronation of king—2 Samuel 15:10.
Day of Atonement—Leviticus 25:9.
In praise of God—1 Chronicles 16:42; 2 Chronicles 5:13.
See Music and Musical Instruments.

Trusting

All who trust in Lord rejoice—Psalm 5:11.
Do not be troubled, trust Christ—John 14:1.
Do not throw away trust—Hebrews 10:35.
Joy in trusting God—Psalm 40:4.
Trust Christ, your High Priest—Hebrews 4:15.
Trust God, He will help you—Psalm 37:5.
Trust God in times of trouble—Psalm 50:15.
Trust in God at all times—Psalm 62:8.
Trust in Lord, not man—Psalm 118:8.
Trust in the Lord—Psalm 37:5.
Trust with whole heart—Proverbs 3:5,6.
Trusting the Lord leads to prosperity—Proverbs 28:25.
Trusting oneself is foolish—Proverbs 28:26.

Trustworthy

Be trustworthy with worldly wealth—Luke 16:11.
Everything God does is worthy of trust—Psalm 33:4.
God guards what we entrust to Him—2 Timothy 1:12.
God is trustworthy—2 Chronicles 6:4,14,15;
    1 Corinthians 1:9.
Guard what God has entrusted to you—1 Timothy 6:20.
In God I trust—Psalm 56:11.
Trustworthy employees—Titus 2:9,10.
Trustworthy people are given more responsibility—Luke
    16:10.
See Dependability.

Truth

Church, pillar of the truth—1 Timothy 3:15.
Faithfully preach truth—2 Corinthians 6:7.

T

Fix thoughts on what is true—Philippians 4:8.
Gently teach those who oppose truth—2 Timothy
2:25.
God desires truth—Psalm 51:6.
Honest witness tells truth—Proverbs 12:17.
If walk in darkness, truth not in you—1 John 1:6,8.
Jesus full of grace and truth—John 1:14,17.
Jesus is the truth—John 14:6.
John the Baptist preached truth—John 5:33.
Live by the truth—John 3:21.
Love rejoices with truth—1 Corinthians 13:6.
No truth in the devil—John 8:44.
Put away falsehood—Ephesians 4:25.
Set forth truth plainly—2 Corinthians 4:2.
Some distort the truth—Acts 20:30.
Speak the truth in love—Ephesians 4:15.
Suppressing the truth—Romans 1:18,25.
The word of truth—Ephesians 1:13; James 1:18.
Truth will set you free—John 8:32.
Worship God in spirit and truth—John 4:23,24.
See Doctrine; Honesty; Integrity.

Tumor

Boils of Egypt—Deuteronomy 28:27.
Plague of tumors—1 Samuel 5:6,9,12.
See Disease.

Twins

Twin sons—Genesis 38:27.
Twins were born—Genesis 25:24.

T

U

Unbelief

Disciples rebuked for unbelief—Mark 16:14.
Do not have doubtful mind—James 1:6.
Do not have unbelieving heart—Hebrews 3:12.
Do not partner with unbelievers—2 Corinthians 6:14.
Doubting Thomas—John 20:27.
Impossible to please God without faith—Hebrews 11:6.
Jesus knew who would not believe—John 6:64.
Unbelief among Jews—Romans 11:20; Hebrews 12:25.
Unbelief and condemnation—Mark 16:16.
Unbelief at Second Coming—Luke 18:8.
Unbelief, despite miracles—John 12:37.
Unbelief in Scripture—Luke 24:25-36.
Unbelief of Jesus' brothers—John 7:5.
Unbelief of Moses and Aaron—Numbers 20:12.
Unbelief, so few miracles performed—Matthew 13:58.

Uncertain, Things that Are

Friendship—John 16:32.
Future—Proverbs 27:1.
Life—James 4:14.
Mens' promises—Psalm 146:3.
Riches—Proverbs 23:5.

Uncharitable, Do Not Be

Do not act better than everyone else—1 Corinthians 4:7.
Do not be judgmental—Luke 6:37.
Do not condemn neighbor—James 4:12.
Do not lack in love—1 Corinthians 13:1.
Do not speak evil—James 4:11.
Those without sin, cast first stone—John 8:7.

Understanding

See Discernment; Knowledge.

Unfair

See Injustice.

Unfaithfulness

Covenant breakers—Leviticus 26:15; Psalm 55:20; Isaiah 24:5; Jeremiah 11:10.

Israel's unfaithfulness—Hosea 10:1,2.

Judgment is imminent—Matthew 3:10.

Marital unfaithfulness, reason for divorce—Matthew 5:31,32.

Peter's unfaithfulness—Matthew 26:31-35,69-75.

Unfaithful hearts and lustful eyes—Ezekiel 6:9.

See Dependability.

Unfruitfulness

Adversity makes us more fruitful—John 15:2.

Fruit of the Holy Spirit—Galatians 5:22,23.

Fruitless deeds of darkness—Ephesians 5:11.

God prunes, so more fruit—John 15:2-6.

Good tree cannot produce bad fruit—Luke 6:43.

Unfruitfulness leads to judgment—Matthew 3:10; 7:19; Luke 3:9.

Unity Among Believers

Agree wholeheartedly—Philippians 2:2.

Live in harmony and peace—Romans 12:16; 14:19; 15:5,6; 2 Corinthians 13:11.

One heart and mind—Acts 4:32; 1 Peter 3:8.

Stand side by side—Philippians 1:27.

Stop arguing among yourselves—1 Corinthians 1:10.

United in the Holy Spirit—Ephesians 4:3.

See Communion, Of Saints; Harmony.

U

Universe

Christ sustains universe—Colossians 1:17.

Design of universe proves Designer—Romans 1:18-20.

Elohim created universe—Genesis 1:1.

Heavens cannot be measured—Jeremiah 31:37.

Heavens tell of the glory of God—Psalm 19:1.
Universe made through Jesus—1 Corinthians 8:6;
Hebrews 1:2.

Unpardonable Sin

Blasphemy against Holy Spirit not forgiven—Matthew
12:31,32; Mark 3:29,30.
Sin unto death—1 John 5:16.
Sins of Eli and sons—1 Samuel 3:14.

Unrighteousness

Eat the bread of wickedness—Proverbs 4:17.
Every sort of evil—2 Thessalonians 2:10.
Godlessness and wickedness—Romans 1:18.
God's wrath imminent—Ephesians 5:6; Colossians 3:6.
Impiety—Exodus 5:2; 2 Chronicles 32:17; Job 21:14;
Proverbs 1:30.
Ungodliness—2 Timothy 2:16; Titus 2:12; Jude 18.
Wrongdoing, sin—1 John 5:17.
See Depravity of Man; Sin.

Unselfishness

Be servant of everyone—1 Corinthians 9:19.
Do not be selfish—Philippians 2:3.
Do not focus only on your interests—1 Corinthians
10:24,33; Philippians 2:4.
Do not just please yourself—Romans 15:1; 2 Corinthians
5:15.
Love does not demand its own way—1 Corinthians 13:5.
Love each other with genuine affection—Romans 12:10.
Love your neighbor as yourself—James 2:8.
See Generosity; Self-Denial.

Unstable

See Inconsistency; Instability.

U

Values

See Priority.

Vanity

Envy is meaningless (vain)—Ecclesiastes 4:4.

Flattering lips and insincere hearts—Psalm 12:2.

Pleasure is meaningless (vain)—Ecclesiastes 2:1.

Turn eyes from worthless things—Psalm 119:37.

Vain boasting—2 Peter 2:18.

Vain discussions—2 Timothy 2:16; Titus 3:9.

Vanity of nations—Acts 4:25.

Wealth is meaningless (vain)—Ecclesiastes 5:10.

Vegetation

Abundant—Psalm 104:13-15.

Farmer who plants few seeds gets small crop—
2 Corinthians 9:6.

Grass and seed-bearing plants—Genesis 1:11,29,30.

Needs rain—Genesis 2:5.

Plant a variety of crops—Ecclesiastes 11:6.

Planting seeds—2 Corinthians 9:6.

Plowing and sowing necessary—Isaiah 28:24.

Vengeance

See Revenge.

Victory

Do not lose the race—Philippians 2:16.

Fight a good fight—2 Timothy 4:7.

In race everyone runs, one gets prize—1 Corinthians
9:24.

Run with endurance—Hebrews 12:1.

Strain to reach end of the race—Philippians 3:14.

Triumph in Christ—1 Corinthians 15:57;
2 Corinthians 2:14.

V

Victory that overcomes the world—1 John 5:4.
We are more than conquerors—Romans 8:37.

Vineyard

Parable of the two sons—Matthew 21:28-32.
Parable of workers in the vineyard—Matthew 20:1-16.
Planting beautiful vineyards—Ecclesiastes 2:4.
Solomon's vineyard—Song of Solomon 8:11.
Vineyard of one lacking sense—Proverbs 24:30.

Violence

Acts of violence in hands—Isaiah 59:6.
Clothed with violence—Psalm 73:6.
Earth filled with violence—Genesis 6:13.
Land filled with violence—Ezekiel 8:17.
Lord, protect me from violent people—Psalm 140:1.
Wicked are violent—Proverbs 16:29.

Virgin Birth of Jesus

Fulfilled—Matthew 1:23; Luke 1:27.
Prophesied—Isaiah 7:14.

Virtue

Fix thoughts on good things—Philippians 4:8.
God likes integrity—1 Chronicles 29:17.
Live with moral excellence—2 Peter 1:5.
Maintain integrity—Psalm 41:12; Proverbs 11:3; 19:1; 20:7.
Man of integrity walks securely—Proverbs 10:9.
Manual of integrity—Book of Proverbs.
Wisdom and virtue lead to honor—Proverbs 3:16; 8:18; 13:18; 21:21; 22:4.
See Conduct, Proper; Integrity.

Volcanoes

Mountain burning with fire—Deuteronomy 4:11; 5:23.
Mountains billow smoke—Psalm 144:5.

V

Mountains burst into flame—Psalm 104:32.
Mountains melt like wax before Lord—Psalm 97:5.

Vow

Be careful in making vow—Proverbs 20:25.
Children dedicated to God—1 Samuel 1:11.
Faithfulness required—Numbers 30:2; Deuteronomy 23:21.
Israel's vow—Numbers 21:2.
Jacob's vow—Genesis 28:20,21.
Jephthah's vow—Judges 11:30.
Jonah's vow—Jonah 2:9.
Nazirite vow—Numbers 6:2-8.
Paul's vow—Acts 18:18.
Peter's feeble vow—Mark 14:29-31,66-72.
Promises to God—Psalm 76:11.

V

Wages

Do not cheat employees of wages—Jeremiah 22:13; Malachi 3:5; James 5:4.

Parable concerning wages—Matthew 20:1-15.

Wages of sin is death—Romans 6:23.

Waiting

Be patient, await Lord's return—1 Corinthians 1:7; James 5:7.

Lord is good to those who wait for Him—Lamentations 3:25.

Those who wait on Lord find new strength—Isaiah 40:31.

Wait confidently for God—Micah 7:7.

Wait for coming of Holy Spirit—Acts 1:4.

Wait for God's mercies—Psalm 52:9.

Wait for God's rescue—Psalm 59:9.

Wait for Lord's help—Isaiah 8:17.

Wait patiently for Lord—Psalm 27:14; 37:7; 40:1.

Wait quietly before God—Psalm 62:1,5.

Walking in God's Ways

Lord protects those who walk with integrity—Proverbs 2:7.

Stay on the path of the Lord—Deuteronomy 5:33.

Walk in all God's ways—Deuteronomy 28:9; Joshua 22:5.

Walk in the godly way—Jeremiah 6:16.

Walk in the Spirit—Galatians 5:16.

War

Be strong and courageous—Deuteronomy 31:6; Joshua 1:9.

Do not go to war without wise guidance—Proverbs 24:6.

End times, many wars—Matthew 24:6; Mark 13:7; Luke 21:9.

God prepares people for battle—Psalm 18:34.

God will fight for you—Exodus 14:14; Deuteronomy 1:30; 3:22; 20:4.

Must we solve differences with swords?—2 Samuel 2:26.

Wardrobe, Spiritual

Be clothed with armor of right living—Romans 13:12.

Be clothed with humility—Colossians 3:12; 1 Peter 5:5,6.

Be clothed with mercy and love—Colossians 3:12-14.

Be clothed with patience—Colossians 3:12.

Put on all of God's armor—Ephesians 6:11-18.

Put on body armor of faith and love—1 Thessalonians 5:8.

Watchfulness

Be careful how you live—Ephesians 5:15.

Be careful lest you fall—1 Corinthians 10:12.

Be careful to love Lord—Joshua 23:11.

Be careful to obey—Joshua 22:5.

Be on guard, stand true to beliefs—1 Corinthians 16:13; 1 Thessalonians 5:6.

Beware, do not be greedy—Luke 12:15.

Beware of yeast of Pharisees—Matthew 16:6.

Diligently obey commands—Deuteronomy 6:17.

Do not let your heart turn away—Deuteronomy 11:16.

Keep a clear mind—2 Timothy 4:5.

Keep alert and pray—Matthew 26:41; Ephesians 6:18.

Keep close watch on yourself—1 Timothy 4:16.

Listen carefully to truth—Hebrews 2:1.

Pay attention to what you hear—Luke 8:18.

Watch out for attacks from devil—1 Peter 5:8.

Watch out, so you do not lose prize—2 John 8.

Watch out, you may be seduced with wealth—Job 36:18.

W

Water

Everything in sea will die—Revelation 16:3.
God divided sea for Moses—Exodus 14:21,22.
Jesus turned water to wine—John 2:1-11.
Jesus walked on water—Matthew 14:25.
Water from rock—Exodus 17:6; Numbers 20:11.

Figurative

Drink deeply from fountain of salvation—Isaiah 12:3.
Floodwaters up to neck—Psalm 69:1.
God is with you through deep waters—2 Samuel 22:17;
    Isaiah 43:2.
Let the thirsty ones come—Revelation 22:17.
Living water from Jesus—John 4:10,14; John 7:37,38.
Springs of water of life—Revelation 21:6.

Wavering

See Inconsistency; Indecision.

Weakness

Accept Christians weak in faith—Romans 14:1.
Burden too heavy—Numbers 11:14.
Disciples cannot bear more teaching—John 16:12.
Disciples too weary—Matthew 26:40.
God strengthens the weak—Isaiah 40:29.
God's strength makes up for our weakness—
    2 Corinthians 12:9.
Jesus understands our weaknesses—Hebrews 4:15.
Not ready for solid food—1 Corinthians 3:2.
Quick to disobey—Judges 2:10-13,19.
Spirit strong, body weak—Matthew 26:41.
Weak consciences, easily violated—1 Corinthians 8:7,12.

W

Wealth

Be trustworthy with worldly wealth—Luke 16:11.
False security, wealth—Jeremiah 49:4.
Fear of Lord brings wealth—Proverbs 22:4.

People who desire wealth fall into temptation—
1 Timothy 6:9,10.

Tax in proportion to wealth—2 Kings 23:35.

Wealth from hard work grows—Proverbs 13:11.

See Affluence; Riches.

Weariness

Do not weary yourself trying to get rich—Proverbs
23:4.

God gives rest to the weary—Jeremiah 31:25.

Growing weary in our present bodies—2 Corinthians
5:2.

We will run and not grow weary—Isaiah 40:31.

Weary of living—Genesis 27:46; Job 3:20; Ecclesiastes
2:17; 4:1,2; Jonah 4:8.

See Rest; Revival; Sleep.

Weeping

God will wipe away all tears—Revelation 7:17.

Plant in tears, harvest joy—Psalm 126:5.

Weeping and gnashing of teeth—Matthew 8:12; 22:13;
24:51; 25:30.

*See Bereavement and Loss; Comfort; Grief; Sorrow;
Tears.*

Wicked

Constant liars—Proverbs 6:12.

Do not envy the wicked—Psalm 37:1.

Far from salvation—Psalm 119:155.

From evil people come evil deeds—1 Samuel 24:13.

God is angry at the wicked—Psalm 7:11.

In pain throughout life—Job 15:20.

No peace for the wicked—Isaiah 57:21.

Plot against the godly—Psalm 37:12.

Wisdom will save you from evil people—Proverbs 2:12.

Prayer of

Confess sin or God will not hear—Psalm 66:18.

W

God does not answer, because of their pride—Job 35:12.

God does not answer, because wrong motive—James 4:3.

God does not listen to sinners—Deuteronomy 3:26; Proverbs 1:24; Isaiah 59:2.

God refused to answer—2 Samuel 22:42; Psalm 18:41.

God shut out prayers—Lamentations 3:8.

Lord is far from the wicked—Proverbs 15:29.

Treat wife right or God will not hear—1 Peter 3:7.

Punishment of

Calamity will overtake the wicked—Psalm 34:21.

Crushed by sins—Proverbs 14:32.

Death—Genesis 2:17; 1 Chronicles 10:13,14; Proverbs 11:19; Galatians 6:8.

Destruction—Genesis 6:13; Psalm 37:9.

Eternal destruction—Philippians 3:19.

Lake of Fire—Revelation 20:15; 21:8.

Light is snuffed out—Proverbs 13:9; 24:20.

Many sorrows—Psalm 32:10.

Memory erased from earth—Psalm 34:16.

No hope—Job 11:20.

Pain throughout life—Job 15:20.

Removed from land—Proverbs 2:22.

Repayment—Psalm 28:4; Proverbs 11:21.

Sent into everlasting punishment—Matthew 25:46.

Shame and disgrace—Proverbs 13:5.

Sudden disaster—Proverbs 24:22.

Suffer from diseases—Leviticus 26:16.

Thrown into fire—Matthew 13:49,50.

Years cut short—Proverbs 10:27.

Wife

W

A treasure—Proverbs 18:22.

Accept authority of husband—1 Peter 3:1.

Husbands must love wives—Ephesians 5:28; Colossians 3:19.

Man leaves father and mother, joins wife—Genesis 2:24.

Must not leave husband—1 Corinthians 7:10.

Must respect husband—Ephesians 5:33.

Not good for man to be alone—Genesis 2:18.

Submit to husbands—Ephesians 5:22; Colossians 3:18.

Virtuous and capable wife—Proverbs 31:10.

Wise woman builds her house—Proverbs 14:1.

Wives must be respected—1 Timothy 3:11.

Woman is responsible to her husband—1 Corinthians 11:3.

Worthy wife is her husband's joy—Proverbs 12:4.

See Divorce; Husband; Marriage.

Wine

Do not be drunk—Ephesians 5:18.

Jesus turned water to wine—John 2:1-11.

New wine, old wineskins—Matthew 9:17; Mark 2:22; Luke 5:37,38.

Wine for medicinal purposes—1 Timothy 5:23.

See Alcohol.

Wisdom

Daniel full of wisdom—Daniel 5:14.

God gave Joseph unusual wisdom—Acts 7:10.

Keep on growing in knowledge—Philippians 1:9.

Lord will give you understanding—2 Timothy 2:7.

Moses was taught wisdom of Egyptians—Acts 7:22.

Pray for wisdom—Psalm 25:4; 27:11; 90:12; 119:12,18,34,125; James 1:5.

Solomon's prayer for wisdom—1 Kings 3:9; 2 Chronicles 1:10.

Wise men from eastern lands—Matthew 2:1.

Wise with spiritual wisdom—Colossians 1:9.

W

Wise Men, Examples of

Belteshazzar (Daniel) was wise—Daniel 4:18.

Solomon was wise—1 Kings 4:29.

Wise men from the east—Matthew 2:1.
Wise men of Egypt—Genesis 41:8; Exodus 7:11.

Witchcraft

Do not consult mediums and psychics—Leviticus 19:31.
Execute mediums and psychics—Leviticus 20:27.
God is against those who consult mediums—Leviticus 20:6.
Medium at Endor—1 Samuel 28:7-9.
Saul banned mediums and psychics—1 Samuel 28:3.
Sorceress must not be allowed to live—Exodus 22:18.
See Occultism.

Witnesses

Complaint against elder requires two or three witnesses—1 Timothy 5:19.
More than one needed for death conviction—Deuteronomy 17:6.

Women

Be modest in appearance—1 Timothy 2:9.
Daughters of Jerusalem, weep for yourselves—Luke 23:28.
Do not be overly concerned with outward beauty—1 Peter 3:3,4.
Eve was deceived—2 Corinthians 11:3; 1 Timothy 2:14.
God created male and female—Genesis 1:27.
Head covered, can prophesy—1 Corinthians 11:5.
Keep silent in church—1 Corinthians 14:34.
Listen and learn quietly and submissively—1 Timothy 2:11.
Made from Adam's rib—Genesis 2:21-23.
No male or female in Christ—Galatians 3:28.
Possible role of deaconess—Romans 16:2.
Serpent tempted Eve—Genesis 3:1-6.
Virtuous wife—Proverbs 31.

W

Wicked
Adulterous wife—Ezekiel 16:32.
Immoral woman—Proverbs 2:16.
Lips of an immoral woman—Proverbs 5:3; 6:24.
Seductive woman—Ecclesiastes 7:26.
Women turned against natural sex—Romans 1:26.

Word of God

Bereans tested Paul's teaching from Scripture—Acts 17:11.
Blessed are those who hear and obey—Luke 11:28.
Correctly explain the Word—2 Timothy 2:15.
Do not add to or subtract from—Deuteronomy 4:2; 12:32; Revelation 22:18,19.
Do not distort Word of God—2 Corinthians 4:2.
God's Word flawless—Proverbs 30:5,6.
God's Word is truth—John 17:17.
God's Word is wonderful—Psalm 119:129,130.
Jesus in the Old Testament—Luke 24:27,45.
Jesus' words never pass away—Matthew 24:35.
Learn Scriptures from childhood—2 Timothy 3:15.
Let word of Christ dwell in you—Colossians 3:16.
Love God's Word—Psalm 119:97-106.
Man depends on God's Word—Matthew 4:4.
Scriptures point to Jesus—John 5:39.
Sword of the Spirit—Ephesians 6:17.
Word inspired by Holy Spirit—2 Peter 1:21.
Word keeps us from sinning—Psalm 119:9-16.
Word of God is living—Hebrews 4:12,13.

Inspiration of
See Scripture, Inspiration of.

Works

Good
Be good example, do good deeds—Titus 2:7.
Let good deeds shine—Matthew 5:16.

Use money to do good—1 Timothy 6:18.
We will be judged for good/evil acts—2 Corinthians 5:10.

Insufficient for Salvation

No one can ever pay enough—Psalm 49:8.
No one justified by law—Romans 3:20.
Righteous deeds are but filthy rags—Isaiah 64:6.
Saved by grace, not works—Ephesians 2:8,9.

Of God

See God, Works of.

Worldliness, Avoid

Be a stranger to the world—1 Peter 2:11.
Do not be conformed to world—Romans 12:2.
Do not be tied up in affairs of life—2 Timothy 2:4.
Do not love praise of men more than God—John 12:43.
Do not worry about everyday life—Matthew 6:25.
Friendship with world is enmity to God—James 4:4.
God's Word can be crowded out by cares of life—Matthew 13:22; Luke 8:14.
If you cling to life, you will lose it—Matthew 10:39.
Set your mind on things above—Colossians 3:2.
Stop loving this evil world—1 John 2:15.

Worldly Pleasures

See Pleasure, Worldly.

Worry

Anxious heart weighs us down—Proverbs 12:25.
Banish anxiety from your heart—Ecclesiastes 11:10.
Cast all anxiety on God—1 Peter 5:7.
Do not be anxious about anything—Philippians 4:6.
God consoles us—Psalm 94:19.
Jesus' advice on anxiety—Matthew 6:25-34.

W

Worship

Baby Jesus was worshiped—Matthew 2:2.

Bow down in worship—Psalm 95:6.

Do not worship angels—Colossians 2:18; Revelation 19:10.

Do not worship human beings—Acts 14:11-18.

Lip-service worship is not enough—Isaiah 29:13.

Obedience is better than sacrifice—1 Samuel 15:22,23.

Offer your body as a living sacrifice—Romans 12:1.

Worship Creator—Revelation 14:7.

Worship God with reverence—Hebrews 12:28.

Worship in spirit and truth—John 4:20-24.

Worship only true God—Exodus 20:3-5; Deuteronomy 5:7; Matthew 4:10.

Worship the Lord with gladness—Psalm 29:2; 100:2.

See Praise.

Of Jesus Christ

See Jesus Christ, Worship of.

W

Yoke, Figurative

Take my yoke on you—Matthew 11:29,30.

Yoke of circumcision—Acts 15:10.

Yoke of discipline—Lamentations 3:27.

Young Men

Do not let people look down on you—1 Timothy 4:12.

Encourage young men to live wisely—Titus 2:6.

Follow advice—Proverbs 7:1.

Prodigal son—Luke 15:11-32.

Purity from God's Word—Psalm 119:9.

Run from youthful lusts—2 Timothy 2:22.

Should love wisdom—Proverbs 29:3.

Should obey law—Proverbs 28:7.

Youth

Bitter memory of youthful sins—Psalm 25:7.

Do not let anyone despise youth—1 Timothy 4:12.

Glory of youth is strength—Proverbs 20:29.

Rejoice in wife of youth—Proverbs 5:18.

Remember creator during youth—Ecclesiastes 12:1.

Run from youthful lusts—2 Timothy 2:22.

Youth is renewed like eagle—Psalm 103:5.

Zeal

Religious

Be diligent and turn from indifference—Revelation 3:19.

Be enthusiastic about Lord's work—1 Corinthians 15:58.

Be ready to die for Lord—Luke 22:33.

Choose today whom you will serve—Joshua 24:15.

Do not put basket over your light—Mark 4:21; Luke 8:16,17.

Longing for God—Psalm 42:1.

Make the most of every opportunity—Colossians 4:5.

Moses an example—Hebrews 11:24.

Never forsake the Lord—Joshua 24:16.

Obey God rather than men—Acts 5:29.

Our spirits are renewed every day—2 Corinthians 4:16.

Serve the Lord enthusiastically—Romans 12:11.

Thirst for God—Psalm 42:2.

Total commitment—Titus 2:14.

Without Knowledge

Apostle Paul prior to conversion—Galatians 1:13,14.

Israelites—Romans 10:2,3.

Some who preach Christ—Philippians 1:15.

Teacher of religious law—Matthew 8:19,20.

See Discernment; Knowledge; Prudence; Wisdom.

Zodiac

Bear, Orion, the Pleiades—Job 9:9.

Constellations—Job 38:32.

Pleiades and Orion—Amos 5:8.

Spirit made the heavens beautiful—Job 26:13.

See Astrology; Constellations.

STEPS TO PEACE WITH GOD

1. RECOGNIZE GOD'S PLAN—PEACE AND LIFE

The message you have read in this book stresses that God loves you and wants you to experience His peace and life.

The BIBLE says . . . *"For God loved the world so much that He gave His only Son, so that everyone who believes in Him may not die but have eternal life." John 3:16*

2. REALIZE OUR PROBLEM—SEPARATION

People choose to disobey God and go their own way. This results in separation from God.

The BIBLE says . . . *"Everyone has sinned and is far away from God's saving presence." Romans 3:23*

3. RESPOND TO GOD'S REMEDY—CROSS OF CHRIST

God sent His Son to bridge the gap. Christ did this by paying the penalty of our sins when He died on the cross and rose from the grave.

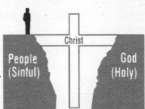

The BIBLE says . . . *"But God has shown us how much He loves us—it was while we were still sinners that Christ died for us!" Romans 5:8*

4. RECEIVE GOD'S SON—LORD AND SAVIOR

You cross the bridge into God's family when you ask Christ to come into your life.

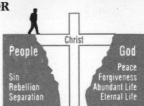

The BIBLE says . . . *"Some, however, did receive Him and believed in Him; so He gave them the right to become God's children." John 1:12*

THE INVITATION IS TO:

REPENT (turn from your sins) and by faith RECEIVE Jesus Christ into your heart and life and follow Him in obedience as your Lord and Savior.

PRAYER OF COMMITMENT

"Lord Jesus, I know I am a sinner. I believe You died for my sins. Right now, I turn from my sins and open the door of my heart and life. I receive You as my personal Lord and Savior. Thank You for saving me now. Amen."

If you want further help in the decision you have made, write to:
Billy Graham Evangelistic Association, P.O. Box 779, Minneapolis, MN 55440-0779